THEOLOGY, ETHICS, AND THE NINETEENTH-CENTURY AMERICAN COLLEGE IDEAL

Conserving a Rational World

Thomas Edward Frank

Mellen Research University Press
San Francisco

Library of Congress Cataloging-in-Publication Data

Frank, Thomas Edward.
    Theology, ethics, and the nineteenth-century American college
ideal / Thomas Edward Frank.
      p.   cm.
    Includes bibliographical references and index.
    ISBN 0-7734-2208-0
    1. United States--Church history--19th century. 2. United States-
-Church history--20th century. 3. Theology, Doctrinal--United
States--History--19th century. 4. Theology, Doctrinal--United
States--History--20th century. 5. Church and college--United
States--History--19th century. 6. Church and college--United
States--History--20th century. 7. Hyde, William De Witt,
1858-1917. 8. King, Henry Churchill, 1858-1934. 9. Tucker, William
Jewett, 1839-1926. I. Title. II. Title: Theology, ethics, and the
19th-century college ideal.
BR525.F67   1993
277.3' 08--dc20   92-44659
                                                  CIP

Editorial Inquiries:

Mellen Research University Press
534 Pacific Avenue
San Francisco
CA 94133

Order Fulfillment:

The Edwin Mellen Press
P.O. Box 450
Lewiston, NY 14092
USA

Printed in the United States of America

To my parents,

Eugene and Wilma Frank,

teachers of Christian character,

models of faith

TABLE OF CONTENTS

FOREWORD

Reading Thomas Frank's perspicuous study of the ideals of a former age, one gets a sense of things having come around again. It is not just that the period of social redefinition we are now going through bears such resemblance to the last two decades of the nineteenth century and the first two of the twentieth. Certainly those resemblances exist. That time, like our own, exerted wrenching forces on the fabric of social life -- the extremes of laissez-faire individualism creating both obscene wealth and brutal privation; a great infusion of immigrants leading to political tension and terrific urban ills; tremendous upheavals abroad bringing both cataclysms of pain and bright possibilities for peace. One has only to think of the Cold War, recently ended, to hear startling echoes in the words of President Henry Churchill King of Oberlin, writing in 1919:

> Who shall declare, for example, the real significance of the Russian revolution? . . . Who shall lay the foundations in righteousness of a Balkan settlement? Who, in short, knows the road to that diviner world for which we really fought this war?

The search for a new world order amid the shifting contours of an older generation sounds eerily prescient.

What is perhaps more remarkable is the magnetism of an older college ideal, just as powerful in our day as it was a century ago. Twice before now in American history, higher education has undergone radical transformation: first, when the colonial colleges and the new liberal arts colleges of the first half of the nineteenth century became defined, under the influence of the Scottish enlightenment, as schools for responsible citizenship; and second, when these very colleges themselves were threatened by the new educational engine of the technological age, the research university. Both these transformations Professor Frank describes with admirable economy.

The social and economic pressures confronting the university today suggest that a "third birth" of American higher education lies around the corner of the twenty-first century. Yet, like our counterparts during the "second birth" a century ago, leaders in higher education and the public generally have turned to the old college ideal as the good fruit that must be preserved. If we perhaps do not believe quite as fully in the inherently obvious sensibleness of moral rules lodged in the framework of the world, we nevertheless share the faith that college is the place where people are formed -- in character as well as intellect -- for playing a responsible part as citizens. Ominously, full access to this training ground for citizens appears threatened as it did when President King voiced concern that entrance to college had become the privilege of an elite defined by class, race, and gender.

If there is much of historical fascination to recommend this study, there is also much from which we might begin to regain our bearings in higher education. We have not gone too far off course that we cannot hear the wisdom of a William Jewett Tucker, who suggested that America's traditional emphasis on liberty must be modified by cooperation, fellowship and mutual regard, and that moral authority lies in the capacity for restraint and self-sacrifice. And after the abuses of technology we have witnessed in Bhophal, Chernobyl, and Prince William Sound, we might learn from William DeWitt Hyde's exhortation to rise above the technical and utilitarian uses of knowledge to an ideal that finds its highest expression in putting knowledge to action in service to the common good. In an age of new accountability in higher education, we could do worse than to conserve something of that older rational world.

James T. Laney
President
Emory University

FOREWORD

The Protestant liberals of the late-nineteenth century viewed themselves as the architects of a "New Theology," and they put their emphasis on the newness. While always insisting that they retained the essentials of the ancient Christian faith, they pressed the point that the old wine needed new wineskins. To most of their contemporaries -- and to most historians who have written about them -- it was their newness, their spirit of innovation, their quest to adapt an ancient tradition to the modern world, that made them seem interesting and important.

It has been easy to overlook the observation of Theodore Munger, a disciple of Horace Bushnell who popularized the term "New Theology," that progressive Protestant thought at the end of the century represented not an abrupt break with the past, not the abandonment but rather the gradual revision of an older system. Like the Boston lawyer Charles Grinnell, another liberal who saw early Protestant progressivism as the result of mild and gradual transitions within orthodoxy, Munger sensed that the new theology was not as new as it might have sounded.

Neither Munger nor Grinnell -- nor anyone else -- took the time to delineate with any precision the traditional (and conventional) assumptions hidden within the bold new assertions of the New Theologians. One of the many virtues of Professor Thomas Frank's *Conserving a Rational World* is his careful analysis of the old within the new, the strands of continuity that tied the Progressives to the certainties of the older culture in which they had grown up.

The towns and cities of ante-bellum America were populated by clerical theologians who viewed themselves as apostles of the unity of truth. They were convinced that God had never enjoined upon men and women the duty of faith without first presenting them with a "reasonable foundation" for it. They believed that a "natural theology," properly limited, prepared the mind to receive the revealed divine truth, and that reason then both validated and interpreted the biblical revelation. It was this confidence in pious rationality that explained the prevalence of Scottish philosophy in ante-bellum Protestant theology, the widespread interest in natural science among ante-bellum theologians, and the conviction that the Christian ethic could find expression in the conceptual forms of the ante-bellum moral philosophers.

What Frank has so nicely described and interpreted is the persistence of such older assumptions within the late-nineteenth century theological movement that supposedly cast so many of them aside. What makes his study even more useful is that he has given his intellectual history an institutional setting by concentrating his focus on the writings of three celebrated presidents of liberal arts colleges: William Jewett Tucker of Dartmouth, William DeWitt Hyde of Bowdoin, and Henry Churchill King of Oberlin. By exploring the interconnections between ideas and institutions, Frank has illumined not only the history of American theology but also the changing character of American higher education.

He writes of a seemingly lost world -- a world that still believed in the capacity (even the responsibility) of an institution to embody a cultural synthesis, a world in which Protestant clergy still frequently occupied the presidency of elite colleges, a world marked by confident leaders who took for granted the rightness of their ideas and the superiority of their culture-- and he charts some of the beginnings of its decline. It seems irretrievable, in many respects even undesirable. Yet who knows? One further virtue of Frank's analysis is that it prompts us to ask how many hidden assumptions we might have inherited from the world that we have supposedly left behind.

E. Brooks Holifield
Charles Howard Candler
  Professor of American Church History
Emory University

PREFACE

The interests that led me to write this book were first generated in a seminar with Brooks Holifield on "Moral Philosophy and the American Conscience in the 18th and 19th Centuries" at Emory University in 1975. Our seminar reading provided my first exposure to the distinctly Scottish Enlightenment that both anticipated and paralleled the epistemological inquiries of the better-known German philosopher Immanuel Kant. The Scottish philosophy put forward first principles of human knowledge and morality grounded in the common sense of all sentient human beings, which as a solution to philosophical dualism of mind and matter may have lacked Kant's speculative profundity but was for the better part of a century more widely read and absorbed in the Anglo-American world. Common Sense Realism was the standard philosophy in ante-bellum America, and academics, preachers, and statesmen at all points on the spectrum from orthodox Calvinism to Unitarian and even deist liberalism were firmly committed to its solutions of epistemological and moral conundrums.

I proceeded in the seminar to write a paper on the "Moral Science" of the leading academic moralist of early nineteenth century America, Francis Wayland.[1] He held, in keeping with his Scottish mentors, that morality consisted of rational right relations of individuals, and that those relations were perceived by the conscience, or moral sense, as self-evident, a priori,

---

[1]My paper was later published as "Contending Values: Francis Wayland's Views on War," *Foundations* 21 (April-June 1978):100-112.

common sense propositions. Thus one's duty was clearly determined by the relations in which one stood to the objects of one's action, and the inducement to perform it was provided by the Moral Governor of the Universe, in whom all rational relations were grounded, and to whom belonged the prerogatives of (rational) reward and punishment.

The practical aim of moral science was the formation of character, which consisted in educating the reason about the rational relations in which the individual stood, and in disciplining the will to perform one's duty. A prime locus for such formation was the liberal arts college. Here one was exposed to the whole rational universe of natural and moral law, subjected to the mental discipline of mastering classical languages and literature, and shaped in opinion and conscience according to the moral principles of the day. The latter task was the particular charge of the college president, who taught a senior course in moral philosophy encompassing everything from politics to economics to family relations. Wayland himself discharged this responsibility with vigor throughout his nearly thirty years as president of Brown University.[2]

My nascent interest in liberal arts education and its focus in religious and moral reasoning having been stirred, I began to explore the fate of the college ideal and its accompanying Common Sense rationality in late nineteenth century America. This era had always attracted me because of its progressive idealism on social issues and its struggle with the problems of human knowledge and moral freedom. Yet as I read along, I was assured by scholars in both American religious history and history of higher education

[2]Francis Wayland, *The Elements of Moral Science*, ed. with an Introduction by Joseph L. Blau (Cambridge: The Belknap Press of Harvard University Press, 1963).

that this period belonged to evolution, German philosophy, urbanization, industrialization, and the rise of large universities. The ideals of the old moral science survived in educational backwaters even into the 1890s, they said, but the intellectual and social world in which it had thrived had been irrevocably transformed. Survey histories of education rushed on from dry episodes of the "old-time college" with its ossified classical curriculum to the unfolding drama of the modern university with its specialized fields of knowledge and impressive new graduate and professional schools. Survey histories of philosophy disposed of Scottish Realism in a few pages, dismissing it as a pseudo-philosophy in the service of religious orthodoxy, and went on to fuller discussions of Idealists and Neo-Kantians whose influence was spreading through all fields. Survey histories of religion picked up Arthur M. Schlesinger's description of the era as a "critical period in American religion" and showed how all the new socio-economic and intellectual conditions made for the construction of a new theology liberal in thought and committed to social change.[3]

Then one day, probably through an accident in the card catalogue, I came across a book entitled *Education and National Character*. The lead article was an address by a college president who spoke of the rational lawfulness of the universe, and the duty of all persons to earnestly seek the will of God in their social relations, to the end of achieving a rational, ethical democracy. This address was delivered by Henry Churchill King of Oberlin

---

[3]Arthur Meier Schlesinger, "A Critical Period in American Religion, 1875-1900," *Proceedings of the Massachusetts Historical Society* 64 (June 1932):523-47.

College at the fifth general convention of the Religious Education Association meeting in Washington, D.C., in 1908.[4]

In the course of further research in King's theological and moral
writings, I was struck by the similarity of the terms of the discussion to the
rhetoric and concepts of the ante-bellum period, and wondered if the rational
universe of knowledge and action conceived by Common Sense Realists had
really been moribund as scholarly opinion assumed. I also noted the
contemporary ring to words describing the college ideal, and wondered if the
pre-World War I period was not somehow anticipatory of the current
collegiate search for identity. Hence I decided to explore the writing of
King, and two other college presidents for the sake of comparison and fuller
discussion, all three of whom were well-versed and articulate in theology,
ethics, and the college ideal.

I have attempted to use the language of these men as faithfully as
possible, in an effort to reconstruct their world of thought and attitude.
Whether quoting, paraphrasing, or describing their ideas, I have necessarily
employed words and references that may be offensive to ears attuned to
contemporary social sensibilities. Particularly noticeable is the overwhelming
maleness of their language in everything from theology to advice on personal
hygiene. Yet this obvious and sometimes even aggressive masculinity was
woven into the idiom of the world-view which they articulated and lived. I
have not attempted to isolate and explore the origins and impact of
masculine attitudes in the progressive era; such would comprise a study in

---

[4]Henry Churchill King, "Enlarging Ideals in Morals and Religion," in H. C. King, et al.,
Education and National Character, Papers of the Fifth General Convention of the Religious
Education Association, February 11-13, 1908 (Chicago: The Religious Education Association,
1908), pp. 7-15.

itself. I have tried, rather, to show that the sexual mores evident in the writings of these authors were an expression of the social order they wished to perpetuate.

In today's pluralistic social order with its diverse understanding of gender roles, appeals to common sense and opinion, basic to the world-view described in this paper, are no longer decisive. Language is itself, of course, a primary reflection of such changes. I have thought it imperative to preserve the integrity of expression of the earlier era, and I hope that the contrast with contemporary discourse may prove instructive.

Candler School of Theology
Emory University
Atlanta, Georgia
September 1992

ACKNOWLEDGEMENTS

My research has been supported by several institutions and encouraged by a number of individuals along the way. I am grateful to the Division of Religion of Emory University for a Graduate Fellowship in Religion which I enjoyed for two years, and to the Board of Higher Education and Ministry of the United Methodist Church for a Dempster Graduate Fellowship which underwrote a third year of full-time study. I could not have completed the writing while continuing in pastoral ministry without the generosity and unfailing support of the congregation of Missouri United Methodist Church in Columbia, Missouri. Particularly I wish to express my gratitude to my colleague and friend Clarence J. Forsberg, who not only arranged for me to take two consecutive summer leaves of absence for research and writing, but also covered my ministerial duties for me so that I would be free to study elsewhere.

The first summer leave I spent on the campus of Emory University, and specifically in the Pitts Theology Library. The Librarian, Channing R. Jeschke, and the entire staff were most helpful in meeting my study needs. I also enjoyed the privacy and quiet of the John Owen Smith residence during those months, and I am thankful to Mrs. Smith for allowing me to use her home in her absence.

The second summer was spent in the delightful environs of Camp Miniwanca in Stony Lake, Michigan. There I was afforded a cabin where I could work in solitude, but could also enjoy the enthusiasm and encouragement of the camp staff. To the American Youth Foundation, and especially to its former Executive Director, now Dean of the Chapel at Syracuse University, Richard L. Phillips, I express deepest thanks.

Among many friends who have been helpful to me, I want to thank particularly June DeWeese of the staff of Ellis Library on the University Missouri-Columbia campus, who went out of her way many times to help me find needed materials. Michelle Adams and Miriam McClure, friends and fellow-workers in many church responsibilities, typed the manuscript, and Janet Gary of the Candler School of Theology staff put it in final form.

Publication of this book has been made possible by the Woodruff research fund of Emory University. I am grateful to Emory, and especially to Dean R. Kevin LaGree, for supporting the project.

Lastly, I express my admiration and gratitude to my three mentors in historical studies: to William Mallard, who revealed to me the force and humor of historical imagination; to Manfred Hoffmann, who grounded me in the discipline of analytic thinking; and to Brooks Holifield, who has not only seen me through this project, but who has constantly encouraged me in my interests.

INTRODUCTION

A THESIS OF CONTINUITY

The first strides have now been taken toward recovering the central place and influence of the Scottish philosophy in the formative period of American culture. As early as the 1930s Gladys Bryson was rediscovering the roots of the field of sociology in the older moral philosophy. In 1955 Sydney Ahlstrom published an article surveying the wide influence of the Scots' moderate Enlightenment on nineteenth century American theology. The next year Wilson Smith brought out a study of the moral philosophy developed by professors and presidents of northern colleges in the ante-bellum period, showing their heavy dependence on Scottish and English authors.

In recent years, the pace of recovery has accelerated. Daniel Howe showed the influence of Scottish Common Sense on the moral philosophy of early Unitarian professors at Harvard. D. H. Meyer reviewed the college textbooks in moral philosophy showing their reliance on a Scottish legacy. Henry May brought the Scots into his study of the Enlightenment in America, albeit in a section on its decline and assimilation, as the expression of a "didactic Enlightenment" intent on formulating moral principle against the skepticism of a more radical strain of Enlightenment. Theodore Bozeman demonstrated the importance of the Scottish epistemology in reconciling tensions between empirical science and religious orthodoxy among Old School Presbyterians. Herbert Hovenkamp more broadly summarized issues of science and religion from 1800 to 1860, with the rational orthodox bases for unity in human knowledge lying in Common Sense Realism. Finally, Brooks Holifield unearthed a forgotten tradition of rational theology and ethics in the South, often assumed previously to be isolated from the intellectual currents of the time and given over solely to revivalism.[1]

The next historical task, expanding from the foundational ante-bellum period, is to show that although Anglo-American Common Sense rationalism, along with its accompanying religious orthodoxy and political conservatism, was pointedly out of vogue in most circles by the 1880s and 1890s, nevertheless many of its ideals, concepts, and even characteristic terms were prevalent in the new context. A philosophy as warmly grasped as Common Sense Realism could not simply disappear from the intellectual scene; its categories and typical attitudes persisted even as a new generation sought to progress

---

[1]Gladys Bryson, "The Comparable Interests of the Old Moral Philosophy and the Modern Social Sciences," *Social Forces* 11 (October 1932):19-27; "The Emergence of the Social Sciences from Moral Philosophy," *The International Journal of Ethics* 42 (April 1932):304-23; "Sociology Considered as Moral Philosophy," *The Sociological Review* 24 (1932):26-36; Sydney E. Ahlstrom, "The Scottish Philosophy and American Theology," *Church History* 24 (September 1955):257-72; Wilson Smith, *Professors and Public Ethics; Studies of Northern Moral Philosophers Before the Civil War*, American Historical Association (Ithaca, N.Y.: Cornell University Press, 1956); Daniel Walker Howe, *The Unitarian Conscience; Harvard Moral Philosophy, 1805-1861* (Cambridge: Harvard University Press, 1970); D. H. Meyer, *The Instructed Conscience; The Shaping of the American National Ethic* (Philadelphia: University of Pennsylvania Press, 1972); Henry F. May, *The Enlightenment in America* (New York: Oxford University Press, 1976), pp. 337-62; Theodore Dwight Bozeman, *Protestants in an Age of Science; The Baconian Ideal and Antebellum American Religious Thought* (Chapel Hill, N.C.: University of North Carolina Press, 1977); Herbert Hovenkamp, *Science and Religion in America, 1800-1860* (n.p., University of Pennsylvania Press, 1978); E. Brooks Holifield, *The Gentlemen Theologians; American Theology in Southern Culture, 1795-1860* (Durham, N.C.: Duke University Press, 1978).

toward a religious and ethical basis for their own world. The late nineteenth and early twentieth century striving for a new rationalism incorporating science and technology and opening the way to an expanded science of moral duty, all under the aegis of theological presuppositions and religious motivations, clearly demonstrated this continuity.

Thus the entire nineteenth century, including the period up to World War I, was marked by a distinctive rationalist strain in American thought, stemming originally from the Scottish Enlightenment. Weaving together assertions about knowledge, nature, human nature, and morality, all based on a common method of philosophical first principles, moderate Christian rationalism formed a complete world-view. So all-encompassing was it, and so laced with interdependent assumptions, that it might best be seen in analogy with a chemical synthesis or compound. That is, it may be broken down into its constituent elements, but in actuality derived its persuasive power from the dynamics created when those elements were brought into a whole.

The synthesis comprised several definite, identifiable elements. First was the certainty that the universe was rational, ordered by the regularity of laws, and accessible to human comprehension. So orderly were the operations of nature -- the changing seasons, the movements of the stars -- that they suggested a unity of plan, which rationalists ascribed to the divine reason or providence. Complementarily, it was equally evident, since all human minds agreed on the rational order of nature, not only that knowledge itself was reliable, but that it was based on universal first principles common to every thinking person. As a consequence, science, the systematic observation of nature, was firmly grounded in the dependability of human sense experience and served to reveal more and more of the divinely founded operations of the universe.

A second element of the synthesis was the assertion that, just as the sensible world was governed by rational law, so also was the moral sphere guided by universal principles of right and duty. So evident were the operations of moral law -- the inevitable consequences of vice, the sound axioms of social order and progress -- that they, too, suggested a single origin in a divine moral governor. Complementarily, the consensus of thinking human beings on the moral order of the universe suggested universal first principles of ethics, perceived and reinforced by the conscience, a natural human faculty. Like natural science, then, morality could also be reduced to laws or maxims defining the relations of things, laws which played out into specific duties and responsibilities in society.

A third major element common throughout the nineteenth century synthesis was the agreed belief that both the theistic basis of the rational universe and the moral order of humanity were best represented in the absolute and highest religion, Christianity. Not only did the Christian religion teach the natural principles of the divine origin of nature and the universality of right and wrong; it added to them the force of divine revelation. Christianity particularly reinforced the essential moral teaching that human beings were responsible for their world and their actions in shaping that world. Further, in connection with the Enlightenment ideology of individual freedom in democratic society, Christianity provided the moral system and incentive that would undergird not only expanding Western societies, but also the emerging colonial peoples.

The chemistry of these elements issued in many by-products, but primary among them was the formation of Christian character. Perhaps one might even say that a basic element of the synthesis was the assertion that, based as it was on universal common sense, it could easily be taught. The person who was educated to see nature as divine providence displayed, to perceive relations with others under clear moral categories, and to devote a lifetime to the practice of Christian virtues, was one who could exhibit the character of a Christian and take leadership in a Christian society. The latter was in fact another by-product of the synthesis, for a society of individuals showing forth the character of Christian rationalism would inevitably become a Christian society and ultimately lead the way to a Christian world.

While the nineteenth century rational and moral synthesis was pervasive in the Anglo-American world, then, it was very clearly evident in educational institutions, in particular the liberal arts colleges. Here the synthesis was especially articulated as an overarching rationale for the unity of all learning, whether natural science, history, or social theory. Here was the synthesis deliberately reconstructed or reshaped when necessary to comprehend intellectual and social expansion and change. And here was the synthesis explicitly advocated as the world-view within which to shape the character of young men (and sometimes even women). In its collegiate setting, the synthesis took the form of the college ideal: the belief that in a community of scholars and students, the order of the universe could be discovered, the duties of the individual in society could be explained, and through disciplined living in the miniature society of the college, character befitting the society at large could be shaped.

To whom should better fall the duty of articulating, reconstructing, and advocating the rational synthesis and its college ideal than the college presidents. In the nineteenth century they were not only the foremost figures on their campuses, but more broadly the axis around which the whole personality of their colleges revolved. They were educators but also philosophers, moralists, theologians, preachers, and leading citizens in American society. Their own comprehensiveness reflected that of the synthesis itself.

The ante-bellum period of the synthesis and its collegiate exponents has been thoroughly researched by others, not only in the works listed above, but also in studies of higher education such as George P. Schmidt's *The Old Time College President.*[2] The task here undertaken is to demonstrate the continuity of the synthesis into the Progressive era of the late nineteenth and early twentieth centuries leading up to World War I.

The case for continuity is not easy to anchor, though, in the tide of "new learning" that began to flow during that period. The generating of new theories itself entailed criticism and rejection of older formulations. Psychologists, for example, were developing the experimental method and refuting the old faculty psychology. Sociologists were demonstrating the influence of environment and social institutions on the individual and casting aside the old laissez-faire individualism in politics and economics. Theologians were breaking with the old theology of God as Governor and Judge and trying to show God's immanence in human life and social progress. In each field scholars saw themselves freed from the shackles of past conceptions and creatively involved with current social and intellectual changes.

---

[2](New York: Columbia University Press, 1930).

Therefore, one is not surprised to find the late nineteenth and early twentieth century liberals in Christian theology and morals interpreting themselves as participants in a movement breaking with the systems of the past. Their recurring calls for theological "reconstruction" and for a vastly enlarged moral idealism accentuated their rejection of the unresponsive formalism of the older "science" and its intellectual assumptions. Thus in 1919, the first reviewer of the liberal field, John Wright Buckham, celebrated the developing theology as a "progressive science" in touch with vital human interests, and began his survey with encomiums to the liberators and pioneers of progressive religious thought, especially Horace Bushnell.[3]

What is surprising, however, is to find that the basic litany of liberal origins that began with Buckham's interpretation was not materially altered thereafter. The list included the Enlightenment belief in human perfectibility and natural rights, Unitarianism, Romanticism, Bushnell, German Idealism and liberal theology in its various forms in Kant, F. D. E. Schleiermacher, G. W. F. Hegel and Albrecht Ritschl, and immediate predecessors such as the American pastors Henry Ward Beecher and Phillips Brooks.

Likewise the assertion that liberal theology was predominantly modernist persisted in all survey interpretations. Arthur C. McGiffert in a 1942 essay identified evolutionism, Ritschlianism, personalism, and naturalism as examples of the "modernist impulse within Protestant liberalism," which impulse he defined as "an interest in coming to terms with specific structures of thought in contemporary culture." Kenneth Cauthen divided the liberals into "evangelical" and "modernist" camps in his 1962 survey. Borrowing these

---

[3]*Progressive Religious Thought in America; A Survey of the Enlarging Pilgrim Faith* (Boston: Houghton Mifflin Co., 1919), pp. 3-4.

terms from Henry P. Van Dusen, he distinguished those liberals who "stood squarely within the Christian tradition and accepted as normative for their thinking what they understood to be the essence of historical Christianity," from those who broke with the historic faith by adopting the "presuppositions of modern science, philosophy, psychology, and social thought." Yet he, too, saw both groups responding to three broadly modern influences: the emphasis on continuity between nature and supernature, human and divine; the autonomy of science and human freedom; and the dynamism of a progressing world.[4]

William R. Hutchison took up the refrain in a 1976 book borrowing McGiffert's phrase, *The Modernist Impulse in American Protestantism*. Finding this impulse "central to the liberal movement," he described it as comprising three primary notions: "the conscious, intended adaptation of religious ideas to modern culture . . . the idea that God is immanent in human cultural development and revealed through it . . . [and] a belief that human society is moving toward realization (even though it may never attain the reality) of the Kingdom of God." While adding the Englishman Frederick Robertson to the list of liberal progenitors, and noting that there were liberals such as David Swing actually practicing their views west of Boston, Hutchison followed the standard line of descent from Unitarian spokesman William Ellery Channing to Bushnell to the new theology of Theodore Munger and the modernism of Henry Nelson Wieman. Rejecting Cauthen's distinction

---

[4]Arthur C. McGiffert, "Protestant Liberalism," in *Liberal Theology: An Appraisal; Essays in Honor of Eugene William Lyman*, ed. D. E. Roberts and H. P. Van Dusen (New York: Scribner's, 1942), pp. 117, 119; Kenneth Cauthen, *The Impact of American Religious Liberalism* (New York: Harper & Row, 1962), pp. 5-25, 27, 29. Lloyd Averill followed Cauthen's typology in his own study, *American Theology in the Liberal Tradition* (Philadelphia: The Westminster Press, 1967).

of evangelical and modernist liberals, he argued that the whole thrust of modernism was to seek continuity of sacred and secular realms in a self-conscious adaptation to modernity.[5]

The only dissenting opinion among the surveyors of liberal theology was heard from Frank Hugh Foster. In a book published posthumously in 1939, he dourly regretted the conservatism of late nineteenth century liberalism, even accusing it of clinging "to everything which it had deemed precious in the past till driven to relinquishing it." The liberals had been too sluggish in responding to the rapid intellectual and social change going on around them, a legacy which Foster apparently saw as a detriment to theological change even in his own day.[6]

While he was certainly not proposing a constructive theory of the continuity of historical development in American liberal theology, Foster seemed at least to be aware of the persistent ties of liberalism to a neglected and rejected past. What no interpreter of liberalism ever took seriously was the heritage of "rational cosmologies and reasonable psychologies" grounded in Common Sense Realism which were pervasive in nineteenth century American thought, and in which the generation of progressive scholars was well-versed.[7] The tendency from Buckham on was to look back at pioneers who labored heroically from a minority position in the early and mid-

---

[5](Cambridge: Harvard University Press, 1976), p. 2 and passim.

[6]*The Modern Movement in American Theology; Sketches in the History of American Protestant Thought from the Civil War to the World War* (New York: Fleming H. Revell Co., 1939), pp. 12, 213.

[7]E. Brooks Holifield, "Reading the Signs of the Times," *Reviews in American History* 5 (March 1977):19-20.

nineteenth century and who finally got the recognition they deserved in an explosion of progressive thought at the turn of the century.

Moreover, interpreters of the history of theology and philosophy agreed that once progressive liberalism emerged in the forefront of American thought, the old orthodoxies were dead. Cauthen claimed that theological orthodoxy "perished" in the tide of a liberalism more adequate to the modern world. Hovenkamp asserted that the American Protestant effort to devise a "scientific theology" was an experiment that "had clearly failed" by 1860.[8] Two major historians of American thought, Herbert Schneider and Stow Persons, treated Common Sense Realism as an unfortunate stage of retarded development, the former calling it an "orthodoxy" not interested in the advancement of the arts and sciences, the latter labeling it "Protestant scholasticism" with a conservative function comparable to the medieval church. Obviously it had to be abandoned in the service of progress.[9]

Whether it really was abandoned in assumptions, attitudes, interests, or even in language, however, is much more open to debate than one would ever surmise from reading the surveys. Examination of the writings of major college presidents who were also theologians and moral philosophers clearly demonstrates that, while it was their liberal assertion that their adoption of the new learning brought a definitive break with the past, in fact the progressive educators were striving to comprehend the new learning in a reconstructed and expanded rational synthesis continuous with that in which

---

[8]Cauthen, *Impact*, p. 5; Hovenkamp, *Science*, p. x.

[9]Herbert W. Schneider, *A History of American Philosophy*, 2d ed. (New York: Columbia University Press, 1963), pp. 195-96; Stow Persons, *American Minds; A History of Ideas* (New York: Henry Holt & Co., 1958), p. 189.

they had been educated themselves and of which their ante-bellum predecessors had been exponents.

The first chapter introduces three college presidents of the progressive era, placing them within the setting of stability and change in higher education. The following chapter presents an overview of the rational and moral synthesis exhibited in the colleges of the ante-bellum period, showing its origins in the Scottish philosophy and its development by American authors. Chapters Three and Four follow the same general topical outline of Chapter Two, taking up first the new theology, its epistemology, grounds, evidences, and consequences, and then the moral philosophy and ethical principles of the presidential authors. Finally, Chapter Five describes the synthesis as its authors intended it to function in the college community and in the society at large. Throughout the latter three chapters the continuity of the new synthesis with the old becomes increasingly apparent, thus opening an angle of vision that has been overlooked by earlier surveyors of nineteenth century American religion and culture.

CHAPTER ONE

THE COLLEGES AND THEIR PRESIDENTS

The nineteenth century liberal arts college provides an appropriate setting for demonstrating the continuity of religious and moral thought in American Protestantism. Up until the 1880s and 1890s, the ideal of most colleges was centered explicitly in the Common Sense Realism and moral science of the ante-bellum era. The traditional college course, with its heaviest emphases on Latin, Greek, and mathematics, was completed, as a keystone completes an arch, by senior year classes in Moral Philosophy and Evidences of Christianity, usually taught by the college president, who normally occupied the chair of Professor of Mental and Moral Philosophy or some similar title. Just as the colleges taught by the method of mental discipline, meaning practically, by rote and memorization, so they trained character by inculcating in students a strict regimen of clear duties logically deduced from a system of rational relations and motivated by love and respect for the moral Governor whose divine reason was displayed in both the natural and moral universe.

By later in the century, however, the limitations of this traditional system were coming into sharp relief against the new learning and methodology imported and advocated by American scholars returning from graduate study in Germany. The specialized departments of German research in every field seemed to put generalist American higher education to shame. U.S. colleges offered little or nothing in the way of graduate or professional education, and gave virtually no opportunity to study modern languages or the work of contemporary scholars in emerging fields such as history, economics, or psychology. The classical tradition of the college seemed increasingly outmoded, confined, and impractical, out of touch with advances in science and research.

Beginning in the 1870s with Charles William Eliot's administration at Harvard (1869-1909), and accelerating through the 1880s and 1890s, a marked change came over the face of American education. Colleges like Harvard and Yale expanded into universities with professional schools and eventually graduate divisions offering advanced degrees. Newer private universities that had been founded in the 1860s, such as Cornell (1865) and Johns Hopkins (1867), began to flourish, and more were chartered, Chicago (1892) being one. Their presidents, Andrew Dickson White, Daniel Coit Gilman, William Rainey Harper, and others, were considered national leaders of the progressive movement in higher education. At the same time numbers of state universities were being organized under the Morrill Land Grant Act of 1862. These began to stress more practical and vocational areas of study such as agriculture and engineering.

As newly specialized academic fields began to develop, associations of scholars and corresponding journals for sharing research were formed. This "new wave of learned societies" included the Modern Language Association

(1883), the American Historical Association (1884), the American Economic Association (1885), and numerous others.[1]

Education itself became a field of study, coming under increasing scrutiny as attention focussed on the basic preparation of American students to do advanced work. The new National Education Association formed a Committee of Ten in 1892, chaired by President Eliot, to formulate a plan for standardizing secondary school curriculum and consequent admissions guidelines for colleges. Change was so rapid, though, that another Commission on the Reorganization of Secondary Education was set up only twenty years later, in 1913. In part the turmoil was caused by the growing public school movement. Only about five hundred public high schools were in service in 1870; the vast majority of the approximately eighty thousand secondary students were in private academies offering training in traditional classical education. But by 1910 over 1.1 million students were enrolled in high school in the U.S., about ninety percent of them in the nearly ten thousand public secondary schools.[2]

Furthermore, new theories of education developed by J. H. Pestalozzi in Europe and by G. Stanley Hall, John Dewey, and others in the U.S., called for classroom content and method to be tailored to the developmental needs of the child or youth, a "Copernican revolution" against the inflexible traditional curriculum imposed on students in the past as a form of mental

---

[1]Frederick Rudolph, *The American College and University* (New York: Alfred A. Knopf, 1962), chaps. 13, 16, 17.

[2]Lawrence A. Cremin, "The Revolution in American Secondary Education, 1893-1918," *Teachers College Record* 56 (March 1955):296,305; Martin Trow, "The Second Transformation of American Secondary Education," *International Journal of Comparative Sociology* 2 (1961):146.

discipline. As part of the new wave of "pragmatism," the educational theorists urged schools to develop persons who could be constructive citizens of their communities, shaped by a school environment that would test their individual skills and ability to adjust to others.[3]

Thus the liberal arts colleges found themselves squeezed from two directions. In one way they were being pressured to compete with the advanced learning of universities by creating specialized departments and offering expansive elective systems, allowing students to omit time-honored requirements in the classics in favor of intensive preparation in one field. In the other direction, they were being forced by the growth of secondary schools to define a purpose for liberal education more advanced than the secondary level and standing between the student and professional or graduate study. From 1890 to World War I general and educational periodicals were laced with articles by defenders of the college, resisting everything from overly lax elective systems to Eliot's proposal for a three-year college course to an ominous trend in admission of high school graduates directly into technical and professional schools. With other added pressures such as the strident demand for more practical, vocational education and more public universities rising to meet the demand, the small, private, often denominational colleges indeed found themselves in a pinch.

But they survived, a fact which is perhaps best ascribed to an abiding and loyal faith in the college ideal. Surveyors of the history of higher education thought that the progressive movement which came to expression in the universities made the old college obsolete. Frederick Rudolph, for example, wrote that "the new era, which was about to dawn, would pass the

---

[3]Cremin, "Revolution," pp. 302-304.

old-time college by or perhaps convert it into a precious preserve of gentility or into a defiant outpost of denominationalism." He went on to state that the "old unity" of the liberal arts college was "utterly destroyed" in the metamorphosis of higher education.[4]

This overlooked the persistence of the colleges in defending themselves, mainly through the outspokenness and national repute of their presidents, against encroachments from both sides. By appealing precisely to the progressive ideal, the colleges refused to let themselves be forced, in the words of a prominent Southern president, Henry Nelson Snyder, into becoming either "quasi-technical school[s]" or "pseudo-universit[ies]." Rather, they kept to their ideal of developing humane character in individuals who would have a "passion for truth as truth," and who could contribute to "the social, the political, the artistic, the industrial, the scientific, and the religious progress of the race." The small college, where boys became men capable of civic leadership and social service under the influence of the mature Christian character of their professors (male language and imagery was normative in these writings), where the social skills attendant to living in a democratic community were acquired, where the applicability of Christian principles to everyday life could be indelibly imprinted on young minds, indeed, where the whole rational universe of knowledge and principles for action could be displayed -- this college had a very definite place in American education between secondary and graduate levels, and had to be

---

[4]*American College*, p. 241. He titled his Chapter 17, "Progressivism and the Universities." See also John S. Brubacher and Willis Rudy, *Higher Education in Transition; An American History, 1636-1956* (New York: Harper & Bros. Publishers, 1958), p. 143, for another example of dismissing the future role of colleges.

preserved for the sake of its influence on the character and progress of the nation itself.[5]

I. The Presidents

Throughout the nineteenth century many if not most college presidents were clergymen; but those in office in 1910 were the last generation of such. This both reflected and reinforced the religious dimension of the college ideal in all colleges regardless of their denominational ties. It would be interesting to know, but probably impossible to determine, when Christian language and referents went out of common public discourse in America. But it is striking to read in national periodicals -- *Nation, Independent, Atlantic Monthly, Education* -- pleas for the college by presidents of some national repute arguing for the development of Christian character modelled on the Great Teacher and Personality of history, Jesus himself. This was by no means a mere ploy to attract the sympathy or support of a wider constituency. On the contrary, it reflected the location of collegiate ideals within Christian faith and teachings, and vice versa, the centrality of Christian faith within the ideal of the college. When they were not defending or administering their colleges, the clergy presidents engaged in discussion of contemporary trends in theology -- biblical criticism, evolutionary thought, social Christianity. Many of them became major interpreters and advocates of liberal theology accommodating the new learning, and of an accompanying moral philosophy encompassing the economic, political, and social changes of their era.

---

[5]"The College Under Fire," *The Methodist Quarterly Review*[South] 62 (July 1913):532-45.

Always presidential theology and moral philosophy was developed and taught for a practical purpose: the formation of personality strong enough to achieve moral mastery of the modern world. Purely theoretical or contemplative pursuits were widely frowned upon. Henry May identified "practical idealism" as the ruling phrase of the early twentieth century, for it combined the two dominant impulses of the age. On the one hand, Americans were seeking ideals and ideas that transcended the material world and gave meaning to human freedom. On the other hand, they were intent on finding the reality of ideas in their pragmatic use and putting ideals to work in progressive society. Thus they would typically borrow the epistemological solutions and moral imperative of Kant, or the Hegelian glorification of family and nation in social evolution, but always with a warning against the speculative and even agnostic abstractions of philosophy. Skepticism and cynicism were intellectual sins, while on the other hand so-called realism in art and literature was an aesthetic offense that could only reflect the low character of the artist.

The peculiar mix of progressive optimism and moral uplift that characterized American culture at the turn of the century gave way to an end of American innocence even before World War I, according to May. But the same dynamics that elevated Theodore Roosevelt to the presidencies of both the nation and the American Historical Association and gave him a forum in religious periodicals also carried the country through an intensely idealistic war under the leadership of a staunch Presbyterian, Woodrow Wilson, and fed the flourishing post-war dreams of national abstinence, international peace based on a league of the nations of Christian civilization, and interdenominational unity in an Interchurch World Movement. The climax of moral idealism was also, however, the beginning of its decline and dissipation.[6] In particular, the war marked an end to the hegemony of the whole rational synthesis so long sustained especially by the colleges, as the ideals of Western Christian civilization fell into disarray and disillusionment amid bitter conflict.

The three college presidents on whose lives and writings this book focuses, William Jewett Tucker of Dartmouth (1839-1926), William DeWitt Hyde of Bowdoin (1858-1917), and Henry Churchill King of Oberlin (1858-1934), exemplified the progressive trends in American education and society between 1885 and World War I. The comprehensiveness of their interests makes it possible to show both the breadth and the unity of the synthesis which they articulated and exhibited in their careers. That breadth, and its consequent superficiality at points, probably explains their omission from survey histories of Protestant liberalism or higher education other than occasional brief mention. But if that breadth was a weakness in terms of particular academic disciplines, it was also their distinctive quality. Like the chemistry of the synthesis itself, their all-encompassing concerns are precisely what makes them stand out in the history of ideas and institutions, which too often isolates specialized chains of thought apart from their milieu. Their catholicity of interests was also an inheritance from a neglected past, from that earlier generation of college presidents who were also synthetic thinkers, builders of Christian character, and leaders of the educated middle class.

When Tucker reflected in his autobiography about his years of administration, he concluded that the college presidency was "an anomaly

---

[6]Henry F. May, *The End of American Innocence; A Study of the First Years of Our Own Time, 1912-1917* (Chicago: Quadrangle Paperbacks, Quadrangle Books, 1959, 1964), p. 14 and passim.

among the professions," for no academic course or other preparation led toward it. The president was simply a leader, a personality to whom others looked as an example of character, or one might say, a personage who inspired awe and respect. Like the old-time college president whose greatest service had been, in Schmidt's words, "education by personal contact," the progressive administrators taught, disciplined, inspired, and challenged their students personally in such a thoroughgoing way that the personality of the institution became their own. Hyde wrote to fellow president Charles Franklin Thwing of Western Reserve that upon assuming leadership of Bowdoin, the college "henceforth would be his alter ego." Given his term of thirty-two years (1885-1917), Tucker's of sixteen years (1893-1909), and King's of twenty-four years (1903-1927), each of the presidents made an indelible impression on their institutions, and in fact shaped them to their own personalities.[7]

All three men were vigorous activists, credited by their institutional historians with completely revitalizing stagnant campuses by adding faculty, reforming the curriculum, attracting new capital for buildings and endowment, and strengthening their college's reputation. Enrollments grew and alumni loyalty blossomed during their modernizing administrations.

At the same time, the presidents gave a personal impression of energetic intensity, although their relentless drive eventually led them to failing health. Tucker was perhaps the most refined or dignified of the three, and was also some twenty years older than the other two. He was described

---

[7]William Jewett Tucker, *My Generation; An Autobiographical Interpretation* (Boston: Houghton Mifflin Co., 1919), pp. 362-3; Schmidt, *Old Time*, p. 229; Charles Franklin Thwing, *Guides, Philosophers and Friends; Studies of College Men* (Freeport, N.Y.: Books for Libraries Press, 1971 [orig. publ. 1927]), p. 311.

as walking with an army quick-step, exhibiting alertness, earnestness, and friendliness in conversation, but always restrained, commanding attention, and never effusive. Thwing remembered him for his geniality, openness, even tenderness, which was combined with a forceful swiftness in making decisions and a capacity for moral indignation at anything cheap or vulgar. A man of keen judgment, delicate temperament, and refined taste, he was, in Thwing's summation, both a democrat and a patrician. His tireless work and extensive travels for Dartmouth unfortunately led to illness brought on by exhaustion in 1907, however, and in the last two years of his term Tucker worked on a reduced schedule, continuing as president only at the insistence of the trustees.[8]

Elevated to the Bowdoin presidency when only twenty-six, Hyde was quickly tagged "the boy president," but left no doubt that he was to be considered a manly personage. His biographers described him as a master in the cult of self-control; he never missed his exercise, and was often seen riding across campus on a bicycle with tennis racket in hand. Yet he was not someone a student or even a professor would slap on the back. In conversation and in public addresses he spoke with an authority and directness that was almost shocking. His brashness sometimes threatened to bring trouble for the college, as when he campaigned against the tariff in the 1888 election, a distinctly unpopular stand in Maine. He struck some people as opinionated, closed-minded, preoccupied and aloof. Yet others thought of him as open in private conversation and witty even in his sharpness; early in life his friends called him "the wily Hyde" for his wry sense of humor. In

---

[8]Ralph Nading Hill, *The College on the Hill; A Dartmouth Chronicle* (Hanover, N.H.: Dartmouth College, 1964), p. 301; Thwing, *Guides*, pp. 411-12; Tucker, *My Generation*, pp. 396-400.

any case, his nervous habits were unquestioned; not only did he possess an unusually firm handshake, but in serious discussion he would chronically shift his eyes left and right in rapid motion. Such intensity focussed on personal efficiency, combined with his persistent need, in a friend's words, to "feel himself seized by a creative enterprise," were perhaps the forces that drove him to illness, possibly a mild nervous breakdown, in 1907. At age twenty he had an illness severe enough to permanently damage his eyes such that he could not read at night; so over most of his life, but especially after 1907 until his death in 1917 at age fifty-eight, Hyde lived with the spectre of ill health.[9]

King was a serious, even severe young man, whose classmates remembered him for insisting on standards "strict, exacting, even puritanical." Acutely religious from boyhood, and later the protege of the restrained rationalism of Oberlin president James H. Fairchild, King was a stubborn conservative on personal matters such as smoking and drinking. He campaigned for the Ohio Senate on the prohibition ticket in 1887 and 1889, and refused to give up the no-smoking rule on the Oberlin campus until World War I. He made the president's home a place of pleasant entertainment for students and faculty alike; but beneath the informality was always a certain stiffness of moral rigor. His biographer characterized him as a "conservative who holds fast to what is good in the past and [a] progressive who presses on to the high calling of the future." King would not have been displeased with such a description. His activism and intensity led him, like

---

[9]Charles T. Burnett, *Hyde of Bowdoin; A Biography of William DeWitt Hyde*, with an Introduction by George H. Palmer (Boston: Houghton Mifflin Co., 1931), pp. 29, 45-50, 110-15, 130-34, 150, 339; C. H. Patton and W. T. Field, *Eight O'Clock Chapel; A Study of New England College Life in the Eighties* (Boston: Houghton Mifflin Co., 1927), pp. 179-93.

the others, to poor health. In the early 1920s he lost a brother, a sister, and his eldest son, and that strain combined with his regular duties brought on a neuro-muscular disease that forced his retirement in 1927.[10]

All three presidents were born into old New England families, although King's had moved to the Midwest in mid-century. All three were raised in religious homes and benefited from the best education available at the time. Only Hyde did not graduate from the institution of which he later became president. The circumstances of their elections to their respective presidencies varied somewhat. Tucker had already had a distinguished career as a noted preacher at Madison Square Presbyterian Church in New York City and as Professor of Sacred Rhetoric at Andover Seminary from 1880 to 1893. He was an editor of the controversial *Andover Review* and was tried in church court along with his colleagues for advocating the "new theology," which they called Progressive Orthodoxy. A board member of Dartmouth, he was elected president in 1876, but declined out of a desire to remain in his parish. Again in 1892 the board elected him, but he preferred to stay at Andover and finish out the trial then awaiting appeal as well as his work with the settlement house movement then gaining public notice.

His colleagues on the trustees, however, with the timeless wisdom of such matters, made Tucker chairman of the search committee. Unable to find a better candidate and forced to acknowledge the resolution of the Andover case late in 1892, Tucker finally agreed to become president the next year. Seven of the eight previous heads of Dartmouth had been Congregational clergy; Tucker's election followed the line of succession, then,

---

[10]Donald M. Love, *Henry Churchill King of Oberlin* (New Haven: Yale University Press, 1956), pp. 1, 19, 52-53, 142, 243-44.

his progressivism being acceptable as long as he remained Trinitarian. His immediate predecessor, Samuel Bartlett, was a staunch advocate of the classics and adamant opponent of modern science, especially Darwinism. He had remained as president till age seventy-five, so Tucker's coming was hailed as a much needed breath of fresh air.[11]

Hyde had begun to build his reputation with a rousing oration on "The Modern Idolatry of Culture" at his Harvard undergraduate commencement in 1879. Continuing as an outstanding student at Andover, where he had classes under Tucker, he went on into the ministry, but found it unsatisfactory, his time frittered away in endless meetings and activities. While a seminarian he had written a letter to Tucker pleading for Newman Smyth to be hired as a replacement for the retiring Edwards A. Park in theology. Smyth was not hired, but a few years later he returned the favor as a board member and alumnus of Bowdoin by submitting Hyde's name for president and Stone Professor of Intellectual and Moral Philosophy. The position was offered Hyde in 1885, after he had only three years of professional experience in the ministry. But his predecessor, Joshua Lawrence Chamberlain, a Civil war general and former governor of Maine, had not been especially popular or satisfactory. He had tried to institute military drill, much to the dismay and vocal protest of the students, had supported an abortive and costly attempt to start a separate scientific department at the college, and had never happily filled the philosophy chair. Bowdoin was at low ebb, and

---

[11]Tucker, *My Generation*, pp. 63-77, 86-87, 213, 222-37; Robert F. Leavens and Arthur H. Lord, *Dr. Tucker's Dartmouth* (Hanover, N.H.: Dartmouth Publications, 1965), pp. 11, 14.

the trustees hoped that a youthful and vigorous administrator could reverse the trend.[12]

King had been student, tutor, instructor, and then professor at Oberlin, teaching first in mathematics and then gravitating into philosophy and theology. Thus he was a familiar personality on a campus that changed presidents three times between 1891 and 1903. He was considered to lack seniority and experience for the position when William G. Ballantine was elected from the faculty to replace Fairchild in 1891. He was thought too parochial when John Henry Barrows, prominent Chicago clergyman and organizer of the World Parliament of Religions, was brought in to lend prestige and influence to the college in 1898. Finally, after serving as dean of the faculty for a year, King moved more or less naturally into the presidency in 1903 and gave it the stability it had lacked. Following the collegiate tradition, many other institutions were represented at his inauguration, and the guest address was delivered by William Jewett Tucker.[13]

The use of full triadic names was customary in higher education at that time, and in part indicated the personage with which chief administrators and often major professors were endowed. Behind each of the presidents was a wife to whom he was devoted, perhaps Tucker especially, having lost his first wife and later remarrying. The roles of these women were largely

---

[12]Burnett, *Hyde*, pp. 72-99; Louis C. Hatch, *The History of Bowdoin College* (Portland, Me.: Loring, Short & Harmon, 1927), pp. 129-80.

[13]John Barnard, *From Evangelicalism to Progressivism at Oberlin College, 1866-1917* (n.p.: Ohio State University Press, 1969), pp. 70, 78-79; Love, *King*, pp. 64, 87-88, 91-111; *Inauguration of President Henry Churchill King of Oberlin College* (Oberlin, Ohio: Oberlin College, 1903).

hidden to biographers and historians, however; one can only surmise that they were supporters of their husbands' ambitions and gracious hostesses in the presidential homes.[14]

The sovereignty of the presidential personage on campus took the form not of modern administrative remoteness, but of personal involvement and initiative in all the affairs of the college. Tucker did not even have a secretary until 1900; Ernest Martin Hopkins, later a Dartmouth president himself, recalled receiving a handwritten note of admission from Tucker in 1896. He commanded respect among the students partly because of such personal touches, partly because of his chapel talks in which he tried to shape the "mind of the college," partly because he made an effort to enter into the lives and interests of his students.[15]

Hyde had personal charge of the discipline on his campus, a task which he took with firm seriousness. He did not lack for a sense of humor in such matters; he asked one miscreant if he were not finding it difficult to study amid all the ruckus on Saturday nights, to which the boy cunningly replied that he went home almost every Saturday. Hyde rejoined him, "Don't you think there would be a little less noise if you went home *every* Saturday?" Nevertheless, Hyde's own moral rectitude often prevented him from displaying "the art or the inclination to relieve the other's embarrassment," especially in a disciplinary interview.[16]

King was a step removed from immediate administration of the various Oberlin departments by a structure of deanships. He was even

---

[14]Love, *King*, p. 32; Tucker, *My Generation*, pp. 229-30; Burnett, *Hyde*, pp. 86-99.

[15]Leavens and Lord, *Dr. Tucker's Dartmouth*, p. 7; Tucker, *My Generation*, p. 339.

[16]Burnett, *Hyde*, pp. 110, 151-60.

further removed from the kind of pastoral presidency enjoyed by his mentor Fairchild, who was remembered for milking his own cow. In fact, if he was in some ways parochial in his life-long attachment to Oberlin, King was exemplary among the three presidents for his wide and varying educational and civic activities. In the late 1880s he not only ran for the Ohio legislature, but traveled throughout the northern part of the state working for cooperation between secondary schools and colleges on admissions standards and requirements. In 1892 he was elected by the National Education Association to its Committee of Ten under Eliot. He served on the Board of the Carnegie Foundation for the Advancement of Teaching from 1906 to 1927, and was president of the Religious Education Association in 1908 and the Association of American Colleges in 1916-17. He traveled through the Orient for the American Board of Commissioners for Foreign Missions in 1909-10, and was active in the Federal Council of Churches and the Religious Work Division of the Y.M.C.A., under which he worked in Paris in 1918-19. President Wilson appointed him as one of two Americans on the Inter-Allied Commission to Negotiate Peace in the Middle East in 1919, which issued a report recommending denial of a Jewish commonwealth in Palestine. As committed as he was, King finally turned down yet another request to serve on a committee, noting that "the number of organizations is increasing beyond all reason . . . I am afraid the only one I should now feel like joining would be one that would be devoted to diminishing the number." In any case, King's reputation brought him wide publication, and he was bestowed with honorary degrees from Western Reserve, Yale, Harvard, and Chicago.

He also turned down offers for the presidencies of Chicago Theological Seminary and Iowa College.[17]

Tucker was in great demand as a speaker and more especially as a preacher. He gave a much-noted Phi Beta Kappa address at Harvard in 1892 called "The New Movement in Humanity," and following his retirement collected a number of addresses on various civic issues. His writing was ponderous and abstract; one group of essays he titled *The New Reservation of Time*, by which he meant the trend toward early retirement that gave him and others like him more leisure time in their old age.[18]

Hyde was anything but ponderous, being rather too simple and direct for some tastes. George Herbert Palmer remembered him as characterized by a "great simplicity . . . which dullards might mistake for ordinariness, but which were really marks of a peculiar originality." His sharp wit, inimitable metaphors, and general candor made him a popular speaker; his address at the 1903 N.E.A. convention was thronged, applauded, almost cheered. A Portland, Oregon, newspaper thought him unsurpassed "in strength of thinking, enticement of style, and especially in moral effectiveness . . . by any man that writes English today, and by few of the great authors of any age." Such encomiums were not isolated, for Hyde was granted an honorary S.T.D. at Harvard's 250th commencement in 1886 (at age twenty-seven) and was invited to consider many college presidencies, including Lake Forest, Oberlin,

---

[17]Love, *King*, pp. 58-61, 116, 133-34, 148, 215-23; Barnard, *From Evangelicalism*, p. 5.

[18](Boston: Houghton Mifflin Co., 1916), p. viii; includes a reprint of "The New Movement in Humanity," pp. 195-213.

and the universities of Illinois, Ohio, and California. He never left Bowdoin, however.[19]

The writings of the three presidents reflected the wide-ranging interests concomitant to their positions. All three published first in theology, during the early years of their presidencies or immediately prior thereto. Tucker published no systematic theology, but contributed articles to the *Andover Review*. Hyde brought out several works attempting the reconstruction of theology in modern terms: *Outlines of Social Theology* (1895), *Practical Idealism* (1897), *God's Education of Man* (1899), and *Jesus' Way* (1902). King similarly published his theological works in 1901 and 1902, *Reconstruction in Theology* and *Theology and the Social Consciousness*, respectively.

The further they moved into their presidential roles, though, the more the authors turned toward ethical concerns. Tucker's weekly Sunday might chapel talks were the guide and inspiration for a whole generation of Dartmouth graduates, and were collected in a 1910 volume entitled *Personal Power*. Hyde attempted a summary of moral philosophy in his book *From Epicurus to Christ* (1904), and continued in a popular vein with such publications as *The Quest of the Best* (1913) and *The Best Man I Know* (1917). Meanwhile, King issued his volume on *Rational Living* (1905), followed by *Ethics of Jesus* (1910), *Religion as Life* (1913), and several other books.

The three wrote extensively for periodicals; in fact, Tucker's only continuous full-length manuscript was his autobiography, *My Generation* (1919). He contributed articles to the *Atlantic Monthly* and other magazines,

---

[19]Palmer, Introduction to Burnett, *Hyde*, p. xvi; also pp. 127, 137, 201.

and his lectures at Yale and elsewhere were also published. Hyde was a popular writer for the *Outlook, Independent,* and *Atlantic Monthly,* and gave his thoughts not only on education and religion, but on politics and economics. He even published a few poems. King also wrote many articles and had most of his major lectures imprinted as well.

A compliment once paid to Tucker would undoubtedly have stirred the hearts of all three presidents. Following Macaulay's comment on Sir William Temple, Tucker's friend described him as "a man of the world among men of letters, and a man of letters among men of the world." The ability of these men to participate in many spheres, to be at ease with different professions, and to synthesize into a sensible whole the learnings and lessons they perceived in the changing society around them, was their pride and their distinction. In their breadth and expansiveness of outlook they conveyed a singular vitality. A friend recalled of Hyde that "he did not so much hold beliefs, as live a faith. Some few thought his broadness had no edges." Yet as generalists in an age of specialization, synthesizers of a world breaking into pluralism, the presidents were uniquely able to become renowned spokesmen for the ideals of a progressive society and the colleges which would prepare its leadership.[20]

II. The Synthesis Preserved

If the presidents were part of the liberal, progressive movement attempting to adapt Christian faith and morals to the modern age, they were at the same time fulfilling a clearly conservative function. Much as they touted their "reconstructions," they were never wanting to break fully with the

---

[20]Tucker, *My Generation,* p. 364; Burnett, *Hyde,* p. 333.

past. They used terms such as "progressive orthodoxy" and the "new Puritanism" to indicate their grip on a middle ground anchored in the past but looking toward the future. What they wished to conserve was a rational synthesis of knowledge, science, ethics, and faith, the same ideal that appealed to the educators of the ante-bellum era.

Common Sense Realism, derived from the Scottish philosophers such as Thomas Reid, James Beattie, and Dugald Stewart, provided the early nineteenth century with a comprehensive world-view. Analyzing human consciousness to find the intuitive principles of judgment common to every human being, the Realists affirmed the reliability of knowledge and the real existence of God, world, and self. They welcomed science based on "Baconian" empiricism, for investigation of the world would only confirm its rational orderliness. They promoted morality grounded in self-evident propositions of duty. They found the Scriptures reliable for spiritual truth and harmonious with human moral sense. They advocated a political economy in which the individual pursuit of self-interest would naturally contribute to the good of society. In short, they wove a whole fabric of suppositions from the thread of humanity's rational apprehension of the natural and moral worlds.

Many of the older assumptions were stretched to the breaking point by the intellectual changes of the nineteenth century. The geological age and origin of the earth underwent radical reinvestigation. The evolutionary theories of Charles Darwin forced a reconceptualization of nature, including the human species. Historical criticism led to a reevaluation of the Bible and its cultural origins. The advance of experimental science encouraged a materialist viewpoint in philosophy. Thus it is little wonder that in his reminiscences Tucker emphasized the "intellectual detachment" of his generation from the past, and like many of his colleagues, quoted A. J. Balfour's recognition of the whole new "mental framework" within which scholars were operating by the turn of the century.[21]

Yet many lines of continuity emerged in the new generation's efforts to develop a rational synthesis of a dynamically expanding world. Just as the older Realists built a scientific theology on rational deductions from points of intuitive certainty, so the new liberals appealed for a theology based on the order and coherence of nature, taking account of current scientific research on everything from evolutionary laws to the principles of psychology. Just as the older Realists founded morality on the universality of human reason and conscience, and put forward a science of ethical duties based on rational relations, so the liberals found society to be evolving toward the good of all through an orderliness grounded in the rational moral activism of virtuous individuals. Just as the older Realists promoted the spread of Christian civilization in the fledgling American democracy, so the liberals encouraged the teaching of Christian democratic values from the immigrant ghetto to the emerging nations of China and Japan. Just as the older Realists formed character through the mental discipline and moral instruction of the college, so the liberals viewed the college years as a prime opportunity to inculcate the practical idealism necessary for progress in modern society.

One of the major problematics of intellectual life in the nineteenth century, following Kant, was the division of the natural and spiritual worlds. With every advance of science and new critique of religious orthodoxy, the material world of nature seemed ever more the only sure reality. Kant

---

[21]Tucker, *My Generation*, pp. 2-4.

himself denied the possibility of certain knowledge in what he called the noumenal or spiritual realm. But while the liberal synthesizers took Kant's dualism for granted, they were never content with his kind of agnosticism. They strove rather to comprehend both worlds by insisting that moral as well as physical laws could be established by rational persons, and by asserting that the individual, seemingly split body and soul by this dualism, could be unified as a natural and moral being. They took as their motto Matthew Arnold's celebrated aphorism concerning Sophocles, that he saw life steadily and saw it whole.

CHAPTER TWO

THE SCOTTISH SYNTHESIS AND THE COLLEGE IDEAL

When Henry Churchill King addressed the Centennial of Allegheny College in 1916 on the subject, "The Importance of the Christian College in the Making of America," he was speaking for a tradition in American higher education that went back to the earliest colonial days.[1] From the founding of Harvard in 1636 through the chartering of hundreds of other institutions in the eighteenth and nineteenth centuries, the college had come to stand for the highest ideals of liberal arts education, moral and religious training, and preparation for responsible citizenship in a democratic society. While it might have been a horrifying leap from such lofty ideals to the reality of most small colleges, the urge to reproduce the collegiate model spread with the expanding nation and became a significant factor in the development of American culture.

At the heart of the college ethos lay several unified convictions: that the world was rationally ordered, that it could be comprehended by educated minds, that it presented the conscientious individual with equally rational

---

[1]In Herbert Welch, Henry Churchill King, Thomas Nicholson, *The Christian College* (New York: The Methodist Book Concern, 1916), pp. 28-48.

moral duties based on clearly defined relations, and that such a sensible
world had a sentient Creator. On the basis of this conception all human
explorations of the natural and moral worlds could be assimilated, for all
would reveal a divine order: science would manifest a rational Creator;
mental philosophy would demonstrate the natural order of human faculties;
moral philosophy would show the universality of principles of right evident
to the conscience. Articulated most compellingly by the Scottish philosophers, a rational synthesis of knowledge and morality under the providential
guidance of a benevolent God became the paramount ideal of American
educators in ante-bellum colleges. They taught from the Scottish works and
penned many books of their own in an effort to educate their students and
the public in a philosophy that would make nature comprehensible, moral
duty apparent, and worshipful respect for God imperative. Their convictions
were profound enough to synthesize the new learning of their own day, and
to lay the groundwork for future generations to accommodate discoveries that
would shake but not dismantle the foundations of a rational world.

I. The College Setting

The prototype of the American "college" was the English institution of
the same name, but without its context. The founders of Harvard, for
example, did their best to reconstruct in 1636 a typical college of the
Cambridge University from which they had come, the deficiency being that
there were no other colleges with which to associate it and provide a broader
foundation.[2] The best they could do was take the name of the town. But

---

[2]Samuel Eliot Morison, *The Founding of Harvard College* (Cambridge: Harvard University Press, 1935).

Harvard was a seasoned and established institution marking its bicentennial by the time of the boom years in college foundation before the Civil War. All across the frontier, in the South, the plains, the (old) Northwest, educators shaped by the liberal arts ideal of the independent college were trying to introduce it as a measure of Christian civilization to their fledgling communities.

Historians have adduced many reasons for the founding of colleges. Donald Tewksbury's standard work on the subject presented the collegiate movement as a democratic force in which higher learning would not be confined to central elite institutions (as in England) but would be made accessible to anyone. He thought the colleges missionary in aspect, "the agent of an advancing civilization and the product of the moving frontier." Tewksbury joined most other historians in proposing that the training of an educated ministry was the immediate motive of their founders.[3] The vast majority of the new colleges being under denominational sponsorship, virtually all listed this as a primary purpose. Yet in general only 20 to 30 percent of a college's graduates went into the ministry; as a case in point, up to 1850 only about 25 percent of Dartmouth, Harvard and Yale graduates combined had become ministers.[4]

A number of other motivations were at work, then. New towns wanted colleges to build civic pride and prestige, and would offer property and

---

[3] *The Founding of American Colleges and Universities Before the Civil War* (New York: Teachers College, Columbia University, 1932), pp. 3-7, 22, 78.

[4] Schmidt, *Old Time*, p. 20.

subscriptions to help them get started.[5] Denominations wanted colleges to complete an educational system, so that young people could be brought up and educated entirely within their sect.[6] Idealistic graduates of New England colleges saw a responsibility to carry far and wide the intellectual and moral training necessary to the well-being and refinement of the rough-edged American culture. The Society for the Promotion of Collegiate and Theological Education of the West was formed in 1843 under the leadership of Theron Baldwin to urge broader support of this responsibility from the well-established East, for the institution founded by the "Yale Band" -- Illinois College -- and others.[7]

Usually, however, high motivations could not make up for meager support. When denominations could not raise their promised donations, when towns were unable to fulfill their subscriptions, when trustees failed to pay the faculty or provide them with facilities, the colleges floundered and often died. Tewksbury estimated that up to 1928, about 81 percent of all the colleges ever chartered in the United States had failed.[8]

Furthermore, the burgeoning of the college movement made for a chaos of standards and terminology. Charles Forster Smith wrote of a boy who attended a "university" in Illinois, then entered Exeter to prepare for Harvard. He also quoted a girl as saying of her Texas school, "It was a

---

[5]Merle Curti and Roderick Nash, *Philanthropy in the Shaping of American Higher Education* (New Brunswick, N.J.: Rutgers University Press, 1965), p. 45.

[6]Albea Godbold, *The Church College of the Old South* (Durham, N.C.: Duke University Press, 1944), pp. 61-63.

[7]Curti and Nash, *Philanthropy*, p. 55.

[8]*Founding*, p. 28.

college before it burned down, for it was *three stories high.*"[9] Tales, perhaps apocryphal, abounded of colleges chartered with one man as president and faculty, or with two men, one professor and one president alternately, so as to bestow honorary degrees each upon the other.

Amid the chaos, however, there was a definite backbone of collegiate tradition grounded in the inherited liberal arts curriculum. This heritage derived from medieval learning, which, following the classical compendium of knowledge devised by Martianus Capella in the fifth century, was organized around the seven Liberal Arts: the Trivium of Grammar, Rhetoric, and Logic, and the Quadrivium of Music, Arithmetic, Geometry, and Astronomy. To that classical format was added the three philosophies, natural, moral and mental, with the rediscovery of Aristotle in the twelfth century. A third element came into the curricular mix in the Renaissance with the advent of *belles lettres* (or *bonae litteae*), the study of history, literature, and aesthetics in the writings of Greek and Latin authors.[10] All three of these groupings, of course, required and assumed mastery of the classical languages.

The medieval heritage persisted in American colleges well into the nineteenth century, having been translated as directly as possible from the English universities. Whether one attended Dartmouth, Bowdoin, Brown or Harvard, in the 1830s one studied variously Livy, Homer, Virgil, or Cicero, Algebra or Arithmetic in one's freshman year, Geometry or Trigonometry, Rhetoric and Grammar, and advanced Greek and Latin one's sophomore year, and in the junior and senior years, Natural, Moral, and Mental

---

[9]"Southern Colleges and Schools," *Atlantic Monthly* 54 (October 1884):546.

[10]Morison, *Founding*, pp. 8, 27, 51-52.

Philosophy, Astronomy, Political Economy, and perhaps even a contemporary language such as French.[11] A well-stocked college would also have a "scientific cabinet" with a collection of rocks to illustrate selected types of geologic formations, or even some apparatus to demonstrate elementary laws of Newtonian physics.

In addition, however, as a child of its Puritan forebears the American college trained all its students in Natural Theology and confirmed their faith with courses in the Evidences of Christianity.[12] While generally avowing their non-sectarian breadth,[13] the colleges assumed the role of building up the piety of their charges not only by classroom teaching but often by campus revivals. Private colleges were fond of contrasting themselves with the "nurser[ies] of crime and vice" that were the state universities, which were to have no formal religious ties. But even the state schools generally feared to hire an "infidel" professor, and even under civil authority people "were still unwilling to divorce education from religion." State institutions often had clergy presidents, and denominational leaders would compete to get on their boards of trustees.[14]

The three Philosophies, Natural Theology, and Evidences became, in fact, the centerpiece of college curriculum everywhere. Here were used, not

[11]American Education Society, *Quarterly Register and Journal* 1 (Andover, Mass.: Flagg and Gould, 1829):229-232.

[12]Ibid.; see also Louis F. Snow, *The College Curriculum in the United States*, Columbia University Contributions to Education, Teachers College Series, No. 10 (New York: Teachers College, Columbia University, 1907), p. 122.

[13]See e.g., Sherman B. Barnes, "Learning and Piety in Ohio Colleges, 1865-1900," *The Ohio Historical Quarterly* 69 (October 1960):327.

[14]Godbold, *Church College*, pp. 150-55, 178.

classical authors, but writers of the moderate Christian Enlightenment, who could make Christianity seem perfectly reasonable, critically irrefutable, and morally imperative. The student, stirred to personal faith, moral righteousness, and a sense of mission by an occasional (or in some colleges by a regular) revival, would hear in these courses the assurance of a rational universe in which citizens with trained mental and moral faculties could find material comfort through dutiful labor in an orderly democratic society, and spiritual comfort through the promise of rewards for goodness in the life to come. In short, "all knowledge, including knowledge of the cosmos, of man, and of society," was drawn "into a consistent and intelligible whole" governed by God and comprehended by the individual.[15] The capstone of this curricular system was the senior year course in Moral Philosophy taught by the college president, in which a climactic effort was made, by mental discipline and exhortation, to build lasting character in students about to enter upon their social responsibilities. The teaching of these courses spawned many textbooks by American college presidents, but the authors never departed far from the rational synthesis of their English, but particularly their Scottish, mentors.[16]

II. The Literature of Rational Synthesis

Up until at least the 1870s, the Scottish Common Sense philosophers, along with certain compatible British authors such as William Paley and Joseph Butler, held sway in American intellectual life, and particularly in the

---

[15]Persons, *American Minds*, p. 189.

[16]D. H. Meyer, *Instructed Conscience*, is the standard study of this genre; see also Schmidt, *Old Time*.

colleges.[17] Such works as Thomas Reid's *Inquiry Into the Human Mind on the Principles of Common Sense*, Lord Kames's *Elements of Criticism*, Dugald Stewart's *Philosophy of Mind*, Butler's *Analogy of Religion*, and the *Evidences of Christianity* of both Paley and James Beattie, appeared often in library and booksellers' catalogues.[18] They were also basic to liberal arts college curriculum. Harvard seniors in 1825 read Stewart, Paley, Butler, and the Edinburgh scholar Thomas Brown. Other schools added Paley's *Moral and Political Philosophy*, Reid, and Kames to the list.[19] Taken together, these books presented a consistent world-view providing the grounds of knowledge, the laws of morality, and the truths of religion. They were "enlightened, moderate, practical, and easy to teach," if not particularly engaging or facile to read.[20] They made skepticism seem foolish, moral turpitude abhorrent. They appealed to the intellectual piety of most educated Americans.

The teaching of Scottish and English authors spawned many works by American educators. Their titles alone indicated the genre: Williams College president Mark Hopkins published his lectures on the *Evidences of Christianity*; Princeton's Scottish-born head, James McCosh, brought out *The Method of Divine Government Physical and Moral*; Thomas C. Upham of Bowdoin wrote two volumes of *Elements of Mental Philosophy*; and Francis Wayland of Brown published the exemplary *Elements of Moral Science*. The latter sold over 100,000 copies, was translated into several languages, and was

---

[17]May, *Enlightenment*, p. 348; Bozeman, *Protestants*, pp. xii, 21.

[18]David Lundberg and Henry F. May, "The Enlightened Reader in America," *American Quarterly* 28 (Summer 1976):262-93.

[19]Snow, *Curriculum*, p. 122.

[20]May, *Enlightenment*, p. 346.

a standard text in nineteenth century colleges, though many other volumes were available, from the *Science of Moral Philosophy* by Asa Mahan, first president of Oberlin, to the *Elements of Moral Science, Theoretical and Practical* by Noah Porter of Yale.

Wayland's education and career may also be taken as exemplary of American presidential authors. He took his college work at Union College in New York, where Eliphalet Nott held forth as president for over fifty years. Nott taught a popular course known among the students as "Kames," his own effort to shape the opinions and character of the seniors based loosely on the Common Sense aesthetics and morals of Lord Kames's *Elements of Criticism* (1763). Wayland took the course, read in Kames and Stewart, and became a protégé of his teacher. Nott was instrumental in his eventual elevation to the presidency of Brown University in 1826, where he expounded in his own senior moral philosophy class for almost thirty years.[21]

In that setting, Wayland, like all the presidents of his era, strove to impress on his students the comprehensiveness and certainty of a rational synthesis of knowledge, and its practical fruit in moral character. His lectures, which provided the basis for his *Elements* (1835), were ever popular. One of his many students was James B. Angell, later president of the University of Michigan, who wrote that, "to nearly every student, the most important event of his college life in those days was contact with the vigorous and suggestive mind of Dr. Wayland, in the senior classroom, and especially during the study of moral philosophy." Another alumnus remembered that in daily student conversation "the president was the prolific theme upon

[21]Joseph L. Blau, Introduction to Wayland, *Elements*, pp. xix, xxxvii, xl-xli.

which all dwelt." His lectures "seemed to us more wonderful than anything we had ever heard. They carried all the conviction of a demonstration. To have believed otherwise would have seemed absurd." Wayland must have been much at home in his presidential role, for, as this student recollected, "the recitation-room was his empire, and he reigned with imperial dignity."[22]

III. The Grounds of Knowledge

The rational synthesis exhibited throughout the literature and teaching of American college presidents was fundamentally both theological and moral in force and intent. A rational theology of divine order was complemented by a science of moral duty and obligation; with these foundations in place, all other human endeavor followed logically. The initial problem, though, resolved so appealingly by the Scots, was the epistemological question of the grounds of knowledge itself.

The Scottish philosophy took its original thrust from Thomas Reid's effort to harpoon the philosophical skepticism of David Hume. The latter's *Treatise of Human Nature* (1739) had carried John Locke's theory of ideas and George Berkeley's idealism to their logical extreme. That is, Hume argued that if the human mind began as a blank sheet of paper, and if knowledge came solely from sense experience mediated to the mind through "ideas" of things, as Locke suggested; and that if, therefore, all ideas of the reality of the world existed only in the consciousness of thinking beings, as

---

[22]Angell is quoted in Schmidt, *Old Time*, p. 139. The alumnus quoted was Silas Bailey, whose reminiscences were reported in Francis Wayland [Jr.] and H. L. Wayland, *A Memoir of the Life and Labors of Francis Wayland, D.D., LL.D.*, 2 vols. (New York: Sheldon & Co., 1867), 1:246-49.

Berkeley concluded; it followed that philosophy could achieve no proof of the existence of anything outside the mind.

In his *Inquiry* of 1764, Reid turned the full spray of sarcasm onto Hume's skepticism, comparing him to the Greek Pyrrho, who was said to be oblivious of attacking dogs or approaching precipices because of his distrust of his senses, but whose friends were fortunately not so skeptical and preserved him to his ninetieth year. Philosophy had lost its way, Reid said; in trying to prove the obvious it had wandered into a "coal-pit." Now it needed to return to be judged and redeemed by Common Sense.[23]

Reid proceeded by the analysis of consciousness; he thought it apparent that "by attentive reflection, a man may have a clear and certain knowledge of the operations of his own mind." Surely no one could seriously doubt the existence of his own consciousness, or demand proof of the existence of a subject being conscious of itself. How a man knew he existed could no more be established by logic than how he knew he was not in a delirium, Reid declared; and if he did not know, he had better seek a cure. For the existence of things, like the existence of the self, was a belief that could not be defined, being a simple and original act of mind.[24] The theory of ideas had been wrong, Reid argued, in making sensation the only source of knowledge; sensation was only a feeling which led at once to a perception of a real object and its qualities.[25] All sense experience was accompanied by

---

[23]Keith Lehrer and Ronald E. Beanblossom, eds., *Thomas Reid's Inquiry and Essays*, The Library of Liberal Arts (Indianapolis: Bobbs-Merrill Co., 1975), pp. 9, 11.

[24]Ibid., pp. 3-5, 18, 152-53.

[25]Ibid., pp. 48-49. Reid illustrated the distinction of sensation and perception by contrasting the hardness of a table (sensation) with its qualities (perception).

judgment or belief: a pain in one's toe was not only simply felt, but met by immediate judgments as to its magnitude and cause. Thus the existence of a thing was never even in question; and its qualities were determined by "original and natural judgments" that were "a part of that furniture which Nature hath given to the human understanding." No one's mind was a blank sheet of passivity but rather all were constituted with principles of judgment by which they actively assimilated experience.[26]

Hume had shown that if knowledge consisted solely of atoms of sense experience, such elementary categories as space, time, motion, or causation, even indeed the assumption of the continuity or identity of the conscious self, could not be ratified by philosophy. Causation could not be seen, nor could one moment be certainly connected with the next. By this reasoning, Reid supposed, one could no longer assume even that the *Treatise of Human Nature* had an author; the book was "only a set of ideas which came together and arranged themselves by certain associations and attractions." Such logic was not only absurd, he thought, but detrimental to science and learning. To the contrary, Reid asserted in his later essays that the existence of objects with qualities, the existence of the self, the categories of judgment such as causation and motion, were all self-evident first principles of philosophy confirmed by the common sense of mankind.[27]

His method of inductive analysis of consciousness once established, Reid moved on to consider the grounds of moral judgment. He was not particularly engaged by the old dispute between rationalists and sentimentalists, for in any case he was going to blend their views by arguing that moral

---

[26]Ibid., p. 118.

[27]Ibid., pp. 21, 266-84.

reasoning was grounded in a moral sense that perceived the moral qualities of things in their real relations. Nor was he interested in quibbling over the term "moral sense," derived from Shaftesbury and Hutcheson, which some had thought too subjective. Whether called moral sense or conscience, it was a faculty of mind, Reid asserted, analogous to the external senses. Just as by the latter one made original judgments about the qualities of bodies, so

> by our moral faculty, we have both the original conceptions of right and wrong in conduct, of merit and demerit, and the original judgments that this conduct is right, that is wrong: that this character has worth, that demerit.[28]

Moral reasoning, like all other, was grounded on first principles, among them, that one knew oneself to be a free agent, that involuntary actions deserved neither blame nor approval, that knowledge of moral duty was to be sought, that one should act towards another as one would judge to be right in the other's actions toward oneself, and so on. Just because some people seemed to lack a conscience altogether was no basis for denying the universality of this faculty, any more than some people's blindness would logically refute the sense of sight. Moral judgments, too, were part of the simple, original furniture of the mind.

Thus did Reid gloss over the hard edges of previous arguments in both natural and moral philosophy, and synthesize into one viewpoint what he held Common Sense to confirm. He thought thereby to rescue the grounds of knowledge from the misguided speculations of the philosophers. Against idealists and skeptics he could show that the real existence of things and relations could be assumed a priori. Against moral relativists he could argue

---

[28]Ibid., pp. 320-321. For a concise discussion of the rationalist-sentimentalist debate, see Howe, *Unitarian*, pp. 45-47.

the universality of a sense of right and wrong, and a common duty to do the right. And against agnostics like Hume who denied that the existence of God could be established from the order or causality of the universe, or that all people had a thought of God, he could reassert the presupposition of a Prime Mover for motion, a First Cause for causality, an Author for moral law, and a conscious Deity known to all thinking beings.[29]

Perhaps because it arose as an effort to affirm the possibility of knowledge, Common Sense philosophy did not succeed in establishing its critical limits.   Once the method of inductively examining one's own consciousness to discover first principles was validated, philosophers and theologians found all sorts of universal maxims self-evident to any sensible person.   Reid's followers Stewart and Beattie were particularly adept at lumping together propositions ranging from "I exist" to "there is a God" to "the sun rose to-day" as all meeting immediate acquiescence in the mind.[30] The method had the stamp of science on it; it appeared to follow the strictures of Lord Bacon, the author of modern empirical method, and to confirm the rational order and lawfulness of the natural and moral universe.

IV. The Harmony of Reason and Revelation

American Protestant educators found in Common Sense Realism the foundation for a synthesis of all human knowledge.   By the method of consciousness they could establish the first principles of epistemology and the intuitive certainty of the existence of the self and the world.   The cornerstone

---

[29]Lehrer, *Reid's Inquiry*, pp. 351-60.

[30]James Beattie, *Essay on the Nature and Immutability of Truth, in Opposition to Sophistry and Skepticism* (1770), quoted in D. H. Meyer, *Instructed Conscience*, pp. 39-40.

of their system, though, was the further self-evident proposition that the order of both the mind and the natural world suggested, indeed required, an intelligent Creator who governed the natural and moral spheres by rational laws, and held all creation in harmony. The human striving to investigate nature, to live morally, and to worship a Higher Being made sense only in such a rational universe.

The authors of the many "natural theologies" issued in the ante-bellum period were intent on assuring their readers, in James McCosh's words, of "the pre-established harmony between the world within, and the world without" by describing the lawfulness by which both nature and human moral nature were governed. Their method both presupposed and proved the existence of a Divine Governor, for they wanted to argue both that belief in God was an intuitive certainty "within" and a demonstrable conclusion "without." McCosh took as his starting point for *The Method of Divine Government, Physical and Moral* (1850) the a priori assertion that belief in God was "universally entertained." He then went on, though, to propose "four natural sources from which the human mind derives its idea of the Divine Being." Two of the sources were internal: the very presence of "intuitive or logical laws" in the constitution of the human mind suggested an intelligent Creator, while the authoritative judgment of the conscience over other mental faculties evidenced a moral law and thus a law-giver. The other two sources were external: the design of nature and the special provision in nature for the needs of mankind illustrated the "wisdom, the power and goodness of God" and his providential care for humanity.[31]

---

[31](Edinburgh: Sutherland & Knox, 1850), pp. 1-9, 328.

Given the wide acceptance of the Baconian method of scientific observation, though, some authors thought it supremely important to discover in the world of nature a reasonable basis for theism. No one put the case for "nature" theology more compellingly or popularly than William Paley, whose *Natural Theology* (1802) was widely read in America. Paley developed a memorable analogy, arguing that just as, if one were to find a watch upon the ground and begin to examine it, one would logically conclude that it had a maker, so one could assume from the contrivance and design of the world a "contriver" with personality, intelligence, power and goodness. Such an assertion was certainly scientific, for it was demonstrable through detailed observation of plants, animals, stars, and human anatomy.[32]

If nature exhibited a God acting intelligently and with wise purpose, then the human activity of exploring nature was necessarily in harmony with divine providence, for every discovery made clearer the wonders of God. The ante-bellum professors believed in a "doxological science" that, rightly pursued, would only add to human confidence in God's lawful government. Any seeming conflict between science and religion arose only when science strayed from its humble task of describing "facts" to the assertion of unsustainable "hypotheses," an undisciplined method that Baconianism itself disallowed. New speculations and theories often surrounded sciences "in their infancy," argued Asa Mahan, "while the same sciences, when they have advanced towards maturity of development, have invariably presented themselves as the handmaids of Religion." Science and religion were not to "be reckoned as opposing citadels," McCosh insisted, for they had the same

---

[32]*Works* (Philadelphia: J. J. Woodward, 1831), pp. 387-90, 462-68.

foundation, with one "the outer and the other the inner court." All learning was united in "the concord of truth," for all was empirical and scientific.[33]

Nevertheless, Mahan was not alone in preferring a more intuitive approach to natural theology. Of course, he viewed his method as equally "scientific," for it was based on examination of the "Universal Intelligence" and the "direct and immediate testimony of Consciousness." In his *Natural Theology* (1867) he suggested that Paley's argument from design was only secondary; the primary principle of theism was an intuitive insistence that "there is *an ultimate reason* why the order and arrangement existing in the universe within and around us are what they are, and why the sequence of events occurs as it does, and not otherwise . . . we call this common and universally admitted reason or first cause, God." The thought of God itself necessarily implied the divine attributes of eternity, immutability, unity, and so on, without reference to nature. Thus natural theology could be substantiated by universal consciousness itself; the conviction of an ultimate cause was joined by the first principles of "Right and Wrong, Duty, Immortality, and Retribution" to provide irrefutable grounds for belief in a divine Creator and Governor.[34]

The theism of nature and the natural mind was not sufficient for most rational theologians, however, and they sought to complement and reinforce it with the absolute truths of Christian revelation. Through pervasive sinfulness, they argued, humanity had muddied its natural knowledge of God, had wandered from the supreme moral laws, and had lost sight of the means

---

[33]Bozeman, *Protestants*, pp. 78, 101-16; Mahan, *The Science of Natural Theology; or, God the Unconditioned Cause, and God the Infinite and Perfect, As Revealed in Creation* (Boston: Henry Hoyt, 1867), p. 227; McCosh, *Method*, p. 451.

[34]Mahan, *Natural Theology*, pp. v, 78-81, 111.

of salvation and immortality. Christianity offered an unmistakable revelation of the truths that nature had always taught: that God in the infinity and eternity of wisdom and goodness ruled the universe with justice, exacted obedience to the moral law, and rewarded those who sought to fulfill it. Thus revelation was both a reasonable and necessary effort on God's part to restore humanity to piety, virtue, and happiness.

The "evidences" for Christianity as an authentic and absolute revelation of God were described at length by English and American authors, and were taught, usually as a required course, in the colleges. Partly in answer to Enlightenment skepticism about the possibility of miracles, Christian apologists tended to focus on the "external," public evidences. They typically argued first that a revelation was necessary, then that a revelation by definition must be extraordinary. Mark Hopkins suggested in his *Evidences* (1846) that "miracles were necessary to give authority to revelation, to give a practical impression of the existence of a personal God, and to indicate the true position of his moral government," that is, that God as a reasoning, willing Being could certainly act beyond known natural law, especially in behalf of a higher moral cause, the salvation of humanity. In "the Protestant paradigm of the universe," in Hovenkamp's phrase, God was certainly supreme over the natural laws by which he governed, and if miracles seemed arbitrary or capricious, they had to be viewed in the higher context of the divine reason and will.[35]

One needed only to consider the rapid and universal acceptance of Christianity by all reasonable people to see that a miraculous revelation was

---

[35]Mark Hopkins, *Evidences of Christianity; Lectures before the Lowell Institute, Revised as a Textbook* (Boston: T. R. Marvin & Son, 1909 [orig. publ. 1863]), p. 61; Hovenkamp, *Science*, p. 91.

no stumbling block to the thinking person. Paley devoted most of his widely read *Evidences* (1794) to the proposition that the truth of Christianity was affirmed by many honest and reliable witnesses in ancient times, and that they could never have been such enthusiastic advocates of it had they not been convinced of the veracity of events attested by Scripture. The Bible was a marvel of consistency anyway, with Old Testament prophecies fulfilled so precisely by the revelation of Jesus Christ. Biblical criticism was investigating the background and origin of the various writings to be sure. But "scientific" criticism was no more of a threat to biblical faith than science in general, for it was to fasten strictly upon the "facts" of grammar, philology, and history, never wandering into speculation about what could or could not be historical, that is, have actually happened. In short, the public evidence for Christianity was indisputable.[36]

On the other hand, though, Mark Hopkins implied that the "internal" evidences for Christianity were less polemical and perhaps even more appealing to a reasonable person. For when one examined Christian revelation internally, probing its actual teachings, one found it completely analogous to the conclusions of natural theology, only clearer and more compelling. Christianity, like nature, taught the eternity and wisdom of God; Christian ethics, like the natural conscience, impressed on every rational being a sense of duty to eternal moral law; Christian teaching was adapted to touch the human mind and emotions, to meet human needs, to offer a means of human salvation. So consistent was Christianity with nature, in fact, that one might say it had always existed. But now the example of Christ,

[36]Paley, *Works*, pp. 274, 295, 326; Hovenkamp, *Science*, pp. 59-60; Holifield, *Gentlemen*, pp. 89-93; Bozeman, *Protestants*, pp. 138-43.

sinless, of perfect moral character and teaching, stood before humanity, in
Hopkins's words, "to show the true worth and dignity of man . . . as an
immortal being, in the image of God."[37]

To argue that Christianity was both reasonable and revelational was to
create a tenuous balance which the rational theologians were at pains to
preserve. The archetypal symmetry had been devised by Joseph Butler, an
Anglican bishop whose *Analogy of Religion, Natural and Revealed, to the
Constitution and Course of Nature* enjoyed remarkable popularity on
American campuses from its relatively early publication (1736) to the end of
the nineteenth century. Butler proposed the dual aspects of Christianity as,
first, a "republication of natural religion," but second, a revelation of the
further duties of humanity toward God, namely, baptism and worship of Jesus
Christ. Christian teaching he found completely analogous to nature; the
principle of resurrection and future life, for example, paralleled the tendency
according to a "general law of nature" for creatures to change into different
states or degrees of life, a worm into a fly or an egg into a bird, for instance.
Whether the claim for human immortality was truly an analogy, though, or
simply another instance of "a natural order or appointment, of the very same
kind with what we have already experienced" in other creatures, that is,
whether Christianity was analogous or identical with nature, Butler was too
circumspect to clarify.[38]

Under the overarching and unifying concept of divine government, of
course, such distinctions were not really crucial. The rational God who
created both nature and human nature would surely have made them

---

[37]*Evidences*, pp. 68-182, 216.

[38](New York: Ivison, Blakeman, Taylor, & Co., 1878), pp. 39-40, 141, 146.

consistent with each other, and in giving a revelation would only have been adding the light of teachings "still in keeping" with natural religion, in Hopkins's words, "as the revelations of the telescope are with those of the naked eye." Such ready analogies avoided the dark paths of speculative metaphysics; rational theologians indulged in no treatises on the ontological possibility of a divine being or on the dual natures of Christ. Rather, they began with the "intuitive convictions of the Universal Intelligence," in Mahan's phrase, and having assumed the first principles of theology, could proceed to make biblical Christianity the story of human moral transformation.[39]

Rational religion made nature itself seem orderly and comprehensible; but far more importantly, it made human activity in the world seem sensible and significant. Christianity revealed, even more than the natural conscience, that human beings were fundamentally moral, with freedom and responsibility for their actions, accountable to the divine moral government which dispensed reward or punishment. Even the revivalist preacher Charles G. Finney, Mahan's successor at Oberlin, began his *Lectures on Systematic Theology* (1846-47) with the claim that "theology is, to a great extent, the science of mind in its relations to moral law," and his book could as easily have been titled a moral philosophy.

As a consequence, Finney interpreted all Christian doctrine in terms of moral law and legal justice. Under the laws of divine moral government humanity was condemned through depravity and ignorance to eternal punishment, his argument ran. The means of salvation had been revealed through Christ's atonement, which was "a satisfaction of public justice" before

---

[39]Hopkins, *Evidences*, p. 354; Mahan, *Natural Theology*, p. v.

the divine assize, as he took the punishment for human violations of eternal moral law to which even God was beholden. Now those who repented and converted to faith in Christ could be saved by divine justification, which consisted in "a governmental decree of pardon or amnesty." They could then be regenerated, undergoing a "radical change of character," of "ultimate intention," of "attitude of the will." Finally, forgiven sinners were to seek "entire sanctification" in holiness of life, living in "full obedience to the moral law."[40]

Finney's "Oberlin perfectionism" was controversial, but his intent to make Christianity the religion of the morally upright was not. Francis Wayland, for example, a denominational leader and preacher of some note, was content to define the church as "a society" made up of "certain individuals," those who repented and received pardon for their sins through Christ's atonement, "united under a common law" of conscience and moral character. For Wayland, as for most ante-bellum rationalist educators, prayer and worship were duties under the more general heading of his real religion: moral science.[41]

V. The Science of Morality

If the divine government was unmistakably evident in the order and lawfulness of nature, it was also tellingly apparent in the moral consciousness of humanity. Moral philosophers in the ante-bellum Anglo-American

---

[40]Revised by the author, Revised and Edited by George Redford (London: William Tegg & Co., 1851), pp. 1, 331-32, 410, 547, 571, 592-93.

[41]Wayland, "The Church, a Society for the Conversion of the World," in *Sermons to the Churches* (New York: Sheldon, Blakeman, & Co., 1859), pp. 65-100.

tradition, drawing on the methods of Common Sense Realism, found the conscience an innate human faculty, the sense of moral duty universal. They concluded that moral law, intuitively apprehended and rationally ordered, could be defined and classified as clearly as the laws of nature. For God intended moral good and evil to be comprehensible, their consequences definite, to the end of the ultimate happiness of humanity.

Moral philosophy was scientific, then, meeting all the criteria of empirical observation grounded on first principles of knowledge. Paley set the pattern for this moral science in his *Moral and Political Philosophy* (1785), which enjoyed widespread collegiate popularity for a time. Defining moral philosophy as "that science which teaches men their duty and the reasons of it," he first explicated the basic terms of the field -- virtue, moral sense, happiness, obligation, rights, and laws -- and then proceeded to a full discussion of the practical duties incurred in ownership of property, contracts, charity, marriage, civil government, and religion.[42] American authors such as Wayland and Mahan reproduced this format, dividing their works into two main sections, theoretical and practical ethics, beginning with definitions and proceeding to applications.

Wayland defined moral philosophy as "the Science of Moral Law," and moral law in turn as "a form of expression denoting an order of sequence established between the moral quality of actions and their results." The consequences of actions were just as "invariable as an order of sequence in physics," he suggested, moral laws just as orderly and classifiable as laws of nature such as gravitation. Butler, from whose *Analogy* Wayland quoted extensively, had held a similar view, describing the world as operating by

---

[42]*Works*, p. 27.

"fixed laws" of action and result; the consequence of moral misbehavior paralleled the pain of touching fire, he had argued. Since vice always eventuated in "poverty and sickness, remorse and anguish, infamy and death," the rational person would always choose virtue.

Wayland was not any more preoccupied with the old rationalist-sentimentalist controversy than the Scots (or Butler) had been. He asserted both that right inhered in the relations of things as established by divine moral law, and that human beings were endowed with a conscience to perceive their duty within those relations. Right was both objective, external, inherent in the moral order of the universe, and subjective, internal, accurately perceived by the conscience; the outer and inner worlds were in harmony under the divine governor.[43]

Some moral philosophers were uncomfortable with Wayland's talk of sequences, however, for fear that doing right would become a "pre-moral," antecedent matter of weighing consequences, and thus a procedure of judging the good, rather than adhering to absolute right. Mahan insisted in his *Moral Philosophy* (1848) on an intuitive position in morals as in natural theology; he considered moral law or the concept of right and wrong a "simple" idea, spontaneous or "primitive," found immediately and necessarily in the fitness of things, and existing universally in all rational minds.

Mahan was even more disturbed by the efforts of his colleague Finney to define the end or sum of the moral law. Finney insisted that if moral intentions were to be right, the end of moral law must be firmly in sight; this he described as disinterested benevolence, "willing the highest good, or well-being of God, and of being in general, as an end, or for its own sake."

---

[43]Wayland, *Elements*, pp. 17-19, 37-42; Butler, *Analogy*, pp. 58, 62, 68.

Finney was as adamant as any "rightarian" that the moral law was absolute under God's governance; but he thought that the rightarian position gave poor grounds for seeking the right. Mahan and most of his contemporaries demanded that the grounds for moral obligation arise from the relations of things themselves, as established by God; Finney thought obligation must arise from obedience to an end resting ultimately in the will of God, namely, the well-being of the universe.[44]

American sensitivity to the grounds of moral obligation stemmed primarily from reaction to Paley's *Philosophy*, which became increasingly controversial in the early nineteenth century and eventually was erased from most college reading lists. Paley had proposed that the ground and end of ethics was human happiness, too utilitarian a proposition for those who identified happiness with fleeting pleasure or self-interest. To be sure, what he intended by "happiness" was the orderly exercise of the faculties toward virtuous ends defined by the will of God, who in divine benevolence wished "the happiness of his creatures," and would ultimately reward goodness with eternal happiness. But Paley appeared to open the way to human judgment of the utility of an action in promoting or diminishing the general happiness. Moreover, he made "violence" the ground of obligation, that is, fear of eternal punishment the chief discouragement of vice, hope of heavenly reward the motive to virtue. Of course, eighteenth century philosophers of all persuasions (except the insufferable Hume) had posed divine rewards and punishments in the afterlife as the final impetus to moral duty. But Paley seemed to introduce a bald expediency to moral action. His critics wanted

---

[44]Mahan, *Science of Moral Philosophy* (Oberlin: James M. Fitch, 1848), pp. 20-28; Finney, *Sytematic Theology*, pp. 124-28, 135.

to insist rather on the disinterested virtue of obeying for its own sake the absolute right intuitively apprehended by the conscience.[45]

Wayland was among the first to take Paley to task; in fact, he devised his own textbook in moral philosophy in part to replace Paley with an adequate alternative. Yet he could not entirely expunge the question of ultimate good from his theory. He tried to establish the grounds of obligation inherently and firmly in the relations of things themselves. But he acknowledged that if one looked even beyond that for grounds, one could see that all relations were established by the will of God, the Moral Governor, who in divine benevolence willed the happiness of all his creatures. The relations of things and their obligations of right were constituted to the end of human happiness, then, in a kind of divine utility. But God's will was beyond human ken; duties were to be fulfilled simply in obedience to moral law.[46]

Thus the tension of right and good persisted in American moral philosophy, the more rightarian position of the inherent fitness of things accompanying a belief that the universe was designed for human benefit and that the individual should seek to contribute to universal well-being. Perhaps the synthesis was best expressed by James McCosh, who was sure that reward for virtue and punishment for vice was built into "the ordinary and natural course of events," but who could see in mere rules no incentive for goodness. Both "righteousness and benevolence," he wrote, "meet and blend in every act

---

[45]Paley, *Works*, pp. 30-39; on the abandonment of Paley, see Wilson Smith, *Professors*, pp. 186-93, and Howe, *Unitarian*, p. 65.

[46]*Elements*, pp. 36, 62, 89-93.

that is morally right, as they meet in the character of every holy creature, and in the character of the holy Creator."[47]

All moral philosophers were agreed on the universality of conscience; human consciousness was endowed with an inherent and immediate sense of approval or disapproval, right or wrong. Thomas Upham argued typically in his *Mental Philosophy* (1841) that human moral nature was reflected in language itself, and in common feelings of remorse or duty even among children and savages. All writers did their best to establish these sensibilities as a separate mental faculty alongside intellect, emotion, and will, but with limited success.

Again in keeping with the Scottish synthesis, Wayland and his contemporaries gave to conscience an intermediary role. Wayland assigned it a threefold office: to discover moral qualities in the rational relations perceived by the reason; to impel one toward the right in governing the will; and to give pleasure in right actions, pain in wrong, guiding the feelings. Upham likewise viewed conscience as the seat of moral emotions of approval or disapproval based on the cognizance or perception of a situation by the reason, and found in conscience the feelings of obligation that would stir the will.[48]

While moral obligation was a distinct and universal feeling, then, the conscience as its locus of awareness was really inseparable from the other faculties. The educators were, of course, convinced that one's perceptions of the moral relations of things and the will to perform the right or good action

---

[47]*Method*, pp. 236, 319.

[48]Thomas C. Upham, *Elements of Mental Philosophy, Embracing the Two Departments of the Intellect and the Sensibilities*, 2 vols. (New York: Harper & Bros., 1840, 1841), 2:248-65, 297-98; Wayland, *Elements*, pp. 42-43, 63, 88-89.

could be educated, trained and disciplined; but these were primarily matters
of reason and will. Following the Greeks, the authors believed that the
practice of good habits built virtues or strengths, and that virtuous intentions,
continually exercised, built moral character. Thus they wanted to sharpen the
rational capacities of their charges, but above all they wanted to reinforce
their wills.[49]

No doctrine was more crucial to ante-bellum moral philosophy than the
freedom of the human will. Obligation to moral law made no sense without
the freedom to perform it; conversely, human freedom made no sense outside
the context of moral responsibility. The will was the seat of decision and
action; it bore the onus of human responsibility for obeying the moral law.
The trained will kept order in the self and built character in moral relations;
the dissolute will led to evil and degradation.

Yet only a free will was susceptible to discipline or to responsibility.
Upham showed that a sense of duty arose only with those objects one had
the power to effect, as feelings of approval or disapproval arose only in
relation to voluntary actions. Wayland put it even more strongly, that God
required of one no duty which God did not also give one the power to
perform. Moreover, the will was to be viewed as a faculty of intention; not
the outcome of will in action was to be judged right or wrong, but rather the
intention behind the action. The most one could be expected to do was to
rationally perform one's duty as one perceived it in obedience to moral law.
Judgment of actions would put too much emphasis on consequences, on
contribution to some good. Judgment of intentions kept the emphasis on the

---

[49]Butler, *Analogy*, pp. 98-99; Wayland, *Elements*, pp. 83-87, 238-43; Upham, *Mental Philosophy*, 2:271-74, 361-63.

rational perception of right relations, while leaving freedom for righteous persons to perform different actions even in similar situations.[50]

A seemingly rigid rationalist moral philosophy was in fact accommodated to human nature, then. The stress on intention and free will helped limit moral responsibility to what a common person could accomplish. Wayland even penned a little book entitled *The Limits of Human Responsibility* in which he suggested that one's duty to do the right was limited by one's own capacities and by the particular situation. Moral obligations limited each other as well; the duty of speaking the truth, for example, did not compel one to violate the duty of respecting others' rights by coercing them to one's own viewpoint. When moral obligations conflicted, he concluded, one should assess the relations of the parties, determine the greatest good, and if necessary follow the greater exigency.

If such prudential considerations seemed to reintroduce utilitarian grounds for morality, it was only because Wayland and his contemporaries never succeeded in expunging utility from either their writings or their thinking. While they may have wanted to teach their college charges an absolute moral duty that would cover all their relations in family, work, and society, they could surely not avoid discussion of the consequences of actions. The collegiate educators were preparing young professionals and merchants for life in a social contract community governed by majority rule and the spirit of compromise in behalf of the common good. Even absolutely righteous behavior had its limits in such a society. Wayland could endorse moral persuasion for political change, but he opposed the aggressive organizing that he saw in the burgeoning voluntary associations of his day.

---

[50]Upham, *Mental Philosophy*, 2:268-69, 303; Wayland, *Elements*, pp. 24-25.

He thought change must be encouraged gradually by those who saw the right. Nothing was to be taken in excess, whether liquor or politics or religion.[51]

That ante-bellum moral philosophers taught an ethic of the middle ground was most evident in their practical morality. The social assumptions of their day were apparent in their attempts to describe what the moral law required in real life situations. They argued that work was a virtue required of all able-bodied persons; they conveyed a distaste for credit, encouraging payment for goods in advance; they decried the giving of charity to those who could do for themselves; they were clear that the husband was "the head of the family," with the wife bearing the "duty of obedience." They spoke out in varying degrees against slavery, but by and large took the gradualist position that manumission of slaves was a moral obligation that rested in the intentions of individual slaveholders. While slavery was both unscriptural -- morally wrong -- and detrimental to society -- of ill effect -- it could only be ended by persuading slaveholders to let their slaves go free. Of course, they should not take such an action if it would create a threat of social or political chaos, a more exigent circumstance.[52]

When civil war finally did break out between slave and free states, the moral philosophers seemed taken by surprise. Like many of his colleagues, Wayland had been a pacifist, arguing in his *Elements* that the duty of benevolence made war unconscionable, even when a nation had clearly been wronged. By the time of the Civil War, however, he was arguing that a

---

[51]Wayland, *The Limitations of Human Responsibility* (Boston: Gould, Kendall, & Lincoln, 1838), pp. 22-43, 118, 188; D. H. Meyer, *Instructed Conscience*, p. 54.

[52]Wayland, *Elements*, pp. 188-98. In the 1865 Edition of his book, Wayland assumed a firmer (but by then commonly held in the North) stance against slavery; see *Elements*, pp. 379-96. See also Mahan, *Moral Philosophy*, pp. 379-80.

nation under attack had a moral obligation to defend itself, especially when a higher cause such as ending slavery was at stake. God required no less, and the North's cause was unquestionably a righteous and holy crusade. Thus did moral principle become moral ambivalence through the dynamics of a rational synthesis holding rightarian and utilitarian considerations in uneasy compromise.[53]

VI. The Persistence of the Old-Time Synthesis

Historians have essayed a number of explanations for the hegemony of Scottish Realism in American colleges and its influence in American culture. Some have been sociological: Woodbridge Riley thought that "the union of church and college" gave Realism an "institutional base" and a "cultural class" to promote it which other philosophies (idealism, materialism) lacked.[54] Some have been socio-economic: Wilson Smith thought that Realism appealed to the genteel middle class, assuring men of education and moral character "the chance to acquire property and the political strength that accompanied it."[55] Others have been theological: Sidney Mead wrote of a "scholastic orthodoxy" dominating Protestantism in a "general flight from 'reason' . . . and the concomitant triumph of pietism."[56] Still others have been cultural: Stow Persons suggested that "the colleges performed an important conservative function" by providing "moral discipline and an

---

[53]*Elements*, pp. 337, 408-12. See also my article, "Contending Values."

[54]*American Philosophy: The Early Schools* (New York: Russell & Russell, n.d.), pp. 478-79.

[55]*Professors*, p. 207.

[56]*The Lively Experiment; The Shaping of Christianity in America* (New York: Harper & Row, 1963), p. 127.

ordered conceptual pattern of experience for the educated class" of a society in which "traditional supports of social order and intellectual authority" were dissolving.[57]

All these were explicitly critical of Realism for being variously fearful of skepticism, "indifferent" to the "intellectual currents of modern Western civilization," and disinterested in advancement of the arts and sciences.[58] As Douglas Sloan argued, however, historians ought to have been more conscious of their perspective. Relative to its times, the Common Sense philosophy was rational, progressive, and at the forefront of intellectual discussion. It could equally be said to have held sway over American institutions for so long because of its sweeping synthesis of knowledge and its compelling reasonableness. It was not anti-scientific; it promoted no religious obscurantism; it lent stability and optimism to a culture just beginning to take shape in a geographically expanding society.[59]

Yet at the same time the Scottish unity was resistant to change and to outside influences. It excluded "idealism on the one hand" and "agnosticism on the other."[60] American Realists wanted no part of Kant, who they by and large found "obscure and scarcely intelligible," and whose critical limitations of knowledge, particularly in the realm of theology, they found

---

[57]*American Minds*, pp. 187-88.

[58]Mead, *Lively Experiment*, p. 127; Schneider, *History*, pp. 195-96.

[59]*The Scottish Enlightenment and the American College Ideal* (Teachers College, Columbia University: Teachers College Press, 1971), pp. 240ff.; May, *Enlightenment*, p. 346.

[60]James McCosh, *Realistic Philosophy* (London: 1887), 1:1-4, quoted in Schneider, *History*, p. 217.

deplorable.[61] But they could not long ignore the engaging debates over Kant and German Idealism any more than they could forever exclude the new Darwinian biology or budding laboratory science or changing economic theory or widening historical criticism.

Fortunately for its descendants, the old synthesis was built on certain methods and perspectives that could be adapted to new circumstances. Its advocates had made self-consciousness the ground of knowledge and so could welcome the development of psychology. They had believed in the perfectibility of humanity and so could reconstruct their optimism in evolutionary form. They had largely converted theology into ethics and so could choose to give less and less attention to abstract doctrines of Trinity, atonement, or sacraments, while continuing to believe in the rational laws of a divinely governed universe.[62] They had based ethics on the consensus of good and rational people everywhere, and so could strive to articulate a morality more adapted to changing social circumstances that everyone recognized. In general they had woven a whole fabric of assumptions to drape over the hard edges of philosophical conundrums, a fabric that would stretch but not tear for many years to come.

---

[61]Samuel Miller, *A Brief Retrospect of the 18th Century* (1803), quoted in Riley, *American Philosophy*, p. 513. Kant did not think much more highly of the Scottish Realists, who he said appealed to the "judgment of the crowd." *Prolegomena to any Future Metaphysics*, quoted in S. A. Grave, *The Scottish Philosophy of Common Sense* (Oxford: The Clarendon Press, 1960), p. 5.

[62]Alhstrom, "Scottish Philosophy." The triumph of ethics over dogma in Harvard Unitarianism is detailed in Howe, *Unitarian*. He concludes that "by the beginning of the twentieth century, most respectable American clergymen had little to say about the Trinity, atonement, or predestination" (p. 7). That this was a long-standing trend in New England Calvinism has been shown by Joseph Haroutunian, *Piety Versus Moralism; The Passing of the New England Theology* (New York: Henry Holt & Co., 1932).

Of course, it was not the older synthesizers but their late nineteenth and early twentieth century descendants who took up the task of unifying knowledge and undergirding moral character in a rapidly changing intellectual and social world. They did so within the stronghold of the liberal arts college, reforming it, too, to meet the demands of the day. Historians have claimed that the colleges "failed to respond adequately to these demands," and that the initiative passed to the universities.[63] But the college ideal of training moral character in a rationally unified world continued to thrive, thanks to the vigor of its new champions.

---

[63]Brubacher and Rudy, *Higher Education*, p. 143.

CHAPTER THREE

RECONSTRUCTING A THEOLOGICAL UNITY

The new intellectual forces of the late nineteenth century seemed to contemporary minds to be dismantling the old rational synthesis of philosophy, religion and ethics. Darwinian biology with its hypotheses of natural and human evolution challenged static views of the classification and permanence of species, threw the traditional biblical story of instantaneous creation into question, and spawned entire philosophies of organic development of both nature and human society. Historical criticism and research with its empirical bent to find out what really happened in history, where documents truly originated, and how change actually took place, put the authenticity of the Bible and the integrity of the Christian tradition on trial. New human sciences of psychology and sociology sought the empirical grounds of human development through physiological analysis and environmental study, making the old faculty psychology awkward and irrelevant and putting human self-determination in an entirely new light. Indeed, the old world seemed infinitely detached from the present. John Fiske's summation had wide currency, with Henry Churchill King among many others:

... in their mental habits, in their methods of inquiry, and in the data at their command, the men of the present day who have fully kept pace with the scientific movement are separated from the men whose education ended in 1830 by an immeasurably wider gulf than has ever before divided one progressive generation of men from their predecessors.[1]

William Jewett Tucker saw in retrospect that it had been "the fortune of [his] generation" to find its own way into the modern world, educating itself into the new knowledge and taking the initiative to find new values.[2]

In the light of the manifold intellectual changes, King thought it "impossible . . . for men of this generation to occupy precisely the point of view of not more than fifty years ago," and similarly "impossible [to] use most naturally and easily the language of the older generation in expressing [one's] deepest convictions on any theme."[3] For its new language and viewpoint the new generation turned away from the old Scottish Realism toward the many voices of German Idealism. Philosophers, theologians, sociologists, intellectuals of every stripe were reading Kant, Fichte, Lotze, Paulsen, Harnack; to quote Reid or refer to Butler would have seemed archaic. This change was so striking it led one historian to conclude that "the disappearance of the older rationalism was almost as complete as the extinction of the passenger pigeon."[4]

---

[1]John Fiske quoted in Henry Churchill King, *Reconstruction in Theology* (New York: Macmillan Co., 1901, 1907), pp. 40-41.

[2]*My Generation*, p. 1.

[3]*Reconstruction*, pp. 38, 41.

[4]Conrad Wright, *The Liberal Christians; Essays on American Unitarian History* (Boston: Beacon Press, 1970), p. 20.

Yet the enthusiasm for German writings and the passion to hear German lectures, witnessed by the mass migration of American scholars to Germany for graduate work, operated within the limits of certain uses to which German philosophy was put. Americans admired the empirical, objective, specialized methodology of the German university, but with typical eclecticism really only grafted laboratory science and critical method "upon the Lockean empirical tradition and upon the a posteriori methodology of the Scottish school," in Jurgen Herbst's words. German Idealism created great excitement, but only insofar as it could be adapted "in the fight against materialism and mechanism."[5] To the extent that Idealism promoted skepticism, determinism, or excessive metaphysical speculation, it was roundly rejected by all but a few.

For the most part American scholars continued to insist, as Henry May wrote, "that scientific truth, properly interpreted, led to moral and idealistic conclusions." They were not ready to surrender the Enlightenment "idea of the unified, coherent universe, understandable as a whole by man through the use of his reason."[6] If this was true of scholars in general, it was especially true of the college presidents charged with bringing the college ideal intact into the modern era. They continued to promote the beneficence of science, the transparency of God's will in the natural and moral world, and the compelling rationality and good sense of religious faith.

What the new generation thought distinguished themselves from the old above all was their consciousness of change, which they sought to interpret

---

[5]*The German Historical School in American Scholarship; A Study in the Transfer of Culture* (Port Washington, N.Y.: Kennikat Press, 1965, 1972), pp. 70, 93.

[6]*End of Innocence*, pp. 224, 226.

with a steadfast optimism. As Tucker put it, "the ruling idea, the dominating purpose, the passionate aim of my generation from first to last was progress."[7] They extended the idea of development in the evolution of nature into other areas, transforming moderate Enlightenment beliefs into progressivism. Modern society was becoming more scientific, knowledgeable, sophisticated, and humane than earlier eras, they believed; advancing education and moral training would appeal to the mind and conscience sufficiently to make all but the extreme miscreant a better and ever-improving person.

Nowhere did change seem more overwhelming nor progress more essential than in theology. The advancement of science and technology threatened to outstrip conceptions of religion entirely. If faith were to remain at the center of the circle of knowledge, then it would have to be articulated anew in modern terms. Thus did Tucker join immediately upon his arrival at Andover in the formulation of a "Progressive Orthodoxy." Thus did King plead for a "developing system of theological truth" that would "grow as science grows." Thus did William DeWitt Hyde describe progressive stages of spiritual development in human history and take education as his fundamental analogy for theology.[8]

The presidential theologians never admitted of any doubt that theology could progress. After all, it was only, in King's rather sloppy definition, "a

---

[7]*My Generation*, p. 449.

[8]*Progressive Orthodoxy; A Contribution to the Christian Interpretation of Christian Doctrines by the Editors of The Andover Review*, Reprint Edition with a New Introduction (Hicksville, N.Y.: Regina Press, 1975 [orig. publ. 1886]). The authors' names were not listed in the original edition, but Tucker gave them out in *My Generation*, p. 142, noting his own authorship of the essays "The Work of the Holy Spirit" and "The Christian." King, *Reconstruction*, p. 2; Hyde, *God's Education of Man* (Boston: Houghton, Mifflin & Co., 1899, 1901).

thoughtful and unified expression of what religion means to us."[9] "Religion" was something broader, more fundamental to human life, underlying all. "Religion is life," King went so far as to say, that is, life in its best activities of reasoning, working, moral endeavor and social service.[10]   As life progressed, then, so did religion. Tucker spoke to an 1893 Boston audience of a religious spirit beyond formal religion, expressing itself as an "enthusiasm for humanity." King told his listeners at the 1904 St. Louis World's Fair that they were witnessing "the great ongoing righteous trend of the universe." Hyde put his ideal for the new century in the first issue of the 1901 *Outlook*: " . . . to recognize God's coming kingdom in every institution and person that helps men to love one another."[11]

Religion was no sphere apart from real life. It was not properly the domain of either metaphysicians or mystics; it belonged neither to the speculative system of Greek philosophy with its archaic formulas nor to the emotional and subjective vagueness of mysticism. It avoided, King declared, both "juiceless intellectualism" and "spineless sentimentalism." Religion could be lived in everyday life. "Real religion," wrote Hyde, "is the offering up of

---

[9]*Reconstruction*, p. 227. King's only definition of theology thus occurred near the end of his first book in the field, and was repeated almost verbatim at the beginning of the second, *Theology and the Social Consciousness; A Study of the Relations of the Social Consciousness to Theology*, 2nd ed. (New York: Macmillan Co., 1902, 1907), p. 6.

[10]"The Fundamental Nature of Religion," *Congress of Arts and Science, Universal Exposition, St. Louis, 1904*, ed. Howard J. Rogers, 8 vols. (Boston: Houghton, Mifflin & Co., 1906, 1907), 8:254.

[11]Tucker, *My Generation*, p. 365; King, "Fundamental Nature," p. 248; Hyde, "New Century Ideals," *Outlook* 67 (January 5, 1901):73.

each man's life, in its concrete setting . . . to the guidance and keeping of God."[12]

Theology was undertaken, then, with the promise that it would get at the meaning behind the traditional dogmas, that it would translate the Gospel "to modern thought in modern terms."[13] King's goal was to "make real to his own generation the great abiding truths of Christianity," Hyde's to bring about a "reunion of vital religion with rational theology." The latter even apologized for those parts of his second major work in theology that might seem "dry and barren of practical results" for some readers, and urged them to skip those sections.[14]

The practical result was finally the whole purpose of theology anyway. Christianity was the preeminently rational and ethical religion, not a creed to which one gave intellectual assent but a way of life and moral relations with real persons. For Hyde, metaphysics was the Alpha and ethics the Omega of a theology "rooted in reason and fruitful in life." Tucker wanted theology to have a deeper sympathy with real human interests. And the phrase "moral and religious" was ever on King's tongue, whether showing the dependence of ethics on religious faith, or showing the necessary ethical fruit of religion.[15]

---

[12]King, *Social Consciousness*, p. 78; Hyde, *Abba Father, Or, The Religion of Everyday Life* (New York: Fleming H. Revell Co., 1908), p. 5.

[13]Editorial in *Andover Review* 1:654, quoted in Daniel Day Williams, *The Andover Liberals; A Study in American Theology* (Morningside Heights: King's Crown Press, 1941), pp. 64-65.

[14]King, *Reconstruction*, p. 3; Hyde, *Outlines of Social Theology* (New York: Macmillan Col., 1885, 1900), p. v; *God's Education*, p. iii.

[15]Hyde, *Outlines*, p. viii; Tucker, *The Function of the Church in Modern Society*, Modern Religious Problems, ed. A. W. Vernon (Boston: Houghton, Mifflin Co., 1911), pp. 3-4; King, e.g., *The Moral and Religious Challenge of Our Times; The Guiding Principle in Human*

In their effervescent optimism the authors thoroughly smudged out any line between descriptive and prescriptive statements about their world. They believed, with Hyde, that God was progressively revealing himself in and through science, art, institutional development, and "the perfection of humanity." Tucker was perhaps more sober than the other two about the distance yet to be traveled toward that perfection, particularly in light of social problems in the cities, but he never ceased to encourage a Christian optimism about humanity's future.[16] King was certain that the new fields of psychology and sociology in particular were producing fundamental truths about the unity and "likemindedness" of persons and the transcendent importance of the personal, indeed the "sacredness of the person" in the modern world. His uncritical standpoint led to a notable circularity, for example, in his *Theology and the Social Consciousness*, wherein he argued both that "the social consciousness itself is a genuine manifestation of the spirit of Christ at work in the world," and that a "proper interpretation" of Christ would show forth the social consciousness.[17] Theology, but more broadly religion, was to progress right along with, in, and through the progress of human enlightenment.

To the service of this religious progressivism the presidents drew any and every author they could lay hands on. In his years at Andover, at least, Tucker tried to write original essays in theology expressing strictly his own thoughts. Hyde and especially King, however, wrote in a style of rampant

---

Development: Reverence for Personality (New York: Macmillan Co., 1911).

[16]Hyde, *Practical Idealism* (New York: Macmillan Co., 1897), p. 283; Tucker, *Function*, p. 38.

[17]*Social Consciousness*, pp. 112, 179.

eclecticism. Hyde was liable to quote anyone from evolutionist philosopher and sometime Harvard instructor John Fiske to English historian and essayist Thomas Carlyle. King was given to long quotations without interpretation or explanation from German philosophers Rudolf Hermann Lotze or Friedrich Paulsen, theologian Wilhelm Herrmann, the English educator Andrew Martin Fairbairn, or the new American psychologists William James or G. Stanley Hall. The poetry of English romantics Robert Browning or William Wordsworth or of Victorians Alfred, Lord Tennyson, Robert Louis Stevenson, or Rudyard Kipling, joined lines from the Americans James Russell Lowell or Henry Wadsworth Longfellow at prominent points in their arguments. Of course, such eclecticism was only a borrowing of just certain ideas or sentiments within certain limited purposes. So the presidential authors would take Immanuel Kant's moral imperative without his agnosticism, or William James's delightfully simple descriptions of human psychology without his serendipitous and sometimes morbid criticisms of religion, or English poet Matthew Arnold's pleasant lines without the gloomy ones. All were to support and enliven a progressive theology.[18]

Their outlook unblemished by the persistence of evil or doubt, the authors welcomed with ingenuous hospitality the inroads of natural and human science on the traditional sphere of the queen, theology. Hyde called his first book in theology an outline because he did not think a new theology could be written until "the returns from psychology and sociology" on which it would depend had come in. King applauded "the principle of freedom of investigation" and was sure that theology had nothing to fear from a science

---

[18]Jurgen Herbst noted the general eclecticism among American college philosophers in *German Historical School*, p. 69.

exploring the facts of nature, humanity and history; for theology would then be able to give the results of scientific investigations their ideal meaning.[19]

However, this was an indication not of a genuinely open-minded theology ready to face the consequence of scientific method, but a theology on the defensive, absorbing as much as it could of the new learning even while broadening its own base of "religion" as fundamental to life. In F. H. Foster's later evaluation, the modernization of theology was "a movement forced upon the minds of our thinkers" by the practical necessity of saving Christianity from what seemed to be "fatal assaults."[20] In denying the ambiguous outcomes of scientific and historical inquiry, these liberal theologians attempted to solidify the grounds of optimism. Yet the plaintive, even querulous tone of their insistence that religious faith was beyond threat was all too evident. Through all this period of criticism and investigation, Tucker asked,

> has there not been an extension of natural and revealed truth . . . in all directions? Is not the thought of God larger, closer, more pervasive than ever before? Does not Jesus Christ hold a more fundamental and central position than he held at the time when Christianity began to be reexamined? Is the Bible less true in its new freedom than when it was in bondage to inerrancy and infallibility?[21]

Neither he nor his colleagues would have considered that the answer to these questions might be no, or even maybe. Only a skeptic would have so replied.

---

[19]Hyde, *Outlines*, p. v; King, *Reconstruction*, pp. 48, 51.

[20]Foster, *Modern Movement*, pp. 11, 14.

[21]*The Making and Unmaking of the Preacher*, Lectures on the Lyman Beecher Foundation, Yale, 1898 (Boston: Houghton, Mifflin, & Co., 1898), p. 17.

But there were skeptics aplenty in America by World War I, and thereafter they abounded.[22]

Presidential theology was liberal, then, in its embracing and adapting of the new learning. Yet it was profoundly conservative in molding that learning into a new rational synthesis that would be morally compelling to its contemporaries. The result was the retention of much of the older rationalism under the new consciousness of change and progress.

I. The Intellectual Inheritance

Tucker, Hyde, and King may have thought themselves completely detached from the intellectual world of the earlier generation "whose education ended in 1830." Yet they were all educated in college and graduate work under the old system, only late in their schooling coming into fuller contact with the new learning, and particularly with German philosophy and theology. Their relationship with "the old regime," in Tucker's phrase, was of course complicated by their personal attachments to their mentors and their need to invoke college tradition to show the continuity of their own progressive ideal of education with the past. But these allegiances were only further indications of the gradual nature of their detachment from the older synthesis; in fact, they never gave up much of its language or many of its characteristic assumptions and evidences.

The presidents were inclined to a general appreciation of the older generation, although Hyde, being a Harvard man, more smartly announced his definite rejection of the past. Tucker thought that "the great gift of

---

[22]May, *End of Innocence*, identified numerous intellectuals who stood outside the progressive mainstream even prior to World War I, esp. parts 2 and 3.

educational value" which had come through the previous era was "intellectual and moral discipline." The rigidity of this system, though it had lost some of its intellectual vigor, was "a steadying force" amid the social reconstruction following the Civil War and the delayed but revolutionary impact of Darwinian biology and other new learning in the 1870s and after. He knew well the old rigors, having once attended an academy in Plymouth, New Hampshire, where his instructor opened the day with the words, "Let the school now preserve tranquillity." Even at the Dartmouth of his student days (1857-61), Tucker reflected, there was little criticism of the traditional curriculum, and it was offered and taken as a whole. Its intent was the mental enlargement of students through training in the classics, which were the gateway to history and thus to human affairs.[23]

Andover Seminary, too, was still imbedded in tradition. Edwards A. Park was teaching the New England theology, albeit emphasizing freedom of the will, while Austin Phelps taught homiletics. The professor of Bible was Calvin E. Stowe, who had taught at Lane Seminary in Cincinnati, then for two years at Bowdoin College before coming to Andover, and who had married Harriet Beecher, author of the best-selling literary plea for an end to slavery, *Uncle Tom's Cabin*. But Andover lacked freshness and passion in theology, Tucker thought, with the faculty intent on holding together a world shaken by the Civil War. Nonetheless he discovered his aspiration to preach through his seminary reading of the recently published letters of the young English pastor Frederick W. Robertson, and found the personal and vital ties of religion to life in the writings of English Romantic Samuel Taylor

---

[23]Tucker, *My Generation*, pp. 1, 7, 13, 19-38.

Coleridge and American pastor-theologians Horace Bushnell and Phillips Brooks.[24]

Hyde attended Harvard some twenty years after Tucker's college days, but found the same traditional curriculum in force even then (1875-79). He studied under Andrew Preston Peabody, the beloved Chaplain and Plummer Professor of Christian Morals, as well as Francis Bowen, the political economist and philosopher. There he found a steadfast allegiance to rationalist natural theology and intuitionist ethics, with Reid and Stewart still required reading, along with Bulfinch's *Evidences*. Hyde looked back none too kindly on "this hidebound uniformity"; it had long since become a "dead prescription . . . [a] dogmatism of second-rate minds . . . elementary from beginning to end."

Fortunately for him President Charles W. Eliot was already undertaking radical revisions of this curriculum, and scholars such as George H. Palmer were beginning to discover and to teach German philosophy. Palmer and Hyde soon became close friends and mutual admirers. Hyde enrolled at Union Seminary in New York upon graduation, but only lasted a year, finding the prescribed Hebrew linguistics tedious and theologian William G. T. Shedd much too conservative in his Calvinist orthodoxy. In 1880 he transferred to Andover, Palmer's alma mater, and became absorbed in the new theology of Egbert Smyth and the homiletic dynamism of the newest faculty member, William Jewett Tucker. But he still found Edwards A. Park clinging too firmly to New England theology, and later claimed that Park never gave "a serious and square answer" to any philosophical inquiry. Hyde found his stimulation from romantic poetry -- Browning, Tennyson --and the

---

[24]Ibid., pp. 55-62; *Making and Unmaking*, p. 53.

inspirations of Carlyle and English critic and artist John Ruskin. He also joined a Palmer seminar back at Harvard on Hegel and German Idealism; Palmer later wrote that "neither he nor I, however, became a Hegelian," but that Hyde's idealism "wrought a great change in the conservatism of his State of Maine."[25]

When King arrived at Oberlin as a college sophomore in 1877 he, too, found the classical curriculum still in force: Greek and Latin, mathematics, political economy, the science of government, mineralogy, chemistry, mental and moral philosophy. He studied Christian evidences, and read Butler's *Analogy* under Judson Smith, later head of the American Board of Commissioners for Foreign Missions. His intellectual and personal mentor, though, was James Harris Fairchild, president of Oberlin since 1866 and professor of moral philosophy. Fairchild helped him choose a teaching career over missionary work in China, and later performed his wedding. Fairchild's theology and moral philosophy were also deeply imprinted on King's mind. When King went to Harvard for an M.A. after finishing Oberlin Seminary, he wrote back to his senior that his professors were "ultra-liberal" and "very ready to tell you all the different views except their own." He was studying under Peabody, Bowen, Palmer and others, some of whom were the very teachers Hyde found so backward. But King was impressed by the continuing debate between "Hedonists and Intuitionalists," or in other terms, utilitarians and those arguing for innate moral judgement, and thought Fairchild's system a useful "meeting ground" of the two.

---

[25]Burnett, *Hyde*, pp. 36, 55-71; Hyde, "President Eliot as an Educational Reformer," *Atlantic Monthly* 83 (March 1899):348-353; Palmer, Introduction to Burnett, *Hyde*, p. xv.

He had his first exposure to the German philosophers, too, reading
Kant and the early Idealists J. G. Fichte and Hegel; and when he returned
to Oberlin in 1884 he found there the first faculty member with a German
doctorate, Frank Hugh Foster. Not until the 1890s, though, did King move
more fully toward study and adoption of German Idealism. In 1893 he went
for a year of study in Berlin, where the themes of liberal theology, stressing
the historical and ethical character of Christianity, were being sounded by the
disciples of Albrecht Ritschl -- Julius Kaftan in theology and Adolf von
Harnack in church history. He also heard lectures from historian Otto
Pfleiderer and the philosopher of method in the natural and human sciences,
Wilhelm Dilthey. Upon his return, King taught a course in German
philosophy, and with his discovery of Herman Lotze, and publication of *An
Outline of the Microcosmus of Hermann Lotze* in 1895, was well on the way
to putting German philosophy to his own uses.[26]

King and Fairchild taught side by side, however, until the latter's full
retirement in 1897. Five years prior, Fairchild had published the final
compendium of his lectures over the years, *Elements of Theology, Natural and
Revealed.* Defining theology as "the science of religion" presenting the "facts
and doctrines of religion," he argued that it was but a species of the genus
ethics; for "religion is duty toward God . . . a branch of general duty."
Religious convictions did provide the "great motives" to all other duties,
though, the most important and comprehensive of which was benevolence.
This derived from the will of God, the divine sovereign and moral governor,
for the well-being of his creatures. Evidence for the existence of God, in
turn, was based on the prevalence of belief in his existence, reenforced by the

[26]Love, *King*, pp. 9-36, 48, 70-77.

universality of the human moral constitution. Evidence for the reliability of the Scriptures was also grounded in their general acceptance in both ancient and modern times, as well as their authenticity and historicity. Belief in a future life could be justified by the faith that a benevolent God would give even greater time for moral improvement. For virtuous persons sought to follow their conscience, that faculty of perceiving the rational, intuitive duty of benevolence, and to apply their duty in particular relations through their judgment. But all stood in need of the divine justification through Christ's legal atonement, and could expect their reward for dutiful faith and faithful duty.[27]

Fairchild's was a Common Sense system, moderately evangelical but of irenic temper compared to the fiery conversionism of his predecessor Charles G. Finney. Fairchild sought to inculcate positive convictions; he brooked no speculative philosophy. George Herbert Mead, later a sociologist of wide repute, was one of his students who loved to pose enigmas against his system, and later described it as "defensive."[28] But King found the concept of benevolence compelling and only gradually added to it his new-found Idealism.

Much as they wanted to break loose from the sterile confines of the old philosophy, then, Tucker, Hyde and King carried their education with them into their own writings. They used Common Sense arguments for the existence of God and the authenticity of Scripture. They spoke of laws, duties, relations, divine will, conscience, virtue, reason. They wanted no speculative doctrine, and did away with what obsolete dogmas remained.

---

[27](Oberlin, Ohio: Edward J. Goodrich, 1892), pp. 1, 111, 115-16, and passim.

[28]Barnard, *From Evangelicalism*, pp. 5, 49.

The main differences in their position stemmed from their consciousness of
change, and their intense desire to gain rational mastery over a world
breaking loose from providence under the investigations of science. To the
"reconstruction" of theological unity they applied every building-block of
Idealism or Romantic poetry or optimistic conviction they could find.

II. The Theological Task

The title "theologian" would characterize the profession of none of the
three presidents in any full sense. Their philosophical pursuits were
truncated by heavy teaching and administrative work, and none of them ever
developed a systematic theology. Tucker never published any work in
theology as such, other than contributions to the *Andover Review* and pieces
on preaching and the church. As an advocate of the New Theology at
Andover he found his role, in Buckham's felicitous phrase, as one in whom
the "personal equation" counted most. That is, he exemplified the "individuality, force, influence," and character of the movement's leaders if not the
best of its systematic thought. With his colleagues he was an editor of the
Review, and stood trial with the rest when charges were brought against all
of them in church court in 1886 and 1887. Accused of unfaithfulness to
creedal Calvinism, all were eventually acquitted.[29]

Hyde undertook his presidency only three years out of graduate school,
but managed to compose three major theological works between 1895 and
1899: *Outlines of Social Theology* (1895), *Practical Idealism* (1897), and *God's
Education of Man* (1899). He wanted to pursue further "the apprehension

---

[29]Buckham, *Progressive*, p. 145; Tucker recounted the Andover controversy in *My
Generation*, pp. 185-213.

and expression of the principles on which man's moral and spiritual life must rest," but admitted to Newman Smyth, his advocate for the Bowdoin post, that what he had done up to 1903 was "of a comparatively popular and superficial character. I have a feeling," he went on, "that sometime I might do something better than this" in the "restful background" of Bowdoin. He never did.[30]

King similarly brought forth a burst of theological writing in 1901 and 1902, *Reconstruction in Theology* appearing first, then *Theology and the Social Consciousness*. Thereafter, as his colleague Foster later reflected, "he wrote many things incidentally, works of great practical value and highly prized; but his work as a constructive theologian ceased."[31]

This restraint of writing was not only for lack of time for study and contemplation, however. It also reflected the presidents' impatience with the theological enterprise, particularly when it became too speculative or too preoccupied with justifying Christian tradition. They professed discontent with the whole contemporary situation in theology; the conservatives were too hidebound in past formulas and ignorant of advances in human knowledge, the liberals too apt to lop off essential elements of Christianity. Hyde warned of a tendency in liberalism toward making theology "a medley of metaphysics and sociology," leaving little but a "vague, semi-pantheistic deification of humanity." King feared the disappearance of religion in the liberal effort to make "religion so like all the rest of life."[32]

---

[30]Burnett, *Hyde*, p. 207.

[31]Foster, *Modern Movement*, p. 185.

[32]Hyde, *God's Education*, pp. 26-27; King, *The Seeming Unreality of the Spiritual Life*, Nathaniel William Taylor Lectures for 1907 (New York: Macmillan Co., 1908, 1911), pp. 16-17.

As a result they were cautious about naming their own enterprise. They wanted theology to be scientific in the sense of being adjusted to modern scientific conceptions and discerning factual data and laws, to "grow as science grows." But they hesitated to name it "scientific theology" if that would mean extending an evolutionary determinism into the spiritual world, of which King especially never ceased accusing Henry Drummond and Herbert Spencer. On the other hand, while they wished to write an eminently rational and ethical theology, the term "rational theology" linked them too closely to their predecessors. Hyde tied the phrase to another one, "vital religion"; King always made clear that he was using "rational" in a new sense derived from the new psychology, and rarely used it at all without the fuller phrase, "rational and ethical."[33]

If Hyde's acerbic remark that "we have no theology to-day" were true, then theological reconstruction must have seemed a colossal task. Yet it proceeded apace on the faith that it was possible, as King said, to "discern the treasure" within historic Christianity and adapt it convincingly to "the thought of the age." Hyde was more given to organic metaphors, and called for a vital approach, discovering the germ of life in the older traditions that would grow a vigorous body of faith. Once find that essential faith and unite it with its embodiments in the historic Christ and the Christian life, he thought, "and all other doctrines of religion follow as logically and inevitably as a geometrical demonstration." Undoubtedly influenced by their reading in Harnack, Herrmann, and others, King and Hyde were certain they could find the essence of Christianity in "Christ's own point of view," and that the "kernel of faith" would grow in the soil of moral life. Never, however, could

[33]King, *Reconstruction*, p. 2; Hyde, *Outlines*, p. v.

this essence be separated from historic Christianity, as some speculative philosophers suggested in their "colossal ignorance."[34]

Not only was the main trunk of Christian tradition still alive and sending off new shoots (albeit with some necessary grafting), in Hyde's metaphor, but Christianity was proving itself real, vital and rational in its connection with all modern movements of thought. Christianity was producing "a new consciousness in the race," Tucker wrote in *Progressive Orthodoxy*, that in turn made "possible the Christian consciousness."[35] Every field, King thought, from sociology to psychology to natural science, was producing new principles that were fundamentally Christian. The spiritual sphere of religious conviction was more alive than ever, and would make possible "a really spiritual reconstruction of theology," rooted in "a central spiritual insight."[36]

III. Reconstructing Natural Religion

"Theology is a circle," Hyde penned revealingly in his *Outlines of Social Theology*, and "we might begin almost anywhere."[37] But it was necessary to begin with some kind of fundamental resolution of the dilemma the nineteenth century inherited from Kant amid the blossoming of science: what was to be the relationship of nature and spirit, law and freedom, science and faith? The old natural theology, which Tucker remembered "our fathers

---

[34]Hyde, *God's Education*, pp. 2, 19, 35; King, *Reconstruction*, pp. vii, 6; *Seeming Unreality*, p. 43.

[35]Hyde, *God's Education*, pp. vii-viii; Tucker, "The Cristian," p. 141.

[36]King, *Reconstruction*, p. v; Hyde, *God's Education*, pp. 44-45.

[37]*Outlines*, p. 85.

preached . . . as easily as they preached the Levitical law," had been shaken to pieces by the changed conception of nature and human nature entailed in theories of evolution. Some new reconciliation of nature and religion was desperately needed, for King feared that many of those who once relied on some form of natural religion now seemed "to have given up any religious basis for their ethical life."[38]

Rethinking the claims of natural theology did not, however, entail a new examination of the grounds of human knowledge. The late-century authors settled into a comfortable mix of Scottish Realist and Kantian assumptions, often using the language of Common Sense epistemology, regularly producing unexamined presuppositions about the natural make-up of the human mind, but no longer concerning themselves with formal argument of the old mental philosophy type. The new psychology, particular-ly the imaginative and expansive descriptions by William James, lent itself to a new syncretism that blended old assumptions with contemporary theories.

Hyde's procedure clearly reflected the eclectic common sense of his day. Echoing the Scottish Realists, he began with what he called the analysis of consciousness. Like the earlier philosophers, he first disposed of the Lockean scheme of knowing; a mind that was only a blank sheet of paper could no more store sensations than a mirror could hold reflections. But then he turned to German philosophy and American psychology, mainly Kant and James, to show that the mind was active in perception, weaving sensations together through processes comparable to the working of cotton cloth out of raw materials in a machine. As Kant had argued, through the forms and categories of the understanding the mind created an ordered,

---

[38]Tucker, *Making and Unmaking*, p. 48; King, *Reconstruction*, p. 25.

lawful, continuous world that otherwise, in James's oft-quoted phrase, was a "blooming, buzzing confusion." Thus forms of perception and laws of relation were inherent as modes of operation in the rational nature of the mind. Moreover, experience was cumulative and the mind moved ever closer to the meaning of things as it grouped them together "according to their more obvious relations"; this building up of wholes was what was meant by "common sense."

To this point, though, the order and rationality of the world would have been purely a mental construct, the correspondence to reality of which Kant had left to an unknowable thing-in-itself. But Hyde could not stop there, for this agnosticism had opened the way to philosophy's becoming mystical and technical, an abstract idealism. He took as the title of his second book what he considered the true task of philosophy: to construct a "practical idealism" that would create an intelligible world and a moral order. "Practical Idealism," he declared, was "simply a presentation of the familiar facts of everyday life in their rational relations, as elements in a logical process and parts of an organic whole."[39]

Modern science had brought that logical process to light and had provided the solution to the problem of Idealist epistemology, Hyde wrote in his *Outlines*. For science had shown that mental notions could be verified by objective standards, that things were really discovered, not created by the mind, and that all minds could agree, given evidence, on one system of "thought-relations," or rational relations. Scientific truth was grounded on the proposition of one natural, objective, rational order of things. This order was "the divine background of truth," he asserted abruptly. If natural law was to

---

[39] *Practical Idealism*, pp. v-vi, 6-38.

be objective, verifiable, and reliable, it required a common ground between nature and the human mind, which ground was "Absolute Thought, the Infinite Spirit, or God." The uniform order of physical events, of which science was the mental equivalent, revealed the Absolute Mind.[40]

The laws by which science proceeded were not merely empirical, mere habits of mind, as Hume had suggested. A scientific law, Hyde said, was a concept that bound two things together in a rational whole, though being universal enough to admit of exceptions. For example, the principle that heat expanded an object was generally true, but not in the case of ice; such did not defeat the law, but only showed the complexity of nature. Science rested on the laws of mathematics and the three laws of logic: identity, contradiction, and the excluded middle. While these were "pure" and science was based on experience, nevertheless scientific law was "as necessary and universal as the laws of mathematics."

The fundamental law of science, though, was that the "world is a self-consistent, rational whole, and consequently everything in it has definite and precise relations to everything else." In sum, science was "the meeting-point of Reason in Nature and the same Reason in man," manifesting the "rational unity" of fact and mind, world and self.[41]

His argument to this point confined to the "natural world," the first division of his *Practical Idealism*, he now moved to the "spiritual world" or "world of persons." The distinctive mark of personality was self-conscious-ness, which Hyde thought had evolved from primitive innocence, in which one was only aware of oneself and one's natural appetites, to the self-

---

[40]*Outlines*, pp. 10-16.

[41]*Practical Idealism*, pp. 68-90, 131.

conscious freedom and responsibility through awareness of the personalities
of others. The Fall had been the "tragic stage in human evolution" when the
knowledge of good and evil entered human consciousness. But man was by
nature a social being, entering into relations with his environment and his
society; and the practical expression of that social nature was love. Just as
reason built up an ordered natural world, so love constructed an ordered
social world through institutions, morality, and religion.[42]

Human society was evolving, too, toward "a harmonious social order in
which each individual shall be at once the servant and the lord of all." This
objective development had a subjective counterpart, namely, the conscience,
an inner moral standard, a fundamental instinct of duty and responsibility, or
in Kant's phrase, a "categorical imperative." The correspondence of these
outer and inner aspects of moral order required a common ground, just as
did the phenomena and perception of the natural order. To the moral
correlation Hyde gave the name "Universal Will," which he saw "embodied
in the progressive evolution of the social order, and revealed in the ever-
expanding ideal of the moral life."

Knowledge of the natural and moral worlds was partial, Hyde admitted.
In his favorite metaphor, each piece of evidence was only an arc of the whole
circle. Yet every arc assumed the circle and made no sense without it.
Without the Absolute Mind and Universal Will "presupposed in the facts"
there could be no science or morals; but since science and morals existed,
"that without which these facts could not be, must exist." That is, the truths
of science being factual and the social order real, the "Absolute Reason and
Eternal Righteousness which they reveal and presuppose must also be real,

---

[42]Ibid., pp. 145-50, 161.

actual, objective." God was no hypothesis, "put under" the facts; God was a hypostasis, "standing under" the facts and giving them reality.

If this reasoning was circular, it was only because the Absolute was a necessary presupposition, a "fundamental intuition" of the rational mind. No argument for the existence of God could be put in a syllogism, for God was "the universal major premise on which all formal reasoning rests." Traditional arguments for God, whether ontological or cosmological, had purported to be either deductive or inductive. The former was not possible since there was nothing greater than God from which to deduce him; and the latter failed because a mere aggregate of evidence from nature could never equal the whole.[43] The simple truth, Hyde argued, was that the Absolute Thought holding the universe in "rational relations," and the Universal Will comprehending all "acts and attitudes of all persons toward each other," was "the inescapable reality which the world agrees to call God."[44]

Lest the evolution of nature and of the social order be identified with God, however, Hyde warned that God was transcendent as well as immanent. God was immanent in every mind and every atom, "yet as an organism is more than the sum of its parts," God transcended the particular as the whole of the reality of which things and actions were only a part. Hyde drew on many analogies for this relationship; God was to the world of facts as a skeleton to bones, the solar system to its planets, the family to its members, the nation to its citizens. Even the laws of evolution themselves demonstrated divine transcendence. The law of natural selection, for instance, showed that the real is always subject to the ideal, for unfit things either became fit

---

[43]*Outlines*, pp. 16-20, 25-29.

[44]*God's Education*, pp. 6-7.

or they perished, which was certainly a merciful, kind and just system, the creation of a rational and moral being.

Hyde was already well along toward concluding that God was not only an Absolute, but a person. If the whole could not be less than its parts, and if the self-conscious personality of man were "the crowning glory" of this "highest of finite beings," then the Infinite could hardly be less "than self-conscious and personal" himself. The divine personality, he argued, quoting Lotze, Paulsen, and Pfleiderer, was the perfect, transcendent one, including all that is positive in human personality.

When he tried to say how one could know this infinite personal God, however, Hyde turned back to the time-honored evidences of natural and moral order. All human knowledge of nature and natural law, all self-consciousness and its expressions in human history and literature, was an expression or revelation of God. God was present and pervasive in the world, so much so that "we know as much about God as we know about ourselves and the world." The increase of Knowledge constituted a progressive revelation of God, now "partially known," but finally "absolutely knowable."[45]

Religion was the ultimate stage in the evolution of consciousness, then, for it offered the complete unification of life in an all-inclusive system of relations, Infinite Thought and Love brought together in one.[46] Its vision of wholeness was not achieved without struggle, however. Life was a constant process of adjusting to a changing environment, of applying perfect ideals to an imperfect real world ever in flux. Religion itself had evolved,

---

[45]*Outlines*, pp. 27-32, 41-42.

[46]*Practical Idealism*, pp. 277-79.

Hyde wrote, from a "promiscuous personification" of natural objects as in fetichism, through the stages of ancestor worship and cultural deities, to the Jewish concept of ethical monotheism, and finally to the Christian understanding of God as Father. Here, in the analogy of god as Father to a human family, religion achieved its wholeness; for a family, like society in general, was composed of the personal relations of its members, and required a Father who asserted the common interests of all as obligatory on the will of each.[47] The progress of religion to this point Hyde viewed as "God's education of man," in which man was progressively taught the duties and mutual obligations inherent in living in an orderly society unified by love. Thus was religion essentially social and ethical, the basis of order in a universe of persons.

Hyde's epistemology, grounded on the universal apprehension of rational relations immediately perceived by the mind, was clearly a continuation of the synthetic method and language of Common Sense Realism. He invoked Kant only as support for the notion of the mind active in perception, and avoided entirely Kant's skepticism about knowledge beyond the phenomenal world. Mind and will required absolutes in order to make sense of knowledge and action, Hyde argued; therefore, the Universal Mind and Will must exist as the unifying bridge between self and world. Such synthetic thinking made for an easy transition to the claims of religion, a facility which Hyde, like his predecessor presidents, exploited to the full.

King also worked within a framework of common sense assertions about the possibility of knowledge and the universality of an ultimate ground for both science and faith. He, too, brought in evidence from psychological

---

[47]*Outlines*, pp. 33-44.

findings, especially from James, that the mind was no longer effectively described by "isolated faculties," but better analyzed as a unity in which all functions and processes of "conception, judgment, and inference . . . induction and deduction" were part of an organic whole and continuity. This emphasis reflected the modern rejection of "abstract atomism" as a model of thinking derived from Berkeley and Hume, he said, and the substitution of the active mind thinking toward relations, wholeness, and unity.[48]

King's theology began not with consciousness, though, but with what he thought was the essential problem of modern philosophy, to bring "into unity the mechanical and ideal views of the world." The true scope and meaning of scientific theories, laws and investigations needed redefinition, for the philosophy of absolute materialism which had made nature a self-contained inexorable mechanism of cause and effect was collapsing under its own weight, even among scientists. At the same time, the grounds of human freedom needed to be more firmly established in a more definitely conceived spiritual world.[49]

For his orientation and approach to these problems King went to the German Idealists, and more particularly to Hermann Lotze. Lotze has been called "the darling philosopher of religious liberals" during the period from 1880 to World War I, but indeed he achieved popularity throughout the Anglo-American world. He was read from Yale to the University of California, and from Oxford to Edinburgh. Ironically, his major works belonged to the 1850s and 1860s, and he died in 1881. But through those

---

[48]*Rational Living; Some Practical Inferences from Modern Psychology* (New York: Macmillan Co., 1905, 1918), pp. 103, 105.

[49]*Reconstruction*, pp. 35-36.

who had heard him lecture, and perhaps also through his influence on the Ritschlians whom later students heard, his fame spread. William James was delighted to have found at last someone "who could write well in spite of being a German philosopher," and joined many who found him among the deepest and most comprehensive philosophers of the day.[50]

Lotze's appeal undoubtedly stemmed from the synthetic scope of his philosophy. His *Microcosmus*, which purported over its 1500 pages to survey the complete study of man, body, soul, mind, nature, history, religion, and life, was translated into English in 1885 by two scholars, one of whom was Elizabeth Hamilton, daughter of William Hamilton, the last of the Scottish Realists. Both Realists and Idealists thought Lotze confirmed their ideas, for he was both an empiricist, founding knowledge of nature on sense and experience, and an Idealist, grounding knowledge of God and moral good on the order and unity of things. He was considered the first philosopher to really try to come to terms with the advance of science, as he was himself trained originally in medicine and appreciated the need for dispassionate investigation of facts and formulation of natural laws. Yet he insisted that any reductionism of all reality into law was a fallacy.[51] Nature was not a self-existent entity explained only by "actually existent things and notions." Rather, it had to have originated beyond itself, and in fact was sustained at every point of its relations by the unity of the Infinite. Laws could describe the interaction of really existent things, but the reality of those relations had

---

[50]Paul G. Kuntz, Introduction to George Santayana, *Lotze's System of Philosophy* (Bloomington: Indiana University Press, 1971), pp. 6-7, 52-55; James quote, p. 65, is quoted from Ralph Barton Perry, *The Thought and Character of William James*, 1:586-87.

[51]Kuntz, Introduction to Santayana, *Lotze's System*, passim.

to rest in the order of a world-ground or Absolute.[52] On the other hand, such an Absolute could not be an independent reality either, from which all natural laws and events were inevitably deduced, as in the Hegelian system. The unity of relations in the One and the pluralism of really existent individual things in the Many were both necessary.[53]

Lotze's synthesis excluded both materialism and absolute Idealism. Yet it left science free to investigate the mechanical interaction of things and opened to theology the whole realm of the Infinite. King was fond of quoting Lotze's claim in the Introduction to the *Microcosmus*, that he would show *"how absolutely universal is the extent* and at the same time *how completely subordinate the significance of the mission which mechanism has to fulfill in the structure of the world."*[54] Science could discover facts and could show how in certain combinations and under certain conditions phenomena must interact, but it could not overextend itself by claiming that what is, must be, and must come into being through certain lines of causality. The ultimate ground of the relations of things was not in the realm of facts or laws, but of worth. In the concept of value, another and transcendent area of human knowledge, the mind could pursue the ultimate origins and purposes of things and of man, thus ratifying the universality of moral duty and the freedom to perform it.[55]

---

[52]Hermann Lotze, *Microcosmus: An Essay Concerning Man and his Relation to the World*, trans. Elizabeth Hamilton and E. E. Constance Jones, 2 vols., 4th ed. (Edinburgh: T. & T. Clark, n.d. [orig. publ. 1885]), 1:372-75, 381.

[53]Ibid., 2:728.

[54]Ibid., 1:xvi.

[55]Ibid., 2:575.

Lotze followed Kant in denying the viability of traditional cosmological or teleological proofs of God, for empirical knowledge was too limited to establish such grand conclusions. But unlike Kant, Lotze, perhaps because he began not with an epistemology (beyond which Kant never satisfactorily proceeded) but with a conviction of the unity of reality, both phenomenal and noumenal, moved on to establish the existence of God from the human impulse to find unity and ethical justice in a transcendent being. Rather than argue for the grounds of such theological assertion, Lotze stated, "we will regard. . . the notion of a Personal God, as being already reached, and endeavor to defend this against doubts as to its possibility."[56] The appeal of such a method to generations of scholars raised on Scottish Common Sense was surely irresistible. For it resonated with the rationalist procedure of assuming propositions such as the existence of God or the necessity of revelation as self-evident to every human mind, putting the onus on critics to prove otherwise.

King leaned heavily on Lotze to establish the proper confines of science. Certain that materialist philosophy had met its end anyway, King asserted that "modern science distinctly disclaims to be either *a priori*, speculative, or ultimate" in its conclusions. Science was restricting itself to "experience, to the tracing of purely causal connections, and to phenomena." It was only interested in the process, not in the "ultimate origin and destiny" of things.

Science should be credited with discovering the "unity of the world," King wrote, for it was finding such universal principles as evolution, in biology, and conservation of energy, in physics. But law was to be affirmed

---

[56]Ibid., 2:672.

in its universality, not its uniformity. Law described things as they were found, not as they had to be, and it was open to correction and expansion based on further experience. No "sphere of eternal self-existent laws preceding or independent of *all* existing being" could be proposed, for laws had no existence of their own "apart from all real existing things." They were only formulations of the way phenomena were observed to interact.

On the other hand, theology was not threatened in any way by the advancements of law, and in fact welcomed law as properly understood. For without law as a means of understanding there could be no growth of knowledge; every fact would just stand alone. Similarly without law as a means of formulating moral values there could be no growth in character; every act would just stand alone. Thus freedom had nothing to fear from law; in fact, the freedom to master the world of nature, the freedom to accomplish moral ends, the freedom to reach spiritual attainments, all depended on the definite conditions and certain results provided by natural and moral laws. Such was a basic supposition of a "rational universe" which both science and religion required.[57]

In the particular case of evolutionary laws, King considered that there was a great deal of misunderstanding. Evolution was universal but not uniform; that is, evolution was everywhere taking place, but it did not operate according to an inexorable, a priori process in which everything was contained in the stage that came before it. Real evolution was "a succession of stages with new phenomena and new laws" coming into being. A really new thing could not have been really present or potential before; it was absurd to argue that a thing's coming into being depended on the pre-

---

[57]*Reconstruction*, pp. 37, 54-60.

existence of all its proper elements and conditions, for if *they* all existed then how could the new phenomenon tarry? Logically, then, the process of evolution required some further ground for its development and some further explanation for the arrival of new phenomena. This King found, as had Lotze, in the Infinite.

Having posited an Infinite, to which he at once gave the name God, King had two immediate problems to dispose of. He first had to argue that God was not brought into the picture simply to fill in "unbridged gaps in the series"; conversely, the extension of lawful knowledge was not a "progressive elimination of God from the universe." To the contrary, every atom was absolutely dependent on God, and evolutionary theory only revealed "a larger view of the method, plan, and aim of God in the universe . . . a far longer sweep of the divine on-going." This was an extension and strengthening of the design argument, for it brought God into closer connection with the world, and gave the whole a dynamic character.

Secondly, though, God was not then to be completely identified with nature in some form of pantheism. God was not the process, but the initiator and ground of the process. God was a person with all the attributes of personality -- freedom, thought, will, character. Pantheism made God "responsible equally and indifferently for everything in the world," which entailed not only determinism, but ultimately loss of even God's freedom of action. An "element of transcendence" had to be retained, then, if God was to be truly "other."[58]

King never really gave any grounds for his move from an Infinite to a personal God. He simply followed Lotze in the conviction that both the

---

[58]Ibid., pp. 82, 84, 88-91, 103.

coming into being of a thing and its purpose or end had to be effected by a Will, which was a quality of a person. He backed away from traditional arguments for God for the same reason Lotze did, that empirical knowledge was too limited and strict proof was impossible. Yet King found in the very struggle to pose proofs a presumed certainty of God's existence anyway, and likewise a need for God in the human constitution itself. He stood not far at all from an older assumption, that any rational person seeking to apprehend a lawful universe would necessarily posit God as a first principle of thought. In truth, while he gave up on formal, logical proofs of God and condemned them to an inadequate "mathematico-mechanical" view of the world, he never surrendered a softer, more common sense conclusion that the lawfulness of the universe was reliable evidence for a divine mind and will.[59]

. If God was a Person, then personality was the highest reality, and King viewed the increasing value and sacredness of the person as an outcome of both evolution and the growing social consciousness. The intellectual, moral, and spiritual life of humanity was the highest stage of evolution, the sphere of "persons and personal relations," which had its own laws beyond those of organic nature. To apply a strictly organic analogy to human life was a bald error, in King's opinion. Any attempt to make society an independent, inexorable reality, or to confine human development to certain necessary stages, as Spencer, Drummond, and others had undertaken, was a denial of the reality of individual persons. Nor was human evolution, like evolution in general, to be identified with God. God was immanent in humanity in the sense of bringing his purpose for Good into being, but God respected human

[59]*Seeming Unreality*, pp. 193, 199-201, 204-5.

autonomy, and revealed himself progressively, according to the human capacity to receive. "God's education of us" marked a developing personal relationship in which every advance of human knowledge would have ethical applications in making love the dominant principle of human life.

Convinced of the reality of persons, which he claimed was the one reality no one had ever denied, King was ready to explore theology as personal relation and leave the problem of nature behind. He never resolved the ambiguities of his concept of nature and natural evolution; in celebrating the human as the realm of freedom he sometimes seemed to sneer at the merely organic laws of nature, as if he had forgotten his insistence on the possibility of innovation. He was also sure that there must be some distinction between God's immanence in nature and in humanity, as if the latter required greater freedom of will and action, whereas God could somehow act directly in nature; but he was not clear on these points.[60]

In any case, for King persons were the most important, most certain, and only eternal facts of human experience, and therefore theology was to be conceived as a personal relation, to God through the analogy of friendship, and to others through the ethic of love. In this he was carrying through what he cited as his mentor Fairchild's intention to make "the organic principle in the system of doctrine presented, . . . the recognition of the distinct and complete personality of God, and a like personality of man."[61] But King wanted to move away from the introspective and closed tone of the older theology, thinking less in terms of "the relations in which I stand," and more in terms of following "the call of the great interests, the

---

[60]*Reconstruction*, pp. 92-95, 104-6.

[61]Ibid., pp. 228-29, quoting Fairchild's *Elements*, p. iv.

great personalities, the great causes and motives" of life. This restive, inflated rhetoric never carried him far, though, from the same general considerations of the older system.[62]

The human relation to God King conceived as a friendship, following the same conditions and laws for developing friendship between two persons. Evolution having come, that is, to the stage of persons and personal relations, and God being the supreme Person in a spiritual world with its own laws, "the essential laws of the friendship with God" would simply be "the laws of any true friendship." In part these laws were based upon general conclusions from the new psychology. King summarized these as the determination that man was built for action and expression, that is, that nothing was real unless it was expressed in action; the evidence of the unity of man, intellect, feeling and will, body and soul; and the importance of association or environment for development. Friendship, then, was an expression of the whole man in association with another.

As King briefly spelled out his laws of friendship in his *Reconstruction*, the basic elements of a friendly relation were threefold. "Mutual self-revelation and answering trust" meant revealing at least something of oneself to the other, and having faith in that part of the person not revealed. Friendship could not be a constant test or exposure of each person, but required trust in the unknown on the basis of the known. For, second, friendship was based on "mutual self-surrender," the giving of oneself to the other, in which the self was affirmed, for the other gave himself in return. The relation to God was the only one, in truth, to which "we can give

---

[62]*The Laws of Friendship, Human and Divine* (New York: Macmillan Co., 1909, 1911), p. 121.

ourselves unstintedly." Third, friendship was based on "some deep community of interests" which followed from self-revelation and self-surrender. "Agreement as to the great aims, ideals and purposes of life" was necessary to any developing relation.

King then named six conditions for deepening a friendship. It had to be for the most part an "unconscious growth," not stimulated by artificial or excessive emotion, but based on trust. It required "association" by staying in each other's presence. "Time" was necessary to growth of the relation, and "expression" in words and sympathy deepened the sharing. A "sacred respect for the personality of the other" meant not riding roughshod over the other person but staying reverent in his presence. Lastly, one had to be "real" and "honest" in the relation, without pretense.[63]

When King expanded this theology in his 1909 lectures at Haverford College, published as *The Laws of Friendship, Human and Divine*, he again began with the assertion that life was "the fulfillment of relations," with relations to things secondary to relations to persons. The relation to God was the highest, and was attainable because "the same qualities, the same conditions, the same means . . . are required for relation to God and relation to men"; one could be "the friend of God on precisely the same terms" as one could be "the friend of another man." He then developed the same laws as in the earlier book, but stressed even more that he did not mean by "friendship" some kind of sentimental, emotional state. Friendship was strongest when pursued in "the objective and self-forgetful mood," he said. It was not introspective, demanded no level of high feeling, insisted on no

---

[63]King, *Reconstruction*, pp. 212, 216-26; King summarized his principles of psychology, pp. 44-45, 171-72, and developed them more fully in *Rational Living*.

constant experience; rather it expressed itself in service, work and achievement of great purposes, grounded not on "emotional states in ourselves" but
on "honest response to objective fact" in the spiritual world.[64]

The apologetic undertow of this theology was evident throughout. In
his classroom and in his audiences (perhaps in himself) King was hearing two
kinds of questions. To the one, why is not God as apparent in the world as
the natural phenomena that are the subject of science -- if he exists, why
does he not reveal himself completely -- King responded that friendship
required time and trust, and that God's respect for the sacredness of human
personality would not permit him to be "obtrusive" or to "force the door" in
violation of human freedom.[65] To the other, must one follow the traditional
approaches to God through conversion experiences and allegiance to creeds,
all of which seemed outmoded in light of modern science, King answered no,
that true religion was objective, active, ethical, and demanded self-giving
service to a progressing humanity which itself bore the marks of God's
immanence.

Thus the new natural theology perpetuated older arguments for the
rational order of the universe intuitively perceived. The lawfulness of nature,
indeed all the relations of things and relations of persons, reflected a
conscious, rational, active, Infinite Being whom all thinking persons
everywhere agreed to call God. The advancement of materialist philosophies
declaring the inexorability of the operations of the universe only brought
forth a broader and more determined response from the theologians of
rational synthesis. They simply asserted even more ardently the personality

---

[64]*Laws of Friendship*, pp. 3, 7, 77, 119-23.

[65]*Reconstruction*, p. 225.

of God, indeed the accessibility of personal relationship to God, now viewed as the divine teacher and friend.

Yet such a personal approach was not to make religion purely internal or subjective. Even as they increasingly stressed the psychological apprehension of God (grounded, of course, on lawful relations), the authors continued to insist on the apparentness of God in nature. Recent scientific theory required theological reconception but not a surrender of foundations. While Tucker admitted that of late, the emphasis had been more on inquiry and less on affirmation, he was also certain that increasing knowledge of the universe was making the immanence of God more evident. The whole concept of God working patiently and with forethought in the development of the world would never have come "into the real apprehension" of human thought had not "modern science . . . prepared the way for it." The findings of Darwinian biology actually brought God closer into the physical conditions of life as their guiding law. This was no mean materialism; not only was evolutionary theory finding as much altruism in nature as it had earlier found amoral struggle for survival; materialism was being effectively challenged by a progressive theology that restored the transcendence of human freedom. The spiritual world was becoming more real as the human spirit sought mastery and control of material forces.[66]

To deny or attack the new findings of science was certainly no solution, then. "It is worse than useless simply to bombard our age," wrote King, without a "sympathetic knowledge" of new facts and theories. After all, "freedom of investigation" had been a basic principle in the advancement of knowledge and modern education, and ultimately derived from a principle of

---

[66]Tucker, *Function*, p. 14; *Making and Unmaking*, p. 19; *My Generation*, pp. 92-94.

Protestantism, the "right of private judgment." Religious progress itself depended on intellectual freedom, Tucker insisted.[67]

The three theologians reconciled science and theology, then, with the declaration that the latter had nothing to fear from freedom of investigation, while the former respectfully limited itself to empirical opinions. The antebellum orthodox rationalists had detailed the same solution. They, too, had insisted that free inquiry based on empirical method, or "science rightly pursued," was no threat to religion. At the same time they had demanded that scientific investigations be absolutely inductive, devoid of theories or assumptions about what could or could not be, making no broad claims for limited discoveries, but exhibiting the virtues of humility and restraint in the face of the factual data. The broader unity of this dual insistence in both the earlier and the later theologians rested in their confidence that the order of the universe revealed a rational and ethical Mind to the common apprehension of human beings. All learning (rightly pursued) could thus be subsumed under God's education of his children.[68]

IV. Rethinking Christian Evidences

Having established the possibility, indeed the necessity, of rational order in the natural and spiritual worlds under a universal, personal God, the presidential theologians were at pains to demonstrate what was their presumption all along, that the highest form of religion was Christianity. To this apology they brought arguments drawn primarily from the "internal"

---

[67]King, *Reconstruction*, pp. 4, 48; Tucker, *Function*, pp. 7, 13.

[68]Bozeman, *Protestants*, pp. 49-50, 107-15.

evidences of the older rational theologies demonstrating the consistency of Christianity with human nature and human need. Christianity was the "ultimate and absolute form of religion," in Hyde's words, because it was rational, ethical, universal, social, historical, developmental, and hopeful.[69]

Tucker wrote in *Progressive Orthodoxy* that Christianity was a revelation of hope and possibility, of attainment of character and destiny; and in later addresses he carried through the same thought, telling the Yale students in 1898 that there was increasing evidence of "a divine order in the world" reflecting the Christian teaching of a sovereign hand directing the universe in love, and declaring to Union Seminary classes in 1902 that Christianity was "the only religion, which undertakes to deal with man as the subject of progress." King agreed that "the world is going to become more and more consciously and avowedly Christian." The new theology could be based on a renewed conviction of the absoluteness of Christianity, for all the "deepest laws and trends of human nature" as well as the rising social consciousness of the value and unity of persons manifested "the spirit of Christ at work in the world." The Christian view was "indubitably connected" with the "realest [sic] trends of our own time."[70]

Not only that, but Christian ideals were advancing with the rising tide of the Christian nations, which, in Tucker's opinion, were "moving under an irresistible momentum" toward responsibility for controlling and directing the very forces of civilization. "We of the more virile Christian peoples have outgrown the lower and more cruel sins of the primitive races," he penned,

---

[69]*Practical Idealism*, p. 286.

[70]Tucker, "The Christian," p. 142; *Making and Unmaking*, p. 211; *My Generation*, p. 369; King, *Social Consciousness*, pp. 112, 130; *Reconstruction*, p. 16; *Seeming Unreality*, p. 180.

but that made the guidance of society toward a higher Christianity an even weightier obligation. King pointed out in his letters for Sunday School teachers that "the most enlightened nations of the world to-day owe their ideal of God to Jesus Christ," and Hyde was sure that "Christ in us in America today is our hope of glory."[71]

The universality of Christianity was apparent as well in that so many people had tried the Christian way of life and found it superior. Their testimony was "a strong presumption in its favor," Hyde thought, for in an experimental, scientific age, if one had not tried something, one could not very well criticize it or say it did not work. "There is no valid intellectual objection to essential Christianity," he wrote with characteristic bluntness; "if a man is not a Christian . . . it is simply because he does not rightly understand Jesus' Way." The Way was hardly something esoteric or other-worldly; to the contrary, it was "one single insight, as a comprehensive whole, of all the virtues, duties, laws, institutions, and ideals which human experience has discovered, enacted, sanctioned, and adored." In short, Christianity was not only universal but more or less inescapable.[72]

Primarily, though, the Christian religion was ultimate because it was the preeminently ethical religion. It was not abstract, general, or metaphysical; it was concrete, incarnated in the human historical and social world where people lived and did their daily duty. The two essentials of Christianity, Hyde wrote in a 1905 Outlook, were the "reverent recognition of One Great

---

[71]Tucker, *Making and Unmaking*, pp. 215-16, 223; *Function*, p. 106; King, *Letters on the Greatness and Simplicity of the Christian Faith* (Boston: Pilgrim Press, 1906), p. 46; Hyde, *Practical Idealism*, p. 287.

[72]*Jesus' Way; An Appreciation of the Teaching in the Synoptic Gospels* (Boston: Houghton, Mifflin & Co., 1902), pp. vi-vii, 27.

Good Will," and the "democratic attitude toward other people." Spiritual development began with consciousness of the world and nature, then moved into the stage of self-consciousness, understanding and will; but the highest development, which Christianity revealed, was God-consciousness, unselfish service of universal ends recognizing the good of all as God willed it. This Good Will for all, he told Yale students in 1916, was "the heart of the Gospel."[73]

King also found it "impossible" to separate the "ethical and religious" any more, for religion was "the one truest way to character." All theology would have to become practical theology, all doctrine would have to be tested in practice, for the "unity of the ethical life in love" would prove itself the fundamental teaching of Christianity in modern society.[74]

If Christianity was preeminently ethical, it also had to be predominantly social in the modern day, the three presidents agreed. Hyde undertook to write a "social theology," arguing that man was fundamentally a social being living in relations, and that Christianity was essentially a social movement concerned with right relations in concrete settings of life. *Jesus' Way* was an enlarging sympathy with others guided by the principles of love: love to the Father who loves all, and love to one's fellow men. Duty and service were the bread and water of the spiritual life, and faith was "wrought out of our own moral and spiritual experience."[75]

---

[73]*Practical Idealism*, pp. 284-85; "The Essentials of Christianity," *Outlook* 81 (November 4, 1905):567; *Outlines*, pp. 3-4; *The Gospel of Good Will as Revealed in Contemporary Scriptures*, Lyman Beecher Lectures on Preaching at the Yale School of Religion for 1916 (New York: Macmillan Co., 1916), p. vii.

[74]King, *Reconstruction*, pp. 169, 181.

[75]*Outlines*, p. vi; *Jesus' Way*, pp. 8-10.

Tucker was the member of Andover's faculty most involved in the building of Andover's South End Settlement House in Boston. In his view, Christianity was social through its sympathy for those of the lower classes and its pity for the helpless poor. The latter could be objects of Christian charity; but for those groups seeking to rise and aspiring to better conditions, the Christian response was a sympathy that was neither pity nor charity, but "the most concrete and sensitive expression of both love and justice." This firm sympathy was the influence of a Christianity which saw a child of God in every person, and so welcomed the rising classes "to the places which they have earned."[76]

King found a social consciousness at the heart of Christianity, particularly in the teaching of the Kingdom of God. That "we are members one of another" united in the coming reign of God, as Jesus revealed, he thought was increasingly apparent in the rising social consciousness of the world in general. "The deepening sense of the like-mindedness of men," their mutual influence, as well as the increasing sense of the value and sacredness of the person -- that is, the constituent elements of modern social conscious-ness -- he found exemplified in the Christian religion. King was cautious, though, about the use Hyde and others made of organic analogies for society. They sounded very scientific, but he feared they would lead toward determinism, the "mechanical." Christianity was "social because personal," King argued. The individual's learning to love was the means to character and the essence of religion; and the Kingdom was the reign of God "in the individual heart." But then, of course, the individual could not learn to love "without recognition everywhere of relations to others," without the "giving of

---

[76]Tucker, *Function*, p. 64; *Making and Unmaking*, pp. 156-57.

self in personal relations," and in that sense the problem of character was necessarily social. The ethical life of love was thus both the means to complete character and the basis of a Christian society.[77]

Thus did the presidents demonstrate the absoluteness of Christianity by its universality, its pervasiveness in the trends of the times, its acceptance by rational and progressive people everywhere, and its superior ethical and social insights. Such evidences echoed the older collegiate rational theology, from Butler's insistence on the supremacy of Christian virtue to Paley's description of the rapid spread and consensus of Christianity in the ancient world to Wayland's belief that the Bible and the United States Constitution were companion guides to human enlightenment.[78] The writers of both periods were determined to defend Christianity against those who thought its claims obscure, irrelevant, or even impossible, by showing that revelation was complementary to the judgments of universal reason and conscience.

To the new generation, though, intellectual difficulties with revelation seemed even sharper. If they were to demonstrate the consonance of Christian religion with modern scientific sophistication, they would necessarily have to shade its more recondite aspects. Consequently the later authors were far less inclined to define revelation by what had formerly been its primary external evidence, the appeal to miracles. They still defended the possibility of miracles and even attached them to revelation as a necessary expression of divine action; but such arguments were more an afterthought, a formality still in place but now subsidiary.

---

[77]King, *Reconstruction*, pp. 238-39; *Social Consciousness*, pp. 9-22.

[78]Francis Wayland, "The Duties of an American Citizen," in *Occasional Discourses* (Boston: James Loring, 1833), p. 41.

Perpetuating the older "Protestant paradigm of the universe," King saw no reason why the God who created natural laws and acted according to them could not further act in a way beyond the laws presently known. No a priori judgment about what could or could not be a fact was justifiable in a scientific world. Moreover, Jesus was "a great new cause" in the human world even as he represented a great movement within the spiritual world; should one not then expect new phenomena, new effects?[79]

The other two authors agreed that miracles were plausible, but found them of little value as evidence of Christ's authenticity. Tucker thought the elasticity and hiddenness of natural forces could account for miracles. Hyde claimed that miracles were actually more believable now that science knew of higher forms of force that might be created in a conflict of laws (physical and chemical, for instance), and now that psychology was discovering all kinds of psychic phenomena. But he also sensed that the scientific credibility of miracles really removed their evidentiary value, arguing that no amount of miracles would establish the divinity of Christ better than his moral teachings.[80] In sum, to the extent that miracles might have seemed embarrassing to the modern mind, they need not be, since they were possible; yet at the same time they were hardly to be on the front line of appeal to demonstrate the compelling moral and spiritual power of the Gospel.

King and his colleagues consequently made no use at all of biblical texts involving healings or miracles. The older generation had already exercised certain selectivity in reading the Bible, distinguishing those parts

---

[79]*Reconstruction*, pp. 61-63, 67; Hovenkamp, *Science*, p. 91.

[80]Tucker, *Function*, p. 46; Hyde, *Outlines*, pp. 67-68.

with timeless doctrinal and ethical significance from passages (especially Old Testament historical accounts) that were limited to the time or viewpoint of their authors. King continued such discrimination by finding texts with an "eschatological coloring" less reliable than others, though it was possible to capture the ethical spirit within them, beneath the "inherited presuppositions of the writers" of that age.[81]

The ante-bellum theologians had in fact already welcomed the whole trend toward biblical criticism, that is, as it operated within its established limits, concentrating on textual philology, grammar, and history. Even in the wake of broadly developed critical method and its occasional excesses at the hands of a skeptic such as David Friedrich Strauss, none of the three later authors viewed biblical-critical method as any threat to the revelation which they wanted every rational, ethical person to face factually and truthfully. Hyde admitted that historical criticism had made a "wreck of the ancient systems," but this had only given Christianity a deeper foundation. The Bible was "the high-water mark of the spiritual life," and the more it was critically tested, the brighter it would shine. The "incidental rubbish" that was no credit to the Bible anyway would be removed to reveal the real faith. The believer could accept the findings of the critics if they were factual; a traditional feature of Christ found invalid would simply have to be eliminated. But this posed no threat to the Christ whom "loyal, loving hearts" had found for nineteen centuries a symbol of "infallible spiritual insight, absolute purity, perfect holiness, sinless sincerity, supreme self-sacrifice and an infinite compassion." In fact, adherence to the ideal of Good Will was the

---

[81]King, *The Ethics of Jesus*, William Belden Noble Lectures for 1909 (New York: Macmillan Co., 1910, 1912), pp. 147-48, 190; Hovenkamp, *Science*, pp. 62-66.

fundamental thing anyway, and Christians could "get along just as well without as with the historical tradition" if it proved unfounded.[82]

Biblical criticism was a product of the Protestant belief in free inquiry, Tucker maintained, and had liberated the Bible from the literalism that had spawned so many sects and schisms. Scholars were leaving the Christian with "a new conception of Christianity, larger, simpler, and more unifying." Dogmatic beliefs were giving way to a stronger and more productive emphasis on ethics, duty and conscience. All this rendered the faith ever more compelling to the modern mind.[83]

King devoted a whole section of his *Reconstruction* to the problems of historical criticism. He was already sure, though, that New Testament criticism was making ever clearer "the solid historical basis of Christianity" and the "incomparable position of Christ as the supreme person of history." The somewhat newer science of criticizing the Old Testament historically would be no threat if it were conducted in a true scientific spirit, free of prejudice, sound in judgment, and modest in the face of the facts. Such a procedure would simply show the facts of how God really did act, thus making faith stronger and the Bible more reliable. The Christian should feel no "obligation to defend anything in the Bible which is unworthy of the spirit of Christ or manifestly not true." Biblical authors were not trying to teach science or history anyway, King argued, but to convey God's self-revelation through real, historical persons, closer contact with whom criticism was actually making more possible. Moreover, critical conclusions would help put

---

[82]*God's Education*, p. 55; *Outlines*, pp. 190-192; "The Christ of Criticism and the Christ of Faith," *Independent* 52 (May 31, 1900):1298; *Good Will*, p. xiv.

[83]*My Generation*, pp. 6, 96; *Function*, p. 22.

a stop to indiscriminate prooftexting in theology, and enable theologians to get back to "the great fundamental principles of the kingdom of God." Of course, King and his two colleagues themselves quoted scripture freely wherever it seemed even remotely relevant to their argument, but perhaps more spontaneously than older theologians, being less beholden to a certain system of doctrine.[84]

V. The Ethical Appeal of the Christian Faith

If the three authors and their audiences were hindered in their faith by any central belief in revelatory miracles or demand for the consistent inerrancy of the Bible, they found in the creeds and dogmas of both the ancient church and the Calvinists a seemingly insurmountable barrier to sensible modern agreement with Christianity. The theologians undertook to show, therefore, that Christianity revealed universally acceptable spiritual and moral realities, and required no doctrine to which a rational person could not accede.

The authority of the modern pulpit, Tucker told Yale seminarians, could not rest on "the impossible or the unreasonable, or upon what may be to most minds the merely external." To the extent that preaching went against "devout reason or reverent scholarship" it would lose its credibility. No, he told a Boston audience, the essential thing in any case was convictions, not creeds, for the great conceptions of God, immortality, the worth of man, the personality of Jesus as the "Master of human service," provided the

---

[84]*Reconstruction*, pp. 110-111, 113, 144, 146, 154-55; *Seeing Life Whole; A Christian Philosophy of Life*, Deems Lectures for 1922, New York University (New York: Macmillan Co., 1923), p. 135.

motive for religion's true practical results: reverence, right-mindedness, and service.[85]

To persuade others of the truth of Christianity, Hyde agreed, one must show them that the faith "is the explanation and the justification and the triumph of all that they now do really believe in" and not ask them to accept creeds symbolic of "the outgrown experience of a bygone stage of human evolution."[86] The current creed, he argued, presumably referring to the Apostles' Creed, possibly to the Westminster Confession, mixed "truth and lies, facts and fancies, intuitions and superstitions, essentials and excrescences," and would have to be sorted out into its essential doctrines and reorganized, not mechanically, but organically.[87] God was no longer to be seen as remote and arbitrary, Christ as a merely sentimental figure, or the Spirit as some vague and mystical entity. "The hard and fast distinctions between earth and heaven, present and future, natural and supernatural, priest and layman, God and man, have completely broken down," he asserted, and a God perceived as setting down rules administered exclusively by the church was no longer any more relevant than agricultural experiments conducted on Mars would be to the farmer.[88] Thus Hyde called for a reorganized faith "rooted in a central spiritual insight," namely, making God's will the basis of character and conduct, with the reconstructed articles of faith

---

[85]*Making and Unmaking*, p. 13; "The Religion of the Educator," in *Personal Power; Counsels to College Men* (Boston: Houghton Mifflin Co., 1910), p. 282.

[86]*Good Will*, p. xxii; *Sin and Its Forgiveness*, Modern Religious Problems, ed. A. W. Vernon (Boston: Houghton, Mifflin Co., 1909), p. 56.

[87]*God's Education*, pp. 1-2.

[88]*Good Will*, p. x; *Sin*, p. 100.

"bound together by logical relations in a rational order of subordination, instead of being tied mechanically together in a promiscuous bundle by the tight cords of blind tradition and unverified authority."[89]

Perhaps because of his ties with Fairchild, King was kinder to the tradition, but equally certain that creeds or outmoded analogies had nothing to do with the basics of Christian faith. No one could hand out a ready-made creed, he told the Sunday School teachers; and he implied that they might wish to follow his example and stop referring to technical theological terms like regeneration and sanctification.[90] He warned against excessive reliance on analogies such as the law and government model of Christ's atonement, and urged believers to come face to face with "the facts of revelation." No other word occurred more often in his writings than "honest"; no one could enter into the spiritual world on a dishonest basis, trying to accept something really unacceptable. One had to make "an honest response" to the "great realities" of spiritual life, which of course he was sure life would constantly verify and justify. But to confine them to a system of doctrines accepted a priori and not based on one's own deepest experiences of life was an invitation to pretense and unreality.[91]

The tradition had some validity for King; he considered the ancient creeds a help toward enlarging one's own point of view through seeing the continuity of Christian history. At the same time, though, he judged the creeds to be riddled with paradoxes ensuing from the ancient method of

---

[89]*God's Education*, pp. 44-45.

[90]*Greatness and Simplicity*, pp. 6, 157.

[91]*Seeming Unreality*, pp. 57-62, 91-92; *Reconstruction*, p. 234; *Social Consciousness*, pp. 172-73.

compromising by putting opposite statements together. The modern theologian could not be content "to leave them simply as paradoxes," but should try to think them through to unity. This task was further complicated by the complete omission from the Apostles' Creed of the life of Christ between his birth and death, and thus of the whole influence of Christianity on the ethical life through Christ's example. Similarly, while he found a strong ethical strain in Calvinist tradition from Edwards to Fairchild, he could no longer put credence in any doctrine of "salvation by divine decree." Again, the test of any dogma was its practical fruit in the life of the believer.[92]

Having scuttled the problem of intellectual assent to creeds, the presidents sought to expand the moral influence of Christianity as the foundation of personal relations. To do so they turned to the personality and teachings of Jesus Christ, who in his life and relations had shown both the character of God and the perfection of humanity. The supremacy of Christ not only within the Christian faith but in all human history and civilization was universally recognized, they thought. King was convinced that the "whole inductive temper" as well as the "deeper moral convictions" of his time were leading "naturally to the recognition of Christ as the supreme person, and therefore the supreme fact, of history and the supreme revelation of God." Evolution was bringing "the distinctively Christian stage" which would give meaning to the whole developmental process, showing in Christ the perfection of character. That virtually all the lives of Christ had been written in the last sixty-five years King viewed as significant evidence of the modern effort to capture "Christ's own mind" as the "one great source of the

---

[92]*Reconstruction*, pp. 5-6, 8, 170, 182; *Social Consciousness*, p. 108.

knowledge of God's character and purpose." As the "supreme datum" of history Christ was thus available to factual scientific historical investigation; but the meaning and value of Christ was of course the sphere which theology was to highlight. This was a happy if easy task, for "by the common consent of all men," Christ was already recognized as "the greatest in the greatest sphere," the moral and spiritual world.[93]

Tucker and Hyde certainly concurred in the supremacy of Christ. Jesus had made it possible, Tucker wrote, "for the spiritual to live in the midst of the tremendous materialism of this century." Hyde found in Christ the historic revelation of the universal will of God brought to personal self-expression in a supreme and ultimate exhibition of God's love.[94]

When it came to defining more precisely the person and work of Christ, though, the presidents found themselves parting ways with ancient tradition in an effort to compose a Christology acceptable to the modern age. They wanted no metaphysical theories, but a compelling ethical portrait that would appeal to the reasonable person. Hyde tried in his first book, the *Outlines*, to argue from an "*a priori* conception" of what a Son of God would be, namely, one who would see nature as Mind, society as Will, the Infinite in the finite, and duties and relations under the Fatherhood of God and the brotherhood of man. The "consensus of the competent in spiritual things has been almost unanimous" that Jesus fit this description and bore this title, he concluded. Not only that, but no matter how exalted a conception of a Son of God one could dream up, Christ would fit it, and it would be no more than the Gospels described. Christ was the perfect man, manifesting all the

---

[93]*Reconstruction*, pp. 185-87, 241-42; *Social Consciousness*, pp. 188-89.

[94]Tucker, *Making and Unmaking*, p. 29; Hyde, *God's Education*, pp. 26-30.

ethical laws and social principles recognized everywhere as fundamental to society and the goal of progress. Since Jesus knew all this as God's Will and purpose, and since "the perfection of humanity" was in itself "the revelation of divinity," it was proper to say that Christ had existed with God from the beginning as the eternal Son or Logos in whom God delighted.[95]

Jesus' human personality, character and life manifesting the divine love and will was the heart of revelation, though; so Hyde soon settled on an "ethical Sonship" as a more accurate term, for it needed no metaphysical or creedal explanations, but could rest on evidence that *Jesus' Way* was ethically superior. Christ could still be worshipped as divine in the same sense that "contact with a perfect conductor is contact with the battery itself," or in another analogy, that a printed book and the mind of the author could be said to be "of the same nature." God's nature was love; Christ's historic expression of love was the highest; therefore Christ was the Son of God.[96]

Tucker was little more consistent in trying to articulate his understanding of Christ. On the one hand, he implied that sonship with God was part of Christian character in general as the believer responded obediently to the call to "diviner forms of service." This call was best heard in relation to the person of Christ, in whom the lines between divine and human faded away as "the perfect humanity of Jesus" became also "the complete expression of his divinity." On the other hand, Tucker maintained that Jesus bore a self-consciousness of his life and being that was not merely the perfection of his humanity, but an expression of eternal divinity incarnate in a man. This was

---

[95]*Outlines*, pp. 50-61.

[96]*Jesus' Way*, pp. 25-29; *God's Education*, pp. 26-30.

a mystery, Tucker conceded, but he claimed to "prefer mystery to insufficiency in my faith."[97]

King found in "the ethical and spiritual personality of Jesus Christ" the "supreme and religiously adequate revelation of God," who being a person, had of course to reveal himself through a historical person existing in personal relations and showing forth character. The considerations about Jesus that weighed most in the modern day were not metaphysical, then, but concerned his "character and personal relations." Jesus was sinless, rising to the highest moral ideal, with a character such as could be transferred directly to God. Moreover, he possessed the "conscious ability to redeem all other men," that is, a "God-consciousness" and "sense of mission" which would have toppled into insanity "any other brain the world has ever seen," but made him "sweet, normal, rational," living a wholesome human life. Jesus was "the Ideal realized" and thereby called out "absolute trust" unlike any other person in history, King concluded.

Thus King considered the ability to adequately phrase some statement of Christ's relation to God in metaphysical terms far less important than seeing God in Christ's life and character. Especially "the metaphysical proposition" that Christ was of one essence with the Father seemed no sensible test of whether a person believed in Christ's deity. For the divinity of Jesus came from his absolutely unique purpose instigated by God, with whom he was morally and spiritually at one. If a metaphysical statement of this were still needed, King thought, one could simply base it on the whole trend in modern philosophy toward defining the essence of a thing teleologi-

---

[97]Tucker, *Function*, pp. 31-33, 38; "'Life in Himself': A Meditation on the Consciousness of Jesus Christ," *Andover Review* 17 (February 1892):195.

cally, in terms of its purpose. Just as the essential quality of a piece of paper, for example, derived from the use made of it, so the essence of Jesus would be based on divine purpose in him; in that sense he could be said to be of one essence with the Father.[98]

The presidential theologians in general presented a Christology of superlatives, demonstrated clearly in King's chapter on Christ in *Fundamental Questions*. Christ represented the best life, the best ideals and standards, the best insight into the laws of life, the best convictions, the best hopes, the best dynamic for living, the best revelation of God. The truly exemplary thing about him, though, was his willingness to sacrifice himself for these ideals, a self-giving which was somehow salvific for the believer.

No traditional manner of expressing the atoning work of Christ was any longer adequate, however, in King's view. The old legal or governmental or forensic analogies had become external and mechanical, obscuring the moral reality of Christ's redemption of personal relations. Even if one no longer thought of judgment coming in some spectacular final assize, though, one still had a sense of falling short and being judged by the standard of moral perfection. At this point a moral interpretation of "propitiation" for sin was helpful, to wit, that God the Father never wanted to give up on his wayward children and would accept the honest intention to do his will as his child grew in character, thus propitiating himself. Christ then represented more explicitly God's long-suffering activity of redemption, through the giving of his life showing how God poured his life into man completely, in an effort to restore man's "filial spirit" in obedience to God's will. God's work in Christ was in a sense a "direct substitute for that punishment" that would

---

[98]*Reconstruction*, pp. 233, 242-49.

come to disobedient man, but it was more fitting to say that God worked in Christ to reconcile the personal relation of man to himself. The Christian life was one of deepening friendship with others and with God, to which Christ's self-sacrificing love pointed the way, and no other, more abstract, definition of his work was necessary beyond this "wholly ethical" process.[99]

Tucker also found in Christ's sacrifice and suffering the great motive necessary to religion; a merely ethical religion lacked the motive that Christianity offered. Jesus' sacrifice was beginning to seem even more real, in fact, as evolutionary theory showed how much sacrifice was necessary to progress even in the fabric of nature. Jesus' sacrifice was thus part of the law of the universe and thereby a source of hope for the spiritual salvation of the world.[100]

Hyde was no more satisfied than King with the old analogical explanations for Christ's atonement, and relied even more than Tucker on a natural, evolutionary understanding of Christ's suffering. Christ had not died to appease an angry God or to vindicate the majesty of divine law and government, he insisted. He died simply because he embodied love, which called for sacrifice in his situation as in every other. Everything of worth required sacrifice, a universal rule which Christ brought to the fore in his faithfulness to his loving Father and friendship with sinful men and outcast women, even to the point of death.

An understanding of Christ's cross required no appeal to doctrines outmoded by human evolution or to the threat of hell and damnation, in

---

[99]*Fundamental Questions* (New York: Macmillan Co., 1917), pp. 96-108; *Reconstruction*, pp. 174-75, 239; *Social Consciousness*, pp. 150-60.

[100]*Making and Unmaking*, pp. 137, 206-7, 211.

Hyde's opinion. Jesus' vicarious sacrifice was simply the best example of the "law of vicarious sacrifice . . . written into the constitution of the moral universe," that is, that if one person did wrong, others suffered for it, since society was organic and required the adjustment of each person to all the others. Jesus saw perfectly how much evil and suffering was being inflicted on his fellow humans, mostly at the hands of "prosperous and respectable sinners," and so he made the "cause of the poor victims his own." He took upon himself the consequences of sin by "appealing to the sinner who . . . caused the sorrow, to be a better man." His enemies killed him for speaking out against evil and sin, crucifying him upon the cross, which was "the naturally selected, divinely appointed method of the salvation of the world" because it showed once and for all the necessity of suffering and sacrifice to the progress of society toward embodying the ideal of Good Will.[101]

Jesus suffered and died for the sake of his ethical teachings, which both Hyde and King thought were clear and comprehensive enough to merit an entire volume. Hyde had already declared in *God's Education* that any "intelligent and thoughtful student of the New Testament" ought to be able to determine with substantial accuracy "what Jesus would say or do" in any given circumstance of life. When he composed his account of *Jesus' Way* a few years later, then, he simply took moral precepts from Jesus' teachings in the Synoptic Gospels, and grouped them together, "freely translated, under a dozen heads, according to their logical relations and common-sense proportions." The chapters predictably reproduced what he had already said in earlier works about love and sacrifice at the heart of God's Good Will for

---

[101]*Outlines*, p. 138; *God's Education*, pp. 121-22, 127-30; "The Cross of Christ in the New Theology," *Outlook* 64 (March 24, 1900):678-79; *Jesus' Way*, pp. 123-29; *Sin*, p. 62.

all human beings as revealed by Jesus. The Bible provided the necessary
corroboration of universal truth that was self-evident to every thinking person
anyway.

King was at least more sophisticated in his approach, basing his account
of the *Ethics of Jesus* on the latest biblical-critical data. The Zurich scholar
Paul Wilhelm Schmiedel had identified twelve passages in Matthew and
Mark that he thought were "foundation-pillars" of historical evidence in the
gospels, mainly on the critical principle that what seemed unfavorable to
Jesus would not have been included in scripture were it not true. All of
these passages King found marvelously indicative of the primacy of Jesus'
ethical teachings; the occasion when he could not heal for lack of people's
faith, for example (Mark 6:5-6), showed the "moral conditions" necessary even
for healing. When John's disciples asked about Jesus' authenticity (Matthew
11:2-6), his reply was the appeal, "beyond all works of healing, that 'the poor
have good tidings preached to them.'"

Putting the Cambridge biblicist Francis Crawford Burkitt's thirty-one
passages doubly attested in both Mark and Q to similar use, King found them
to provide Jesus' statement of the "fundamental laws of life," such as the
inwardness of morality, the necessity of self-sacrifice, the need of simple
living, the inevitability of cause and effect in relations with others, the call
of service, and reverence for the person. King then went on to closer study
of the Sermon on the Mount, particularly the Beatitudes, which demonstrated
Jesus' striking originality and supremacy over other teachers in the insight
and fresh spirit of his moral teaching. The Beatitudes were Jesus' "map of
life," showing the qualities of highest character, the personal elements of
humility, penitence, self-control, and eagerness for achieving character, and

the social elements of sympathy, reverence, love, and sacrifice. In his *Laws of Friendship* he showed how the qualities of the Beatitudes were also, of course, the means for deepening friendship with others and with God.[102]

Thus the new theologians, determined to show forth Christianity as the ultimate ethical religion based on personality and personal relations, put far more emphasis on Jesus' life and teachings than had their predecessors. They took full advantage of critical efforts to recover the historical Jesus, while incorporating the basic assumption of the "lives of Jesus" movement, that the character and intent of the real man Jesus had been obscured by the superficial and time-bound religiosity of his day. They were persuaded that one could look beneath the miraculous and eschatological coloring of the Gospels to discover Jesus as a teacher of moral freedom and duty, the revealer of the ethical will of God. Yet in their stress on Jesus' precepts and example they were largely carrying forward the moral bent of the older theologians. The latter had also found in the sayings of Jesus the principles of conduct for family, political, and economic life. The rather abstract legal theory of the atonement on which rational theology had insisted certainly lacked the personal persuasiveness of the later moral influence theory; but the intent of both was the same. Jesus had lived and died to reveal and reinforce human freedom and responsibility under the sovereignty of divine will, both generations argued; and if both God and Christ seemed friendlier, closer, more personal, to the later theologians, it was only because such a God was more believable to the rational mind focussed on human progress toward a visible kingdom of duty fulfilled in all social relations.

---

[102]*Ethics of Jesus*, pp. 33, 41-42, 57, 73-77, 198, 206, 213-14.

VI. Living the Christian Life

If Christianity was the preeminently ethical religion, then the concomitant movements of sin to salvation, law to grace, justification to sanctification,
would seem to have deserved a prominent place in the theology of the
presidents. Actually, though, these doctrines were so readily subsumed under
the category of the moral character necessary to fulfilling the will of God in
personal and social relations, that at least the classical approach to such
questions occupied a relatively minor position. King hardly touched on the
problem of sin in his initial *Reconstruction*; Hyde wrote only a short volume,
Sin and Its Forgiveness. Older questions about human ability, the irresistibility of grace, and so on, were implicitly rejected even as subjects of discussion.
The new authors moved away from moral government theology toward a
thoroughgoing emphasis on ethical personality.

At the same time, however, in their intent to define sin and salvation
simply as matters of moral choice, the three men were carrying forward the
older impulse toward converting theology into moral philosophy and dogma
into ethics. King's predecessor Finney had already defined salvation as a
change of will evidenced in moral character, and more widely, discussions of
such doctrines as the atonement and predestination had long since dropped
from prominence in theological discourse. In their place came broad appeals
for Christianity based on its ready accessibility to the conscientious, well-
meaning person. No abstruse definitions were needed when the pattern for
Christian life was apparent in the common human experience of living in
modern society.

King thought the rising social consciousness, especially in its emphasis
on the mutual influence of men, was leading to a "deepening sense of sin."

As personal relations took on more value, the social conscience became keener. People became more aware of what was due to others, and of their failures to fulfill the Golden Rule in all their relations for lack of love. Unlike the "self-tormenting and fanciful sins" typical of devotional literature, though, the sense of failure of judgment spurred by the social consciousness was a "good, honest, wholesome sense of sin" growing from the judgment of Christ himself. While the fear of sin was diminishing with the receding vision of hell, the shame of it increased as one compared one's actions to the moral standard Christ set, or took to heart his words that in doing things to others, "Ye did it unto me."

Conversion from sin to righteousness King grounded on "the contagion of the good"; that is, Christ redeemed a person through his "immediate influence" and complete giving of himself to the sinner. This manifest self-sacrifice and patient suffering could hardly fail to win the "cooperative will of the other" to desire the same spirit and to accord his will with "God's own righteous purpose." Thus was one launched on the journey toward "right relations" with others and "attainment of character." If King's method seemed to provoke its converse, that moral character, not Christian experience, was the locus of salvation, King was worried not the least. The world was seeing a lot of "unconscious Christianity," he asserted, and he was not one to exclude from his company anyone doing good, or to say that Jesus could not work "in the consciousness of men far beyond the limits of our feeble faith."[103]

Tucker began his essay on "The Christian" in *Progressive Orthodoxy* with the same question, whether people whose lives were Christ-like could be said

---

[103]*Social Consciousness* pp. 130, 139-50.

to be saved by Christ. He first argued that salvation must be by faith, not by character, that Christ could not save without the person's consciously seeking and knowing it. But then he went on to argue more or less contrarily that through the "development of moral agency" even the heathens could be "brought into conscious relations to Christ" and could "personally appropriate his redemption." This process operated through God's unity of method by which his "moral government" was no longer divided into law and grace, but rather wholly intent on granting to every person a Christian opportunity. Here Tucker seemed to hint at affirming the controversial Andover doctrine of probation, in which every human being was to be granted the chance here or hereafter to know Christ before facing judgment.

In any case, a unified moral government meant that God intended all his children to enter into a "filial relation" with him. Sin was simply inconsistent with that relation, and the believer resisted sin out of gratitude for a relation from which could develop Christian character.[104]

The movement from sin to salvation, from law to grace, Hyde viewed as a divine education of man along evolutionary lines. In his first article on the matter in an 1890 *Andover Review*, he confined law and sin to the lower ideals of man's animal self, and perceived grace and salvation as adherence to the higher ideals instituted by God. The divine education, detailed in *God's Education of Man*, covered three stages, from the state of nature in which man was self-sufficient and self-assertive as Thomas Hobbes described, a state which had to come under the control of law; to the state of grace in which one was part of the organism of society; to the state of service in which one found one's specific role in the organic whole. More succinctly,

---

[104]"The Christian," pp. 133-145; see also Williams, *Andover Liberals*, p. 81.

law was the dam controlling natural desires, grace the channeling of them toward awareness of others, and service the ideal drawing man toward self-forgetful love.

Quoting Kipling's "Law of the Jungle . . . Obey!" Hyde argued that human evolution necessitated law, for in the complexity of social relations man was well-adjusted here, ill-adjusted there, from which the evil of man's lower state arose. As natural selection made examples of the good (the well-adjusted) more numerous, they were made into law. The highest form of law, because universal and progressive, was found among the Jews, whom God taught the lesson of his will for "the impartial and universal good." The law established right relations between persons as well as harmonious relations between man and his environment, and so led to universal good.

At the same time, though, law was only man's "primary school condition" of conformity and restraint. The attainment of the higher character of which man was capable came through grace, to quote Browning, making "the low nature better." Where law was merely restraining, grace taught "what others have done for us; and in turn suggests how we should feel toward them." This "new disposition in the individual, a new dispensation for the race," brought the realization of gratitude for a good and beneficent moral order. While it was difficult for man to overcome old habits and associations, he was helped by the "glad message" of justification by faith, which assured him that the desire to follow Christ and to suffer in behalf of others for the larger life of love was sufficient for redemption.[105]

---

[105]"What Is Salvation?" *Andover Review* 13 (April 1890):372-79; *God's Education*, pp. v-vi, 36-40, 59-71, 74, 114-17, 167-171.

In his later book on sin and forgiveness, Hyde accused the "new theology" of failing to develop a sufficient doctrine in this area, and so remaining "vague, sentimental, inchoate, inefficient: a halfway station on the road to soulless secularity." He argued that theology should help people see how much sin and forgiveness were part of the fabric of everyday life experience, and so fundamental to morally relevant Christianity. Sin he saw as a common failure to maintain "that constant kindliness, that sensitive sympathy, that strenuous rectitude, that disinterested benevolence, which the love of God" required. To experience sin, though, was to experience forgiveness, for the two were virtually inseparable. One knew of forgiveness through the experience of forgiving others, which was "proof positive, assurance absolute, that God, and Christ, and all Christian men so far as they know the facts, forgive us our sins." To have a forgiving spirit was to know that God forgave, for God was at least as good as the best in man. The only unforgivable sin in Hyde's book was to reject proffered forgiveness; the unrepentant sinner deserved punishment, the other half of a virile, effective Christianity, and should suffer society's condemnation and nature's retribution until he repented his offense. Hyde was sure, though, that sinners would give up their sins if they were earnestly confronted with the grief and suffering their actions were causing to others and to society.[106]

Sin was no esoteric doctrine, then, the presidents argued, nor was salvation from it limited to some elite who had gained favor with God. Law and grace were thoroughly interwoven with the evolution of human nature and society. For modern persons living at the highest stage of civilization, sin was simply the poor moral choice, the refusal to live in appropriate social

---

[106]*Sin*, pp. 10, 16-17, 19-20, 74, 90.

relations and attitudes. God's salvation worked through improved character; there was nothing strange or mystical about turning toward the moral life in a spirit of seeking God's will. One might even unconsciously qualify as a Christian.

Thus no peculiar spiritual experience was required of the Christian, either. Hyde rejected earth-shattering conversions as unnecessary; studies had shown that these were simply associated with puberty and growing up anyway, that is, the stress caused by the "ramification of nervous tissue" in the brain and the consequent "ability to grasp general ideas." On the contrary, regeneration and spiritual growth was a gradual process of development through the influence of one's environment. Spiritual life was inseparable from one's relations to others in society through the family, business, politics, and community in general. The spirit of those who accorded their lives with the will of God and entered into the "self-transcending life of social service" was in fact the Holy Spirit, working for the realization of God's will in the life of humanity. The Holy Spirit was divine as the will of God working through individuals, and as Christ's life multiplied into individuals; therefore it was part of the Trinity, proceeding from both Father and Son.[107]

Christian spirituality took the form primarily of social service, then, in Hyde's view. Certainly he brooked no mysticism, condemning it in a 1902 *Independent* as a primitive trait carried over from man's early days as a "jelly-like" form seeking union with the world around it, in short, a form of pantheism. The person who performed the concrete duties of everyday life was far greater than any mystic. Nevertheless Hyde thought that prayer was not only possible but appropriate; for it called upon new forces to be brought

---

[107]*God's Education*, pp. 142-66; *Outlines*, pp. 80-84.

to bear upon a situation through the workings of a rational will. To deny the possibility of prayer was to deny divine personality, for God had to be free to act in the realm of causality and law. In fact, since prayer was the communion of the will of man with the will of God, answer to prayer was as inevitable as any cause and effect in nature. Hyde's analogy for this was prayer as a keeping of "the car of life in constant connection with the spiritual trolley," so that God's will could not help being done in the individual will.[108]

Tucker also described regeneration as the "reconstruction of character" along the lines of Christ's, and found it to be the work of the Holy Spirit which motivated man to faith in Christ. The Spirit was universal in making effective Christ's atoning power, but was inseparable from Christ. Again, Tucker thought it fallacious to argue that the Spirit was working toward universal understanding of Christ without Christ himself being necessary; at the same time he admitted that regeneration occurred outside of Christianity, just without its higher and more definite standard. In any case, the Holy Spirit worked through individuals and through society for "the elevation of the race," furnishing the "direct material for all progress and all reforms."[109]

King's vision of the spiritual world was so thoroughly ethical that he could find little role for the specifically Holy Spirit, even in the regenerate life of the believer. In his *Reconstruction*, he criticized those who were trying to apply personalism to the Trinity, for he feared they would emerge with three Gods, three complete persons. Yet when he wrote out what he

[108]"Mystic or Christian?" *Independent* 54 (January 2, 1902):10-11; "Mystic Morality," *Independent* 54 (January 9, 1902):74-78; *Outlines*, pp. 121-29; *God's Education*, pp. 154-55.

[109]"Holy Spirit," pp. 116-129.

considered the true biblical creed, God revealed in Christ and making himself known in the believer through friendship, he did not even mention the Holy Spirit. In his second book he at least used the name, in going over the same ground, calling God's presence in every individual heart that opened itself to association with him and his will, the Spirit. "What metaphysical theory" might be used to describe the Trinity was not "of prime importance," to King; the simple reality was all that mattered.

An excessive spirituality, what earlier rationalists had labelled "enthusiasm," was clearly not a legitimate part of the Christian life, in King's opinion. He was constantly warning against sentimental or emotional religion. Quoting Herrmann, he condemned false mysticism that was "unrational, unhistorical, and so unchristian," in its appeal to possession of the soul by God or emotional excitements. Any such state, "half a swoon and half an ecstasy" was a "swamping of clear self-consciousness" necessary to moral life. It was indicative of the whole "neo-platonic" system that operated by negative method, making God unknown and irrational. As against emotional, subjective, vague, misty, and pantheistic mysticism, the true Christian mysticism was based on honest faith, ethical surrender to God, and reverence for persons, a real love that led to moral duty.[110]

Likewise King warned against the excesses of revivalism; the method should not become coercive in overrunning the sacred personality of the believer, nor should it demand one type of sudden experience as a mark of true conversion. Modern psychological studies of religion by C. C. Starbuck, George A. Coe, and William James seemed to cast instantaneous changes from gloom to happiness in the skeptical light of subconscious motivations,

---

[110]*Reconstruction*, pp. 191-93; *Social Consciousness*, pp. 55-65, 70-77, 222-26.

King suggested, and conversion should not be made to depend on excessive emotional states. Yet with a collegiate ancestor like Charles G. Finney, King could not and did not turn completely against revivalism, only indicating its proper place as an occasional stimulus to the human feeling of personal relation to God in a religion real, rational, and ethical. This middle ground had once been occupied by his mentor Fairchild and other moderates like Wayland.[111]

King defended the possibility of prayer on the grounds of personal relations. If God was a person, then surely he must have access to human persons in the spiritual sphere. Again, even the natural laws by which the material world operated were only modes of God's activity, and certainly if evolution had led to the personal stage, it also allowed for further development of the spiritual under a creative God. Prayer was effective, of course, as the growth in moral unity with God and the development of character; but further, it manifested a growing social consciousness as people were drawn to see their mutual influence for good upon each other through intercessory prayer.[112]

All three authors understood the church to be the community of those seeking to follow God's will in organized service to humanity. Tucker accused existing churches of being too institutional, too concerned with saving themselves through exclusivist doctrines of election, and too beholden to the upper classes to be in sympathy with the working classes.

---

[111]"Christian Training and the Revival as Methods of Converting Men: A Historical and Psychological Study," in *Personal and Ideal Elements in Education* (New York: Macmillan Co., 1904, 1908), pp. 129-235.

[112]*Reconstruction*, pp. 71-72; "Difficulties Concerning Prayer," *Biblical World* 46 (September 1915):131-34, and *Biblical World* 46 (November 1915):281-84; *Social Consciousness*, pp. 164-67.

He was particularly aggravated by the persistence of the American
Board of Commissioners for Foreign Missions in requiring all missionary
candidates to subscribe to the doctrines of the "universal perdition of the
heathen" and of "restricted opportunity" for salvation, as the rationale and
basis for mission work. By contrast, he called upon Christians to identify
with the world, to communicate Christian sympathy "in the democratic spirit"
to those seeking to rise but suffering injustice. If the church really lost itself
"in the life of humanity" it would find unity in the brotherhood of man
beyond all petty sectarianism.[113]

Tucker acknowledged Hyde's role in promoting church unity much
along the same lines. The latter wrote numbers of articles faulting excessive
sectarian spirit and preaching of abstract doctrine for the "impending
paganism in New England." The churches needed to open their doors by
simplifying their confessions of faith and demonstrating the connection of
Christianity to the life of the community.[114] He blamed the seminaries for
measuring ministerial candidates by "morbid, narrow and inadequate tests,"
thus keeping out "youth and manliness, and letting only effeminacy and
sentimentalism in." He urged the use of a case system in educating ministers,
for nothing could be done in the abstract -- only in the particular could the
universal be found -- and the application of Christianity to real life was
urgent. He was so strident in his demand that theological schools stop
educating candidates into a dry formal creed "concocted before modern

---

[113]"The Christian," pp. 148-52; "The Church of the Future," in Rossiter Raymond, ed., *The
New Puritanism* (N.Y.: Fords, Howard, and Hulbert, 1898), pp. 223-29; Buckham, *Progressive*,
pp. 151-52; Tucker, *My Generation*, pp. 144-45, 152-58.

[114]Tucker, *My Generation*, p. 183; Hyde, "Impending Paganism in New England," *Forum*
13 (June 1892):519-28; "Church or Sect?" *Outlook* 66 (December 8, 1900):889-94.

philosophy was born," that a professor from his own alma mater inquired why, "if the heads of our seminaries and their professors were such fossils," New England colleges kept calling them to be their presidents.[115]

Undaunted, Hyde called upon the churches to give up their spiritual exclusiveness that discouraged from membership "the strong, brainy, forceful men of affairs" as well as those who did not "wear their hearts upon their sleeves." The church at the highest stage of God's education should be the "training-school for righteousness" and the fellowship for education in social service. Not to join it ought to be seen as comparable to a soldier refusing to fight with his regiment. On the other hand, nothing in the institutional church could be said to have "magical virtue or mysterious efficacy" in and of itself. Joining the church for the sake of joining made no more sense than trying "to warm a room by breathing on the bulb of the thermometer." Action in the world for which the church prepared one was the crucial purpose of the fellowship. The sacraments simply assisted in the struggle to put God's will into moral action; baptism was a kind assurance of God's blessing, for which common sense commended sprinkling over immersion, especially in the cold climate of Maine; and the Lord's Supper was a renewal of fellowship with Christ who was present there in the same sense that an author was present when one read his book. The clergy certainly had no special role except as exemplary servants; they needed to guard against an "idolatry of eloquence" in their preaching, and simply lead people to service, for "laymen, and ministers acting as laymen, that is as individual men in

---

[115]"The Minister Who Is Wanted," *Independent* 55 (August 20, 1903):1960-62; "Reform in Theological Education," *Atlantic Monthly* 85 (January 1900):16-26; "The Case System in the Ministry," *Homiletic Review* 57 (February 1909):95-96; "College and Seminary," *Independent* 61 (August 2, 1906):264-68; Burnett, *Hyde*, pp. 248-49.

personal relations with other individual men, do the real work" of advancing the Kingdom on earth.[116]

King joined the others in declaring the church a "priceless, living personal fellowship, in which alone Christian character, Christian faith, and Christian confession can arise and can continue." Christians would discover their unity beyond sectarianism in their common life and experience of Christ which would find expression through moral action. King was particularly exercised to rid the church of excessive sacramentalism; rather than putting faith in mechanical means only, he argued, the Christian should be seeking God in all his personal relationships.[117]

Thus in their apology for Christian faith and life the presidents were determined to remove all barriers to rational assent and moral compliance, all distance between spiritual grace and ethical will. The Christian was not asked to believe what he could not already accept as rationally necessary, nor to do what he could not already accept as morally desirable. The church was but a society of those who sought improved personal character and the good of the social order. No narrow requirements of spirituality were to be maintained -- conversion, contemplative prayer, sacramental practice. On the contrary, Christianity was for everyone who believed in the moral progress of an advancing civilization.

Finally, as Butler had always insisted, even the ultimate blessings of Christian faith were not to be limited to the chosen few or to those who

---

[116]*Outlines*, pp. 179-86, 193-95, 200-1; *God's Education*, pp. 41-43, 158-59, 190-95; *Good Will*, pp. 229-31; *Sin*, p. 95.

[117]*Social Consciousness*, pp. 174, 177-78; *Reconstruction*, pp. 176-77. The trend toward a rational, ethical view of the sacraments in the ante-bellum rational theology is detailed in Holifield, *Gentlemen*, pp. 155-85.

trusted in narrow dogmas. In a concluding rush of sentiment in no less than three of his major books, King reassured his readers that immortality was not only possible in a spiritual world of persons, but necessary to the character of God. If God annihilated his children, or simply let them perish, this would surely be more punishment to him than to them, as devoted as he was to their upbuilding in Christian character. Christ's work of bringing men into closer communion with God, too, was eternal and abiding. No historical evidence of his resurrection was necessary to establish his Lordship in the moral and spiritual realm, or his living presence with those striving to do God's will. The more one so strove to produce in his life the qualities that "ought to endure," the more one could "believe in immortality." Human ignorance of the facts of the future life was just another indication of God's reverence for the sacred personalities of his children and his unwillingness to intrude on their moral freedom to struggle toward the good.[118]

Hyde thought that immortality was implied in the very thought of the final triumph of God's kingdom, which was being progressively fulfilled "in the multiplication of disciples over the whole earth, in the deepening of the spiritual life, in the transformation of social institutions, and the elevation of moral standards." In his book of prayers entitled *Abba Father*, he joined in King's feeling that God was withholding knowledge of the future life for man's own good, and that it would turn out to be a life of even further growth in character. "As Thou has made this life of ours on earth a closed circle, free from violent interruptions," he prayed, so may I do my duty here,

---

[118]*Reconstruction*, pp. 249-50; *Social Consciousness*, pp. 239-46; *Seeming Unreality*, pp. 245-50.

trusting in Thy power "for future growth in character and progress in blessedness."[119]

VII. Conserving a Reasonable Christianity

The three presidents unquestionably intended their theology to be a complete break with an older Calvinism based on ancient creeds and divine decrees, and it was in terms of this discontinuity that the whole "new theology" was generally interpreted. As a reviewer of Hyde's *Outlines* in an 1895 *Critic* put it, "a theologian of twenty-five years ago would never have suspected the author of orthodoxy."[120] Tucker's address calling for the church to abandon its sectarianism and seek unity in service to a progressing humanity appeared in a collection entitled *The New Puritanism*. King took the same title for an essay in his volume on *The Moral and Religious Challenge of Our Times*, in which he implied that Puritanism had preached an arbitrary and judgmental God in a cold, intolerant religion disconnected with real life.

Yet the actual purpose of King's chapter was not to condemn Puritanism out of hand, but to preserve its best qualities for the new age. He warned against an overreaction from the Puritan heritage that would lead to false sentimentalism, false tolerance, false realism, or false aestheticism. Modern Americans needed to keep "the great positives of the Puritan spirit": its sense of the reality of God, its calling to a divine vocation, and above all, its feeling of accountability to the will of God in moral duty. Without such

---

[119]*Jesus' Way*, pp. 195-97; *Abba Father*, p. 69.

[120]Review of *Outlines of Social Theology*, *Critic* 27 [n.s. 24] (October 5, 1895):211.

an ethical heritage of self-control and self-denial in behalf of the moral unity
of society, generations to come would be "vacillating, flabby, self-indulgent,"
lacking the vigorous will to serve necessary for the good of persons and of
the community.[121]

The preservationist instinct showed itself throughout the presidents'
theology. Of course, they attacked creedalism, sacramentalism, mysticism,
and metaphysics, in short, anything that could not be put to a direct moral
purpose. But in this they were only carrying to fuller development the
strongly ethical bent of the Calvinism of their predecessors. In reference to
the genre of his mentor Fairchild's *Elements*, King asserted that "the days of
the great theological systems are doubtless past." Indeed the settled order
and ready deductions of the old rational theology had been thrown into
disarray by the new learning. Yet the presidents were sure that a theology
could be reconstructed around the "treasure" or the "germ" of truth in
Christian tradition, and that new doctrines could be just as scientific, that is,
factual and lawful, as any of the rest of the new knowledge. The result
would be, in a phrase of Hyde's strongly flavored with the older method of
analogy, a dogma that was to religion "as astronomy is to the stars."[122]

For their grounds of certainty, for their evidentiary arguments, for a
consensus on their moral purpose, the presidents went right back to the
rational theology in which they were educated, only applying it to new
problems. Even the most acerbic critic among them, Hyde, consistently
adduced Universal Reason and Will as an intuitive first principle of
philosophy, referred constantly to right relations among persons that were as

---

[121]*Moral and Religious*, pp. 235-82.

[122]King, *Reconstruction*, p. 2; Hyde, *God's Education*, p. 50.

certain as the laws of the universe, and virtually trumpeted his abiding faith in divine benevolence. He was joined by Tucker and King in finding evidence for God's existence in the natural and moral order, and evidence for the absoluteness of Christianity in its universal acceptance among the enlightened, its historicity, its moral superiority, and its connection with the higher, more progressive and civilized nations. While the miracles associated with biblical religion had dropped lower in the scales of data for revelation, their possibility was still defended largely on the grounds of a transcendent creator God's ability to act in ways beyond present knowledge of natural law. Passages on the probability of immortality as a state of blessedness in moral improvement were only transfigured arguments right out of Butler's *Analogy*.

Like their predecessors, these new theologians made ethics the heart and soul of religion. They were just as resistant to an "enthusiasm" of emotional religious experience or a "sacramentalism" of necessary divine grace as their forefathers in the faith had been. They were just as sure that humans could rationally, straightforwardly, honestly, and sincerely both know and do their moral duty, since God would never require them to do what he had not also granted them the means to accomplish. Unlike the older generation, they drew heavily on a Jesus whom they claimed to know historically rather than a Christ limited to creedal piety. But for all their sophistication in biblical science, the Jesus they educed merely endorsed their theological conceptions and ethical assumptions. If Jesus was made more personal, it was only because he was thereby more persuasive to rational minds intent on human moral progress.

The new generation was generally restless with the cold logic of the older rational theology. They were no longer interested in reasoning through questions of human moral ability or the irresistibility of grace. The precise deductive logic of a theology moving from sin to atonement to conversion to justification to sanctification with all its carefully rationalized assumptions no longer engaged the imagination or the will of the new authors. Yet disinterest in doctrines of divine grace or more broadly of the Godhead was only the natural outcome of an earlier theology written as a subheading of moral science. If religion was in the service of moral duty carried out in the rational relations of human society, then obviously human beings by nature had the necessary ability and knowledge to carry out their responsibility. Revelation was but a compelling supplement, and its new apologists sought only to make it more persuasive by appealing to the sensibilities of their own generation.

The striking difference between the old theology and the new emerged in the latter's struggle to respond to questions arising from the overwhelming consciousness of change in their era. Would new conceptions of nature, rising dependence on scientific data, historical criticism of the Bible or widening secularity in American life bring the decline of Christianity? The presidents responded with a resounding assurance that not decline, but progress, lay ahead for the Christian faith. They showed how closely it was connected with every new theory of nature or society (that is, the ones that affirmed human freedom). They argued that Christians had nothing to fear from science properly conducted, nothing to lose in criticism of their historical revelation. They suggested that God could be seen working in the evolution of nature, human nature, and advancing civilization. They dispensed with troubling metaphysical doctrines and outmoded analogies, professing to worship a God devoted to the friendship and moral education of his children, pointing to the supreme example of a divine moral life in Christ.

So sure were they that the modern era was expressing the very convictions of religion -- as King stated them, the reverence for the person, the unity of the ethical life in love, the recognition of Christ as the supreme person in history -- that they thought it unnecessary and detrimental to maintain any longer, again in King's terms, the "separation of the sacred and secular."[123]   Man could know as much about God as he knew about himself, Hyde argued, and God's Kingdom could be fulfilled in a society truly seeking to follow his will.

The source of all this optimism arguably lay in the absolute certainty of divine providence in the older theology. The government of a rational, lawful God had then incorporated the whole natural and moral order. The new theologians were equally sure of God's control, only adding qualities of dynamism and immanence in an age of change. But of course, these additions themselves evinced the anxious doubts that disquieted the presidents as well as their students. The world seemed to be breaking loose from providence in autonomy from religious assumptions once thought necessary.[124]

The presidential theologians rose to deny such a possibility, but in tones increasingly strident with intellectual assertions and cloyed with social complacency. "The universe must be on the side of the ethical will," King demanded with desk-pounding certainty in one of his last books, *Seeing Life*

---

[123]*Reconstruction*, p. 45.

[124]For a broader view of this problem, see William R. Hutchison, "Cultural Strain and Protestant Liberalism," *American Historical Review* 76 (April 1971):386-411.

Whole. "God's purpose in the universe and in its constitution must be such as shall be in line with man's own highest purposes . . . there could be no possible adequate religion otherwise." Ironically, he had already complained in his introduction that a new thirty-volume history of American civilization had just come out in which there was no mention of religion. The world was changing, but Hyde and his colleagues still clung to their vision of seeing life clear and seeing it whole. Look at "our railroads and furnaces . . . our comfortable homes . . . our hospitals for the sick . . . our settlements in the slums . . . our churches . . . our missions," Hyde clamored; they all "proclaim us a very religious people."[125] Nothing could be stronger evidence of the conservative defensiveness of such claims than the disappearance of the intellectual and social world which they were meant to evoke.

---

[125]King, *Seeing Life*, pp. 5, 123-24; Hyde, *Practical Idealism*, pp. 323-25.

CHAPTER FOUR

THE ETHICS OF RATIONAL LIVING

The era of published works in the old academic moral philosophy came to a close in 1892. In that year appeared James McCosh's *Our Moral Nature* and James Fairchild's *Elements of Theology*, the latter of which was as much an ethical as a theological tome. Within the next twenty years the entire genre was to disappear from public view. When the psychologist and later university president G. Stanley Hall surveyed college catalogues in 1894 to find what textbooks were being used to teach logic, ethics, psychology, and "allied subjects," he discovered that Wayland, Stewart, Reid, and Butler were still hanging on in some places, while Lotze, Kant, Hegel, and Spencer were coming into wider use. By 1910 John Dewey and James H. Tufts brought out a whole textbook on *Ethics* without so much as a mention of the older works, which vanished from college curricula as well.[1]

As Gladys Bryson showed in her 1932 studies, the old collegiate moral philosophy that had been the capstone of liberal arts education, incorporating

---

[1] D. H. Meyer, *Instructed Conscience*, pp. 130-31; G. Stanley Hall, "On the History of American College Textbooks and Teaching in Logic, Ethics, Psychology, and Allied Subjects," *Proceedings of the American Antiquarian Society* [n.s. 9] (April 1894), 137-194.

political science, economics, sociology, psychology, and ethics, broke up into its component parts in the late nineteenth century as each area became its own field of specialization. Sociology, for example, developed the study of social forces and movements, while psychology moved in two directions, toward laboratory experimentation exploring connections of mind and body, and toward developmental studies of the individual and its environment.

Yet as Bryson was at pains to show, the new fields still bore the imprint of the older unified method. Works in sociology especially still proceeded from general postulates about human nature and generalized pictures of the historical emergence of society, then described social forces presently at work and proposed schemes for the "quick amelioration of society." One of the first recognized sociologists, Albion Small, called sociology "a moral philosophy conscious of its task," and from his college presidency at Colby to his later professorship at the University of Chicago continued to maintain the unity of his field as an empirical yet also moral and religious undertaking.[2]

Thus, even though specialized studies were breaking off from the older unity, a definite movement was still afoot to sustain a moral purpose and consensus in the new fields. The traditional emphasis on individual character and responsibility would have to be maintained, if in new forms, to prevent psychology from falling over into behaviorism, or sociology from converting to collectivism or determinism. Chief among the advocates of preserving a personal if progressive ethic were the college presidents.

---

[2]Bryson, "Comparable Interests," "Emergence of the Social Sciences," and "Sociology Considered"; Small is quoted in the latter. See also Jurgen Herbst, "From Moral Philosophy to Sociology; Albion Woodbury Small," *Harvard Educational Review* 19 (1959):227-44; and Barnes, "Learning and Piety in Ohio Colleges."

Hyde, King, and Tucker were as sure of the primacy of personal morality as any of their predecessors had ever been. A changing intellectual and social world only made all the more important their affirmation of the ultimate ground of goodness and its reflection in the rational, self-controlled, properly motivated, and productive individual. Modern persons might have to adapt and adjust to a new world taking shape around them, but with a solid and resolute core of righteousness within, they could also and above all be shapers and masters of it.

Certainly the presidents·recognized the passing of the old systems in which they had been educated. Moral verities logically deduced from intuitive metaphysical or theological first principles seemed out of touch with the new learning and irrelevant to modern life. Practicality was the code word for a new moral philosophy. Just as in his *Practical Idealism* he wanted to show that the grounds of knowledge were inherent in the experience of things themselves, so Hyde intended in his *Practical Ethics* to demonstrate the reality of duty through a method of comprehending "in a rational and intelligible order the concrete facts with which conduct has to do." King took it upon himself to reduce modern psychology to its basic principles in order to apply them to *Rational Living*. They both joined Tucker in seeking to produce in their students a sense of truth that would establish them as right-minded and active citizens.[3]

Yet if the old moral philosophy now seemed sterile and old-fashioned, it had nevertheless been practical and *au courant* in its own day. Wayland's *Elements* began with a section on theoretical ethics, but the latter two-thirds of the book were devoted to practical ethics, and moral instruction of

---

[3]*Hyde, Practical Ethics* (New York: Henry Holt & Co., 1892, 1893), p. iii.

students was far more his purpose than abstract debate about ultimate right. He and his generation built on a faculty psychology that was then thought to order the human psyche, with the division into intellect, emotion, and will being universally accepted in Anglo-American "mental philosophy." Thus in a general sense the late nineteenth century presidents were only carrying forward similar impulses toward practicality and relevancy in moral theory.

Moreover, the new authors were just as anxious as their predecessors had been to convey a rational system of duties and laws and to invoke a universal conscience to apprehend right and wrong. They were just as sure that a well-motivated individual could determine what he ought to do, and do it. And if it could not be done, then they were just as certain that the effort to accord one's will with the will of God was all the moral governor of the universe could possibly require. For ultimately all morals were of divine origin, as revealed in the exemplary life of Christ, which the devout, good man sought to apply to his own life. Morality was inseparable from religion, then, in the syntheses of both the older philosophy and the new.

I. Teaching and Writing a Popular Morality

The title "moral philosopher" would not be much more applicable to the three presidents than "theologian" was. While they did all in their power to impart a moral philosophy to their passing classes of students, none of them wrote a systematic work comparable to Wayland's or Paley's, beginning with first principles and basic definitions and passing on to specific relations and duties. They were content to let stand the general grounds of ethical knowledge as presented in their theological works, and to devote their moral writings to the means and purposes of Christian character. Their moral views were for the most part far more hortatory than analytical.

Tucker lacked even the traditional presidential forum of the senior classroom, employing most of his time in administrative work and travels among the alumni. He later wrote of the "painful contrast" he felt with Hyde, who had made "his chair of instruction a seat of power." Tucker did fulfill a task which he thought went beyond the ordinary accomplishments of the classroom, though, by addressing the student body virtually every Sunday evening in chapel talks that he hoped would impress on them the truths and religious sense fundamental to intelligent action in the wider world. Many of these addresses were collected in a volume entitled *Personal Power*.[4]

When he was elected to the presidency of Bowdoin, Hyde also assumed the professorship of mental and moral philosophy. His former seminary professor Tucker wrote in support of his candidacy that Hyde was suited for the "chair of Metaphysics in any of our colleges," being possessed of "singular insight . . . genuine originality and . . . large resources." Indeed his teaching did bring him notable popularity with students, for he was more than willing to combine more formal recitation with open discussion of the issues of the day, always impressing his own opinion and course of action on their minds, to be sure. Some students later reminisced that they often incorporated his judgments into their own decisions, and one considered Hyde "my ideal of what a man ought to be."

On Hyde's arrival in 1885 the senior moral philosophy course was still using Noah Porter's *Elements of Intellectual Science* with its faculty psycholo-

---

[4]*My Generation*, pp. 318, 339-46; Leon B. Richardson, *History of Dartmouth College* 2 vols. (Hanover, N.H.: Dartmouth College Publications, 1932), 2:744ff.

gy, and comparable works in moral science and Christian evidences. Within ten years, though, Hyde had moved away from those and adopted contemporary studies such as William James's *Principles of Psyhology*. Soon the course was dropped as a senior requirement, no one textbook was followed, and presumably the class turned even more into a presidential forum.[5]

Hyde published two books more or less directly out of this class, *Practical Ethics* (1892) and *From Epicurus to Christ* (1904). The latter, like King's *Laws of Friendship*, was given in the form of lectures at Haverford College, and provoked widely different reactions which themselves reflected the synthetic nature of his work. *The Nation* called it a "popular study" conveying an "eclectic system of ethics" that disregarded historical considerations in favor of practical ones. Theodore Roosevelt, on the other hand, praised it in *The Outlook* for its "lofty nobility of ethical concept" which was combined "with the most practical and straight-forward common-sense treatment of the ways in which this concept should be realized in practice." *The Independent* took the middle ground, saying that Hyde discoursed in "a familiar and breezy sort of way," indicative of "the new method of writing philosophy in the language of the street," a trend which would please some and offend many. In any case, Hyde edited the book for republication in 1911 under a new title, *The Five Great Philosophies of Life*, an edition which was reissued as late as 1959.[6]

He also wrote several other short books in an even more popular style, including *Self-Measurement* (1908), later translated into Japanese as "How to

---

[5]Burnett, *Hyde*, pp. 84, 108-9, 226.

[6]Review of *From Epicurus to Christ*, *Nation* 80 (March 16, 1905):212; Theodore Roosevelt, "The Search for Truth in a Reverent Spirit," *Outlook* 99 (December 2, 1911):819-26; review of *From Epicurus to Christ*, *Independent* 58 (May 11, 1905):1075.

Cultivate One's Mind and How to Adjust Oneself to One's Environment,"[7] *The Quest of the Best* (1913), and *The Best Man I Know* (1917). The latter was part of a whole Macmillan Company catalogue of popular ethics that included King's *Fundamental Questions* and other works.

King began to teach philosophy courses in the 1890s that blended his mentor Fairchild's general theory of benevolence with themes from German Idealist authors. When he assumed the presidency he took over the course popularly known as "Senior Bible" and became a much acclaimed teacher and chapel speaker. Washington Gladden visited Oberlin to hear King, and remembered "the volley of sustained applause" upon the conclusion of King's remarks to the students.

In the classroom King used the textbook he published in 1905, *Rational Living*. His more devoted followers even formed a club called the "Rational Livers" to discuss his ideas. Their more cynical rivals soon countered by announcing with typical collegiate wit the forming of another club, the "Radical Gizzards." The *Dial* reviewer in 1906, Mr. Cockerell, would probably have joined the latter, for he thought the book at best "a collection of amiable platitudes." King was not discouraged by this, though he did not make further forays into ethical writing except in lectures published in *The Moral and Religious Challenge of Our Times* (1911), *Fundamental Questions* (1917), and *A New Mind for a New Age* (1920).[8]

In sum, while the late century presidents authored no new systems of ethics, they still assumed a time-honored role as moral spokesmen on the

---

[7]Burnett, *Hyde*, p. 294.

[8]Washington Gladden, "Henry Churchill King: Leader in Theological Thought," *Outlook* 85 (January 26, 1907):223; Love, *King*, pp. 70-73, 184; T. D. A. Cockerell, Review of *Rational Living, Dial* 40 (March 1, 1906):151.

issues of their day. Before their students and the general public they
presented what they considered a rational, common-sensical, practical, and
progressive morality. That they would be among the last college presidents
to fulfill just such a civic function they apparently did not imagine.

II. The Ground and End of Morals

The presidential moralists did not systematically articulate what they
considered to be the grounds of morals as such. Scattered throughout their
writings, however, were compacted statements of the universality of goodness
and ethical will, the comprehensiveness of love, and the necessity of moral
freedom. Their vagueness at this basic level both reflected and contributed
to their implicit synthesis of rightarian and utilitarian ethical views, a mix
inherited from their predecessors.

Hyde's first book on the subject, *Practical Ethics*, was but little removed
from the older moral science. Echoing the ante-bellum moralists, he
described ethics as "the science of conduct, and the art of life," which
consisted in "the maintenance of relations" through fulfillment of duty which
formed virtue and built character. Most of the book detailed specific duties
in the twenty-three fundamental relations of life: work, property, sex, friends,
family, and God, among others. *The Critic's* reviewer thought all this an
excellent discussion of "the various duties of men," but found the theoretical
dimension lacking. "What opinion he really holds as to the ultimate basis of
morals," the reviewer wrote, "we cannot quite make out."[9] The main
difficulty was that Hyde combined an Aristotelian definition of virtue as the

---

[9]Review of *Practical Ethics*, *Critic* 21 [n.s. 18] (September 24, 1892):163; Hyde, *Practical Ethics*, pp. vi-vii, 1-3.

mean between two extremes with a seemingly absolute right duty in every relation. For example, everyone had the duty to belong to a family, the fulfillment of which duty was the virtue of loyalty. The vice of defect in this duty was self-sufficiency, the vice of excess self-obliteration in complete identification with the family. How one found the middle ground was presumably a prudential matter.

Hyde moved toward establishing the grounds of morals in his next three works. In the *Outlines* he argued that just as the correlation of natural facts and science required an Absolute Mind as their common ground, so too did the social order and the individual conscience find their correlation as outer and inner aspects of the one Universal Will. Hyde thought that the moral standards of a given social order were but "arcs of the infinite circle" of Universal Will, and thus that individual goodness consisted of adjusting to one's social environment by progressing from pure self-interest to concern for the well-being of others and society. The law functioned as a restraint on self-interest while man developed toward a higher stage of seeking the greater good of others. Evil consisted of the absence of good, sin of the choice of lesser goods.[10]

In his *Practical Idealism* Hyde continued to hold that evil was the choice of lesser goods and could be overcome by choosing the greater good of social responsibility. As one moved toward self-conscious freedom of choice, a freedom which Hyde apparently assumed as part of common human experience, one strove for the moral ideal of realizing oneself as part of a social order with a specific function to perform for the common social good. One's individual role was rationally apprehended through consideration of the

---

[10]*Outlines*, pp. 20-21, 42-43, 90-91, 96, 226.

good of others, with the conscience acting as the arm of reason in approving
or disapproving actions. The highest form of the moral ideal so monitored
by the rational conscience was the Golden Rule. Man's social nature found
its ultimate expression in love, which created the social world. Neither
Kant's imperative of duty for duty's sake nor a hedonism of pleasure and
good feeling were adequate, then, for love went beyond either to seek the
highest good in sympathy and identification with others.[11]

God's Education of Man added some more succinct statements of
Hyde's view. He considered man a social being defined by his relations; one
could no more think of a purely individual person without society than of a
mountain without valleys. All human relations inhered rationally in a
Universal Will that included all "acts and attitudes of all persons toward each
other." More specifically, all moral judgments

> inhere in and partake of a single system of spiritual obligation
> and moral judgment, the existence and universality of which is
> attested by the tendency of all minds, in proportion as they are
> intellectually and morally developed, to come to an ever closer
> agreement concerning what is good and what is evil, what is right
> and what is wrong.

The law binding the conscience Hyde viewed as necessary to a lower stage
of human development than the beneficent vision just stated. Humanity
progressed from a Hobbesian state of nature in which self-interest reigned,
to a society ruled by love in which every individual sought first the good of
all other persons. Any potential conflict between his assertion of human

---

[11]*Practical Idealism*, pp. 140, 143, 145-46, 150, 226-27, 235-36, 239, 263.

sociality and his reference to Hobbes's belief in natural human anti-sociality Hyde seemed to resolve with an evolutionary scheme.[12]

To this point, then, Hyde maintained that human morality expressed in social relations and order was grounded in, in fact was a direct reflection of, the Universal Will. Individual moral growth in responsibility consisted of moving away from self-interest toward consideration of the good of others, which movement reached its highest expression in love. The same movement was reflected in the evolution of the whole human race from primitive societies to progressive civilization, as modern institutions more and more embodied the good of all under universal love.

Hyde expounded a similar developmental pattern as he traced the history of ethical thought *From Epicurus to Christ*. Quoting sources profusely and often without explanation, he sought to move toward quick general conclusions about five different ethical viewpoints. The Epicureans taught the simplicity and desirability of pleasures without fret or anxiety and banished melancholy and unhappiness as an illusion, all of which Hyde thought admirable. But a person was more than passions and appetites seeking gratification, and the good of society required more than this sort of parasitism. Epicureanism could create "the club man" or the socialite flitting irresponsibly about Europe, but it could not produce chaste husbands, devoted citizens, efficient workmen, or brave soldiers. Hyde accused J. S. Mill of promoting such hedonism by defining right and wrong in terms of pleasure and pain. Each person seeking his own happiness would no more lead to social good, Hyde argued, than (to quote Carlyle) each pig at the

---

[12]*God's Education*, pp. 2-7, 74-85.

trough grabbing all he could get would lead to every pig getting his fair share.[13]

Hyde next dispensed with Stoicism, which was commendable for its emphasis on universal law and unemotional devotion thereto, but was too impersonal and fateful to accommodate real human relations. He deemed a Stoic woman "a contradiction in terms," and delighted in W. S. Gilbert's satire of Stoic philosophy, "Roll on, thou ball, roll on." Moving on to Platonism, Hyde expressed admiration for its earnest ideal of reason in supremacy over passions and appetites, which he illustrated by arguing the relative merits of eating breakfast: was it merely gluttonous such as to clog the mind or would it make one think more clearly all day? He judged Plato too idealistic, though, with his head in the clouds exalting the universal and infinite, without sufficient attention to the realities of everyday life and duty.[14]

Coming now to the fourth stage which he considered only a step below Christianity, Hyde called Aristotle the master moralist who recognized the social nature of the self and the inherence of the good in the well-being of society. Aristotle taught, said Hyde, that "the good man is he who, in each act he does or refrains from doing, is seeking the good of all the persons who are affected by his action." The individual achieved virtue in relation to larger social ends, and chose only such means as would achieve those ends. Virtue always consisted in moderation, or the mean between two extremes. This point Hyde illustrated with the choice a football player must make on the night before a big game: should he go to the dance and wear himself

---

[13]*From Epicurus*, pp. 32-44.

[14]Ibid., pp. 101-9, 123-131, 161-167.

out or should he conserve energy by listening to a concert of cheery glee club songs, thus being more ready to play the next day.[15]

Aristotelian ethics needed only the Christian principle of love for persons to form a complete system. The essence of Christianity, Hyde said, was "Universal Goodness reproduced in our reverent and obedient wills," the fruit of which was love effected in all one's relationships. Out of such good will came all higher forms of service and self-sacrifice necessary to the well-being of society. When he brought out the new edition of his book, Hyde rewrote the chapter on Christianity to put even more emphasis on it as the "final philosophy of life" incorporating all the best features of the other four, but making love the supreme law of life -- love toward the Father whose goodness was reflected in the advancing social and moral order, and love toward one's fellows who were sacred persons as God's children. The chapter became a paean to the blessedness of love and joy, consolation, righteousness, self-sacrifice, and courage.[16]

Hyde's later writings further solidified and formularized his moral viewpoint. *The Quest of the Best* required the sacrifice of lesser goods for greater; in the upbringing of boys into men, for which the book was a volume of advice, the first stage would be their natural badness in choosing self-interest, which led to slovenliness, smoking, laziness, tardiness, vulgarity, vindictiveness and even murder. Restraining laws and enticing rewards would create in them an artificial goodness, but at the next level of development they would truly quest after the fulfillment of all interests of all persons, the

---

[15]Ibid., pp. 176-81, 194-96.

[16]Ibid., pp. 215-18, 247; *The Five Great Philosophies of Life*, 2nd ed. of *From Epicurus to Christ* (New York: Macmillan Co., 1911, 1914), pp. vi, 218.

supreme moral good. The worth of every individual interest was to be
judged by its inclusiveness in considering the "worth and claim, of all interests
of all persons," through which men would reach "the best."[17]

In his last two books Hyde had arrived at the slogans which characterized his whole view. *The Best Man I Know* was the Christian man who lived
out his will for the good of all. That will was in turn both grounded in and
a practical reflection of the Universal Will for the good of all, which Hyde
shortened in his *Gospel of Good Will* to simply the universal Good Will. He
now argued that the benevolence of a Christian could be placed in a
syllogism with the major premise being Good Will, and the minor its
particular application. Since every Christian subscribed to the Good Will, all
that was necessary for the ethicist was to "show him where the most good
lies" in each case. Hyde had no doubt that such a task could be accomplished with ease, for he had once stated that "righteousness is simply fitness;
goodness is what right-minded people want to have done."[18]

In sum, while Hyde conceived Christianity to be the highest ethical
system because of its doctrine of love for persons in social relations, he also
retained explicit elements of Aristotelian ethics based on teleology and the
virtue of the mean. In fact, his synthesis of the two traditions put so much
emphasis on benevolence in moral action that his critics accused him of
making virtue "exclusively utilitarian." But of course, Hyde was taking for
granted a moral consensus on what "right" actions would lead to "good" ends,
and he never wanted to dissociate ethics from religion. Their relationship he

---

[17]*The Quest of the Best; Insights into Ethics for Parents, Teachers, and Leaders of Boys*
(New York: Thomas Y. Crowell Co., 1913), pp. 4-5, 17-48, 83-84.

[18]*The Best Man I Know; Developed out of the will for the good of all* (New York:
Macmillan Co., 1917), pp. xi-xii; *Good Will*, pp. 30-31; *Jesus' Way*, pp. 172-73.

variously stated in references to religion as "the consummation, rather than the foundation of ethics," or religion as the root from which ethics branched, but this contradiction was inconsequential anyway, since whether it stood at the beginning or the end, the bottom or the top, religion invoked the whole range of assumptions necessary to the moral life, baptizing goodness in the will of God and the example of Christ. As Hyde condensed it in a poem, "The Strenuous Life,"

> We see the end at which we aim --
> The blessed kingdom of the Right . . .
> The goal may ever shine afar;
> The will to win it makes us free.[19]

Hyde had clearly inherited, then, the tension between rightarian and utilitarian views characteristic of the older moral philosophy. He was if anything even less rigorous than earlier generations, though, in distinguishing the two arguments for the ground of morals. Echoes of the old complaints about both viewpoints could still be heard: he was displeased with any legalism associated with rightarian assertions, and critical of the hedonism implied in utilitarian thinking. Yet on the whole, he had settled into an easy synthesis best expressed in the benevolence of "right-minded people." Such was only the logical outcome of a moral philosophy which had long purported to stand simply on the ground of common sense.

King was much more concerned than Hyde to declare the grounds of human moral freedom, and objected to his colleague's type of organic analogy for the relation of the individual to society. All Hyde meant by the individual finding his fulfillment in his social role for the well-being of society

---

[19]Review of *Outlines of Social Theology*, *Critic* 27:211; Hyde, *Practical Ethics*, p. iv; *Quest*, p. 202; "The Strenuous Life," *Outlook* 74 (May 9, 1903):119.

was that everyone should do what befitted their station in life, and live in moderation. But King saw in sociological language a danger of lost human moral freedom and responsibility, and spoke much more of laws ordering the facts of the spiritual world according to the will of God.

King's first two books in theology established the higher reality of ideals and values in the spiritual world of persons. Above the mechanism of organic nature, persons were capable of perceiving the rational order of the universe that inhered both in factual data and in the worth and value of things. Just as nature operated lawfully, so the moral sphere had its own conditions and laws of action. The ground of each was the Infinite or God, who was the "source of the moral constitution" of humans; for God's very existence constituted a moral universe of laws expressed in every individual as "a recognition of the eternal distinction of right and wrong." God was the supreme person, out of "right personal relation" to whom came all other "right relations" with others, as shown by the two great commandments in the New Testament.[20]

If the world was to be "a sphere for moral training and action," King argued, it had to root in universal laws that could be fulfilled by actual moral initiative (freedom) in the mutual relations of persons. "This *is* no play-world," he warned, for human actions had definite consequences for oneself and for others according to laws as real as natural cause and effect. As he explored this further in *Fundamental Questions*, he declared that law and liberty were not at odds but absolutely essential to each other. The laws of one's moral constitution were as necessary to one's self-realization as the manufacturer's directions "for the running of a superb automobile." Law

---

[20]*Reconstruction*, pp. 207-9.

pointed the way to freedom, for it showed the lines along which one would develop one's own being to the fullest; and conversely, the person who was true to the laws of his own nature would take responsibility for acting lawfully.[21]

King seemed to suggest two related ends of moral action according to law. One was the common good of everyone in society, to which the individual contributed by achieving his "individual highest good." If the world was to be a cosmos, not a chaos, then each person had to act lawfully under "steady self-discipline" and obedience, working toward a society that would recognize the sacredness of persons.

The other and final end was the fulfillment of all relations in love. God was not will alone, but personal, loving will; God's laws imposed on the individual and reflected in society were not so much constraining as leading to one's highest self. Ethical commands were "a revelation of the love of God" opening the way to "a steadily enlarging life" of relations with others.[22] To the extent that one entered into a loving relation with God by conforming to the holy purposes of his Infinite Will, one would also enter into loving relations with other persons; and vice versa, to the extent that one recognized the value and sacredness of other persons, one was fulfilling the divine will. Love was the unity and sum of the ethical life.[23]

The fullest revelation of God's love was in Jesus Christ, whose character bore the imprint of the divine will and whose teachings laid open

---

[21]*Social Consciousness*, pp. 30-32; *Fundamental Questions*, pp. 140, 145, 150.

[22]*Fundamental Questions*, pp. 137, 148, 168.

[23]*Social Consciousness*, pp. 45, 98-99; *Reconstruction*, pp. 169, 208.

all the fundamentals of moral law. Thus ethics had to root in religion, King wrote, morality reaching its highest form in communion with God. Only in self-giving love, exemplified in Christ and articulated in the Golden Rule, could man achieve perfection of character.

King believed the older analogy of moral government unnecessary to an understanding of the ground of ethical law in God's will; he hoped to replace it with his model of personal relations culminating in love. He thought his own system made morality more immediate and real through actual relational living, rather than seeming abstract and remote as in the older view. Yet his very emphasis on love reflected Fairchild's overarching theme of benevolence, both supporting a divine purpose for the well-being of all creatures; and King was not averse to referring to moral government in connection with the providence of God. In fact, in his explicit use of the language of "rational relations," King, like Hyde, showed himself not far removed from the conceptual world of the older moral philosophy. If his rhetoric had now become more personal, appealing to sentiments of love and good will, it was only to make arguments for the laws of rational living more convincing. The existence and cause and effect relations of such laws, he was as determined to prove as his predecessors had ever been.

Tucker also used the phrase "moral government of God," but viewed it as evidenced by the unity and order revealing itself immanently everywhere as human knowledge expanded. The human search for truth was in accord with the mind of God, even as advancing society mirrored a widening human sympathy that manifested God's unfolding will. Moral commandments had little impact any more, Tucker told his students; the authority of law handed down from above was giving way to Jesus' sense of the human. Moral maturity consisted not in obeying commands, but in seeking the way of life toward which Jesus pointed, especially in his articulation of the Golden Rule. Following a way and not an edict was riskier, Tucker admitted, but it promised greater tests of character and opportunity for influence. The measure of a "morally well-bred man" in the days ahead would be his sense of justice, his ability to recognize his commonality with others and to accommodate his actions to their rights and interests, combined with a sense of sympathy and fellow-feeling. Tucker acknowledged that the young people of his day were less sure what they should do in given situations, but he was convinced that the virtues of humility, obedience, trust, sympathy, and justice could be learned and applied with renewed clarity.[24]

All three presidents, then, sought to avoid the appearance of a legalism or moral absolutism smacking of the older system in the ethical philosophy they imparted to their students. They made love or fellow-feeling the highest form of morality, and set up the Golden Rule as the standard of social relations. All were aware of the inadequacy of a purely individualistic ethic and alerted their classes to the common good of a changing society. In short, they appealed to the optimistic convictions of their day and advanced a morality of persuasive invitation over one of coercive restriction.

Yet if they replaced an outmoded Absolute Right with Universal Good Will or Love as the foundation of their systems, and made benevolence and the well-being of all an even more prominent feature of their ethic, they were still positive that only certain forms of behavior were in harmony with the good to be achieved. Righteous ends still played out into specific duties the

---

[24]"The Christian," p. 135; "The Capacity for the True," "The Morally Well-Bred Man," and "Moral Maturity," in *Personal Power*, pp. 114-63.

fulfillment of which would build individual character, the foundation stone of the stability and improvement of society. Thus did one generation's verities become legalisms for the next. Thus did the next generation's liberalism veil an impulse to hang onto absolutes no less unquestionable than those of their predecessors.

III. Conscience, Duty, and the Motive of Love

The presidents considered the universality of conscience as primary evidence for the benevolent will of God. Unlike the earlier moral scientists, however, they were less inclined to try to define the conscience as a specific faculty of human makeup. Hyde described conscience simply as "the knowledge of our duty, coupled as that knowledge always is with the feeling that we ought to do it." Conscience was not some mysterious faculty, he declared, but simply the thought of duty and the feeling accompanying it. The source of duty, in turn, was God's will as expressed in the most generally applicable way in the great commandments to love God and neighbor. Duty was simply the inward voice of that divine will, the consciousness of obligation to obey God's laws. Those laws did not take the form of eternal edicts, of course, but rather were expressed through the requirements of social well-being. In short, duty was "the affirmation of the universal interest as binding upon the individual will," prompting the choice of the greater good, the larger interest, and finally the good of all over one's self-interest.[25]

The older moral science considered the duties taught by conscience to be fulfilled in right intentions. The person who intended the right action was judged good regardless of the actual outcome of the action. This emphasis

---

[25]*Practical Ethics*, pp. 179-81; *Practical Idealism*, pp. 252-55; *Jesus' Way*, p. 14.

on intentions reflected the older system's insistence on obedience to absolute right and its fear of utilitarian or prudential considerations. In Hyde's view, however, the focus on intentions was a form of legalism, for he considered the intention to be part and parcel of the action; bad actions expressed bad intentions and the purpose of the law was to restrain such evil. He argued instead that the good or evil of a person was judged by the motive; the good man, he asserted, always had universal good, or the good of all who were affected by his action, as his motive. Jesus himself had taught the distinction of intention and motive, and showed that poor intentions could be redeemed by good motives. "The only thing we need be concerned about is the purity of our motives," Hyde wrote in *Jesus' Way*; "if these are right, if the tree is good, the fruit will follow in good time," or as he elsewhere put it, "the earnest purpose in the end always manages to make itself outwardly effective." He illustrated his distinction rather ineffectively with the example of a boy who blew up a mailbox with a firecracker; his intention, to blow up the mailbox, which his action carried out, was bad; his motive, to have fun, was good, or at least harmless.[26]

The motive of the good of all, or what was the same thing, the motive of love, fulfilled one's duty, then, in Hyde's view. But if the motive of seeking good seemed too sweeping, Hyde was determined to confine good motives to certain forms. Invoking a "principle of limitation," he stipulated that every individual had a specific place or function within which he could make his best contribution to society, so that his good will was best fulfilled through his station in life and the duties and opportunities pertaining thereto.

---

[26]*God's Education*, pp. 130-32; "The Definition of a Good Man," in *The Message of the College to the Church*, Addresses in Lent, 1901, Old South Church (Boston: Pilgrim Press, 1901), pp. 41-66; *Jesus' Way*, pp. 100, 150.

For example, he opposed any "so-called emancipation of women" that would remove them from their proper place in the home; and he was equally critical of "promiscuous charity" performed by those whose good motives did not discriminate the real needs of the poor from the things for which the needy should work.

Moreover, Hyde narrowed the scope of good will by devising four practical principles for limitation of effort. One could identify one's highest and best duty as being the nearest (for example, the mother's role in the home), the one best expressing one's individual aptitude or specific excellence, the most urgent, and the one incorporating the larger good consistent with the first three principles. Thus Hyde sought to prevent the erosion of his philosophy into utilitarianism by retaining a wall of certain duties and limitations on which he thought there was, or should be, a consensus in society. His procedure unmistakably echoed the manner of reasoning of Francis Wayland.[27]

King also wanted to reduce the conscience from a faculty to simply the sense of duty. The conscience represented the "demand of God" impressed on the person as a "sense of obligation . . . . a sense of facing a clear duty," an experience that was part of the common consciousness of mankind. The distinction of right and wrong, or divine law, was written into the moral constitution of every human being. Everyone sensed the indications of conscience, although in a free moral universe one could choose not to obey and thus to defy God's will. If one followed one's conscience, though, one would be fulfilling what was best for one's own self-realization, and could be

---

[27]*Practical Idealism*, pp. 241-49; "Definition of a Good Man."

assured that under a righteous God, in the end duty and happiness would coincide.[28]

In keeping with his interpretation of the new psychology, King tried to purge his thinking of older faculty categories. He stressed that "the whole man" was involved in every thought or action, that intellect, feeling, and will were interdependent in the unity of the mind, and that mind and body were mutually influenced. What he meant by the duty to follow the will of God, then, was not intellectual assent or awareness but expression of the love of God in actions that fulfilled one's relations with other persons. The "genuine rationalism that knows the whole man" took account of the whole self in a plan of "rational living." Such a plan was not constituted by rules and regulations but built on "the dynamic of the single motive of love" for God, for Christ, and for others. That motive, however, played out in specific duties present to the consciousness as God's holy will and purpose.[29]

Tucker linked "the consenting reason and the awakened conscience and the kindled emotion" together as the fruit of religion. If reason were at work broadening its understanding of the world, it would lend greater authority to Christian principles, which would impress moral duty upon the individual through the conscience or "moral sense," and feed a renewed emotion or motive of sympathy for others. Tucker called for moral education that would lead to intellectual growth, a rightly adjusted will, and a fit motive, and called

---

[28]*Reconstruction*, p. 207; *Social Consciousness*, pp. 86, 90-91; *Fundamental Questions*, pp. 114, 118.

[29]*Reconstruction*, p. 172; *Rational Living*, pp. 106-7; *Seeming Unreality*, p. 105.

upon religion to provide the motive for responsibility and consecration to the advancement of humanity.[30]

Thus the presidents were aware that all human faculties need to be brought into unity, and at the core of that unity they placed the motive of love. Like the older moralists, however, they still maintained that duty was universally present to common human consciousness as an expression of the will of God, and that devotion to the divine will marked a definite way of living. The self-evidence of duty they still called conscience, which they wanted to make less a faculty or organ of sense and more simply an internal moral arbiter. But even here they occupied virtually the same middle ground as Wayland and other synthesizers, who never really detached the conscience from other faculties, even while insisting on it as the name of a mental function. The new generation wanted to comprehend the new psychology, then, but they were not about to surrender the claim of the universality of a sense of moral duty, which tied them to the older systems.

IV. Will and Character

In his 1902 *Atlantic Monthly* article interpreting "The New Ethics," Hyde noted the passing of the old faculty psychology focussed on conscience and will and their governance by cut and dried rules. The new psychology was demonstrating the unity of the person, he argued, and a new ethics would need to show how to create a coherent, unified individuality, an organic whole capable of expanding to absorb new interests and new materials of life. When he and his colleagues fully described that unified person, however, they fell back on language they thought to leave behind. The habitual practice of

---

[30]*Making and Unmaking*, pp. 6-7, 141-43; *Function*, pp. 53-56; *Personal Power*, pp. v-viii.

duty, they said, formed virtue, and the concert of virtues formed character. The primary virtue they considered to be self-control, and thus the backbone of character continued to be the will.[31]

King's textbook on *Rational Living* consistently illustrated this train of thought. Of course, attainment of character was the continuing theme of all his writings; the whole point of theology's establishing the grounds of moral freedom in the sphere of persons was to make character possible through the choice of practicing duty. Religion was "the one truest way to character," for it impressed the ethical will of God upon the individual, offered the supreme example of character in Jesus Christ, and presented love as the perfection of character.[32]

In *Rational Living*, King reduced the results of modern psychology to four major teachings in order to show how they could lead to growth, character, happiness, and influence (meaning influence upon others). First, psychology was revealing how much more complex man's life was than previously thought; modern man had wide and broadening interests and experiences, exposure to many more phenomena than ever before. This heightened the "paradoxes of life" that were already complicated: in order to be active, one had to rest; in order to make an urgent decision one still had to weigh all alternatives; in order to assimilate new knowledge one still had to be discriminating, balancing old ideas with new.

Secondly, psychology was showing that despite the complexity of life, man was a unity in body and mind. While warning against a materialism that would make physical processes too determinative, King adapted the results

---

[31]"The New Ethics," *Atlantic Monthly* 90 (November 1902):577.

[32]*Reconstruction*, pp. 181, 238.

of physiological psychology from Wilhelm Wundt, considered the founder of experimental psychology, and others, to show particularly how bodily conditions affected the mind, rest and exercise and "well-oxygenated blood" being necessary to alert thinking, for example.

The third finding from modern psychology brought King closer to the theme that not so subtly pervaded his whole book. Psychology was stressing the "central importance of will and action," he claimed, for the "natural terminus of every experience" whether physical or mental was action. King drew from James to show that the mind actively attended to an object, and that attention would bring about a corresponding action. Thought and feeling had little meaning if they were purely internal, King believed; they reached their full expression only in activity. The emphasis on action carried over into the whole philosophical trend toward practical interests, King thought; everything was being defined in terms of its purpose or end in the contemporary resurgence of teleological philosophy. The essence of a thing lay in the purpose of the Infinite for the part it would play in the world. The essence of man, then, was action.[33]

Man being a free creature, however, responsible for his own self-development and activity, was above all a creature of choice in whom the faculty of choice, the will, was primary. Man could make his own environment, he could choose to what he would attend and thus how he would act, in short, he was responsible for creating his own character. The means to character, King argued, was above all the trained will, and the preeminent strength or virtue of the trained will was self-control. "The chief differentiation of men from animals," King wrote, was self-control, the "root-principle

---

[33]*Rational Living* pp. 9-10, 23-38, 57, 64, 153-59, 161-64.

of all virtues." Mature character, then, comprised wilful mastery of the self, the dominance of the lower impulses, passions, and appetites by the higher ideal ends and purposes attended, chosen, and put into action. The man who was master of himself could in turn be master of his environment; a whole society of self-controlled individuals could come to embody all the virtues of the righteous Kingdom, and achieve mastery of a changing world.

Will-power was built up and strengthened along the way by the choices one made and the habits one formed. Here again, muscular activity and exercise helped strengthen volitional power, as did habits of rest and avoidance of fatigue. King thought the new psychology was showing how habits actually shaped one's nervous system. The nerves were plastic and flexible early in life. But as one established a pattern of activity the nerves themselves formed equivalent habitual responses. King warned his students that "all your habits are setting like plaster of Paris," and that if they did not exercise their power of will to shape themselves while they were young, they would not be able to change very much later.[34]

King's fourth learning from contemporary psychology became a catch-all for his characteristic opinions. Under the rangy title of "the concreteness of the real -- the interrelatedness of all," he again stressed that absolute idealism was neither a meaningful philosophy nor an adequate description of man. "Life is always more than thought; the concrete, than the abstract," as he put it. For that matter, no one-sided view of life could account for its wholeness; a materialist philosophy that neglected the sphere of free persons, or an organic analogy for society that absorbed the individual into some social mind, or an excessive realism in literature that ignored nobler human

---

[34]Ibid., pp. 59-62, 159-61, 237.

ideals, all were partial, and detrimental to the extent that they claimed absoluteness. The whole man could only be addressed by a rationalism that took account of his individual unity and his social relationships. The mind actively perceived relations and wholes; the will expressed thought and feeling in actions; the trained body enabled clear thinking and definite action; and the only true, comprehensive emotion, love, manifested itself in activity according to the Great Commandments and the Golden Rule.[35]

King's conception of wholeness, though, was no more than an interrelatedness, and in describing what parts were interrelated, he used the language of the faculty psychology. Moreover, by making wholeness or character an achievement for which the individual was responsible, King had to make the will, and its virtue of self-control, the center of human personality. Thus his ethics still fell out into a set of rules for rational living, "rational" meaning the "rationalism of the whole man," meaning the choice any person with common sense would make based on the evidence from modern psychology and the inevitable effects of one's activity on oneself and others.

For all his talk of personal relations, King's ethic of character came out markedly individualistic. But of course, what he meant by personal relations was simply the relationships in which individuals learned from each other and influenced each other. A constant theme of his moral advice was association with the best, keeping oneself in the presence of the best; for character was caught, not taught, and the young man particularly would learn virtue through association with mature men. Association was not a mere rubbing-off of something good on to one's forming personality, though; it was only fruitful

---

[35]Ibid., pp. 220-35, esp. 234.

to the extent that one attended to the right influences and environment; and attention was a matter of choice.

The primacy of the will emerged even more stridently in King's addresses to young people.   For example, he urged Y.M.C.A. students gathered at Northfield, Massachusetts, to make a "rational fight for character" by heeding the laws of their natures which were "the laws of God."   The moral life was made up of a series of volitions, he told them, "that involve the definite choice of definite means to definite ends." He inveighed against "vagueness of thought, vague promises, vague aspirations" that contributed nothing to "that kind of direct, definite willing that belongs to character." Precisely the unity of man, he suggested, the influence of body upon mind especially, made self-control the root virtue. Warning them against any form of determinism in which the environment was said to make the man, he charged them with responsibility for thinking intentionally, for choosing to what they would attend, and for combatting the temptations of their lower moments.   At such times, he cautioned, one must "fight or die" to keep oneself at one's best, for, he cried with rhetorical flourish, "you have no right to have these lower moments continually breaking in upon your life." Make a habit of duty, build the virtues that make for character, he pleaded, for such was "the strenuous life" (in Hyde's very phrase) that God willed for his children.[36] If King had supplanted the dry rules and regulations of the old moral science with a new appreciation of the whole man, he made it clear here and everywhere that exhortation to moral duty had not lost its place.

Hyde likewise mixed traditional definitions of character and its accomplishment with the findings of the new psychology.   On the one hand,

---

[36]"How to Make a Rational Fight for Character," in *Personal and Ideal*, pp. 236-72.

he described character as the form of virtuous conduct, the product of the trained, habitual will performing its duties. "Character is a storage battery," he penned in yet another metaphor, "in which the power acquired by our past acts is accumulated and preserved for future use." He composed two books, *Practical Ethics* and *Self-Measurement*, purporting to show what were the duties and virtues pertaining to the basic relations of life. "Man stands in a system of relations," he stated in the latter, and the moral principles inherent in them "are so well known that it is useless for a writer to try to tell the reader anything about them which he does not know already." To this moral science he added only the Aristotelian quality of which he was so fond. The virtue in every case was the mean between two extremes, with the cardinal virtues apart from religion, as he wrote in the *Atlantic Monthly*, being wisdom, justice, courage, and temperance. To these religion added the spiritual dimension and motive.[37]

On the other hand, Hyde was restless with the old model of conscience and will understood as faculties governed by "intuitions and categorical imperatives." Such an approach was bound to make the person lifeless and passive. Modern psychology had shown that the mind was active, assimilating experience, open and attentive to a wide range of interests. Individuality was formed out of the manifold of experience which in modern life was increasingly complex.

When he described how such personality came about, though, Hyde, like King, put the onus on the individual. The challenge of a person's life was to bring unity out of diverse interests by choosing to what one would

---

[37]*Practical Ethics*, pp. 182-84; *Self-Measurement; A Scale of Human Values with Directions for Personal Application*, The Art of Life Series, ed. E. H. Griggs (New York: B. W. Huebsch, 1908, 1916), pp. 7-9; "The Cardinal Virtues," *Atlantic Monthly* 88 (July 1901):121.

attend, and by ordering oneself to a single moral purpose. The very essay in which he celebrated the new psychology was entitled, "The Career of Self-Conquest," for moral purpose was to be found in aligning oneself with the Good Will of God, an achievement which required self-control and adherence to moral law. In a commercial metaphor, Hyde called the moral laws "the coined treasures of the moral experience of the race . . . the only terms on which [one] can be admitted to a free exchange of the moral goods of society." The task of the moral life, then, was to do one's specific work well for the good of others, living in the influence of fellow strivers in "the strenuous life."[38]

Tucker's addresses to students exhibited similar sensitivities. Decrying the current trend to "life in the now, live to the full," he called upon his listeners to seek the freedom of a wisdom that looked to further goals and to intellectual integrity. No one could grow in the life-long search for truth without limiting one's desires, or better, elevating them through the trained conscience and refined taste. Tucker outlined the "self-government" necessary to organize one's life toward a goal. The man of duty recognized the actions that would build up his personality in intellect, conscience and will, leading him to full growth in decisive action, controlled desire, and devotion to truth.

Personal power, he argued, was not measured by rampant aggressiveness, but by qualities of restraint, refinement, and even sacrifice. Such moral sanity was the mark of maturity. A person's greatness, he told the cadets at the Naval Academy, lay in his originality, his authority, and his beneficence.

---

[38]"The Career of Self-Conquest," in *The College Man and the College Woman* (Boston: Houghton Mifflin Co., 1906), pp. 81-82, 109; *God's Education*, pp. 19, 174; *Quest*, pp. 7-8.

The man who had control of himself could better perceive the truth and put forcefully into action his concern for the well-being of others.[39]

While all three presidents adopted the new psychology's teachings of the wholeness of personality, then, they continued to stress the building of character as the task of an ethic psychologically informed. The emphasis of the new learning on absorption of wider interests and their translation into action only made the seat of choice, the will, and its virtue, self-control, all the more important. The perception and impress of duty, for which the authors could find no other name than conscience, maintained its role as the mirror of divine law and the monitor of will.

V. Practical Morality and Self-Control

When they came to advising their charges and the public about specific moral duties, the presidents manifested somewhat varying interests. Tucker was preoccupied with business life, charging his listeners to conduct their business honestly and honorably and to maintain any private property they owned for the public good. Such would be a contribution to the well-being of society. He criticized the vulgar display of wealth as demoralizing to others, and urged the responsible use of money and capital in the public interest. A true gentleman he viewed as devoted to the efficient performance of duty, subordinating private interests to the public good, and relating his

---

[39]"Provisional Self-Government," "The Estimation of Power," and "Wisdom the Principal Thing," in *Personal Power*, pp. 3-44; "The Study of Contemporary Greatness," in *Public-Mindedness; An Aspect of Citizenship Considered in Various Addresses Given While President of Dartmouth College* (Concord, N.H.: Rumford Press, 1910), pp. 336-56.

own business or profession to the welfare of the society whose opinions he would help to shape.[40]

Hyde and King also stressed the importance of honorable work to a healthy society. Hyde even called work a form of worship as each person's offering to the economic life, a way of bearing one another's burdens by each one doing his task well. The worker living by Good Will did his work gladly, thinking of the benefit others would receive from it, and collecting his pay gratefully in return. Hyde attacked laziness in both the rich and the poor, calling the idle and irresponsible rich the parasites of progressive society, and attributing poverty to idleness produced by debility and discouragement. The phrase "get by" he condemned in *The Outlook* as "moral poison," for every person was responsible for giving something back to the society on which he depended. The Christian, or good man, should not respond with charity for the person who would be improved by self-support, but should try to influence the lazy for the better. "We must bring our earnest lives into close contact with their frivolous and indolent ones," he wrote, "showing them at the same time that we care for them, and care for better things than they have learned to care for."[41]

King called for constancy, perseverance, and promptness in work, which was "one of the profoundest needs of our nature." Work was especially noble in enabling the person to forget self-interest and self-concern in favor of "the

---

[40]"The Distribution of Personal Power" and "The Moral Training of the College Man," in *Personal Power*, pp. 81-96, 195-262; "The Ownership of Land," in *Public Mindedness*, pp. 156-57.

[41]*Practical Idealism*, pp. 202, 208-10; *God's Education*, pp. 85-90; *Good Will*, pp. 114ff.; *Self-Measurement*, p. 17; "A Poisonous Phrase," *Outlook* 101 (May 18, 1912):122; "Cost and Consecration," *Outlook* 62 (July 29, 1899):713-19; *Best Man*, p. 41; *Sin*, p. 53.

objective mood." He was worried that excessive emotion detracted from the motives of action. The hysterical, strained, fatigued, or moody person could not think clearly or perform well. "We need to escape fag," King told his students, to avoid a continuous nervous pace that allowed no rest. Dangerous thoughts and poor decisions lurked in the darkness of one's worst hours; at those times the spiritual ideals seemed most unreal, and one might even consider believing in material atheism.

Keeping oneself at one's best for hard work and clear thinking required not only rest but healthy exercise, King taught. The proper mastery of one's body was not some kind of pale asceticism, but wholesome exercise that made the body more useful for work in the world. Muscle-tone he related to will-power, inactivity to vague thinking. For example, he said, he looked forward to an end of "morbid religious questionings" and the coming of the "muscular minister." Idleness and self-indulgence was a menace to the community, but healthy exercise, while also a form of leisure, went to a useful purpose. The personal efficiency thus gained contributed to self-control, and once recognized for its benefits would undoubtedly lead to abstinence from drinking and smoking. "The record of Saturday nights in this world of ours," he was prone to declaring, "would make tragic reading." The time had come to stop "fooling around" and to take life seriously.[42]

Hyde zestfully concurred in the admiration of bodily fitness and exercise, leaving asceticism, he said, to the "emaciated hermits and psalm-singing pietists." No pleasure or relaxation should be excessive, though, or come at others' expense, he warned. For example, one should not patronize

---

[42]*Rational Living*, pp. 58-60, 73, 77, 89, 135, 138-40, 197, 203; *Seeming Unreality*, p. 136; *Moral and Religious*, p. 274; "It's All in the Day's Work," *Biblical World* 45 (May 1915):259-67.

an opera or drama in which a woman had to put off her modesty, for such would be buying leisure with "the stained whiteness of a sister's soul." Hyde was convinced, as he put it in a prayer, that God had made health "the normal condition of every child of obedient parents, who himself obeys [the] laws of diet, exercise, rest, recreation, cheerfulness, trust, and love." Certainly illnesses resulting from vice or overwork would never come to Christian people, he said, so it would not be "altogether untrue or unjust to call them the penalties of sin and disobedience." Hyde especially liked a vision of wholesomeness he quoted from Herbert Spencer's *Data of Ethics*:

> Bounding out of bed after an unbroken sleep, singing or whistling as he dresses, coming down with beaming face ready to laugh at the slightest provocation, the healthy man of high powers enters on the day's business not with repugnance but with gladness; and from hour to hour experiencing satisfaction from work effectually done, comes home with an abundant surplus of energy remaining for hours of relaxation. Full of vivacity, he is ever welcome. For his wife he has smiles and jocose speeches; for his children stories of fun and play; for his friends pleasant talk interspersed with the sallies of wit that come from buoyancy.[43]

Temperance in the use of alcohol would best fit in with "the best man," Hyde suggested, though probably here the mean between extremes was not enough. Complete abstinence was most likely better for oneself and for others. Certainly one ought to oppose the vice spawned by the saloons and try to get the saloon-keeper to see the misery and degradation he was causing.[44]

Hyde identified the saloon as one of the forces breaking down not only the work ethic, but loyalty to family life. Saloons and associated vices fed

---

[43]*God's Education*, pp. 90-94; *Abba Father*, p. 30; *From Epicurus*, p. 259; Spencer quoted in *Practical Ethics*, p. 27.

[44]*Practical Ethics*, p. 12; *Quest*, pp. 90-91; *God's Education*, pp. 133-35.

licentiousness, which Hyde denounced almost more than any other sin. Sex was not intrinsically bad; it was one of nature's prizes. But it belonged in the sanctity of the home. The family he viewed as the foundation of the moral and social order, "the primary school of character." Any force that broke down the sacredness of the family built up over many centuries by self-control and moral struggle was abhorrent. The noble and honourable man included "the sanctity of the home, the peace and purity of family life, the dignity and welfare of every man and woman, the honest birthright of every child," in the social end to which he aimed his life. The one who did not was "a disgrace to the mother who bore [him]."[45]

The sexual assumptions implicit in much of Hyde's writing, he made explicit in his definition of the roles of men and women in modern society. Man was the producer, researcher, laborer, politician, decision-maker. Woman was the consumer, for whom overwork would lead to nervous exhaustion and "flat-chested sterility." Woman was to mould sentiment and hold to moral verities, and let men do the hard-nosed compromising in the world of business, law and politics.[46]

Hyde tended to define strength of character in terms of manliness, too. He feared that rearing a child without proper moral training would produce "a poor, effeminate, namby-pamby, unsophisticated weakling" with a "feeble, flabby will." Those who stood high on his chart of *Self-Measurement*, by contrast, were "men of splendid physique and personal magnetism; drawing others after them as the moon draws the tides; men who find new ways of doing things and make fortunes in the process." *The Quest of the Best* would

[45]*Practical Idealism*, pp. 163-69; *Quest*, p. 127; *Sin*, p. 27; *From Epicurus*, p. 203.

[46]"The Worth of the Womanly Ideal," in *College Man*, pp. 194-218.

never lead a boy to fussy, punctilious, soft-hearted subservience, but to refinement, loyalty, chivalry, and magnanimity, not to the point of being pushed around or overrun, but to the peak of sincerity, honesty, and necessary bluntness.[47]

King also condemned the "free lovers" who let uncontrolled passion reign outside the marriage bond, and feared that those advocating "feminism" were a threat to traditional family life. Moral self-control required marital fidelity and devotion to the home. The alternative was a flood of selfish pleasures and indulgences that would inundate the Christian society that had taken centuries of struggle to build. One of the advances of civilization was the increasing value and sacredness of the person, which ought to be a protection for women, children and dependents in a society of families.[48]

Finally, the presidents wanted to get across the importance of just plain decency and good manners. Whether through Tucker's admonition of the gentleman to acquire refined taste, or King's instructions to students to watch their table manners, their style of dress, their cleanliness, and their language, or Hyde's painting on the Bowdoin stadium the motto, "Fair Play and May the Best Man Win," the three tried to reflect and reinforce the moral and social standards of their day.[49] In fact, they suggested that only a "well-bred" man could rise to the kind of character that would have influence in American society; and breeding began in the home and continued in the school with the training of manners and morals.

---

[47]*Practical Idealism*, p. 173; *Self-Measurement*, p. 14; *Quest*, pp. 73-74, 199-201.

[48]*Fundamental Questions*, pp. 158-62; *Rational Living*, p. 245.

[49]King, *Rational Living*, p. 62; Hyde, *Quest*, p. 175.

In their devotion to gentility, and the consequent mundaneness and even banality of their moral advice at points, the authors were but little removed from their predecessors. Wayland had exhorted his charges to avoid even "*the appearance of evil*," and to stay away from licentious theatre and "immodest dancing." They were to shun lying, disobeying parents, breaking oaths, or collecting excessive interest on loans, while enjoying the benefits of rightful ownership of property and commercial exchange.[50] In short, nineteenth century collegiate ethics were written by and for the propertied, educated, and refined inhabitants of the orderly homes of a tidily harmonious small-town or small-city America. The discord of such a view with the realities of urbanization and racial and economic conflict would soon become apparent.

VI. The Paradoxes of the New Morality

In its informal, unsystematic, sometimes rambling eclecticism, the presidential moral philosophy resonated with paradoxes inherent in the thinking of a generation that wanted the moral certainty and authority of their predecessors without the dogmatic method that originally accompanied it. Their very lack of system indicated the first of these paradoxes. The presidents decidedly did not want to write another plan of divine moral government. They did not want to perpetuate the concept of a remote God issuing decrees of right and wrong and the rewards or punishments ensuing therefrom. Nor could they any longer advocate the postulate of an Absolute Right intuitively known to every human conscience and governing the intentions of every act. On the contrary, they thought of God as a friend, a

---

[50]Wayland, *Elements*, p. 278.

teacher leading his pupils to see how they could join him in working for universal good. By making the end of one's actions the general interests of everyone affected, one could align oneself with God's beneficent will for the well-being of his creatures.

On the other hand, like the earlier generation, the presidents continued to emphasize that the relations in which one stood were governed by definite laws. Any rational person could perceive his situation and know his duty, for his conscience would impress it upon him. The consistent performance of duty would develop the virtues which comprised his character. God might be a teacher, but an exacting one at that, and the laws of rational relations were still the basis of moral action.

Yet this opened up a second paradox. Was one to obey one's conscience because one could introspectively or intuitively sense its rightness and concomitant obligation? Or did one obey because one could see the good that would be effected by one's action? The presidents seemed to shift the grounds of obligation from an inward to an outward-looking perspective. One fulfilled one's duty, they said, out of love or sympathy for others in order to participate in a more humane society in which everyone acted out of love for the good of others. Not the negative constraints of law, but the beckoning grace of love made one want to follow God's will. The glad result would be joy and happiness for oneself and for everyone.

On the other hand, like the ante-bellum moralists, the presidents were very cautious about happiness if it would tend to flow back and undermine the foundation of duty. They made happiness a by-product of achieving character, and attributed character to the systematic carrying out of one's inherent sense of right and wrong on which all people everywhere agreed.

Obligation was apparent in the very consensus of right that belonged to everyone's innate moral constitution.

The authors' stress on conscience and character led them to yet a third paradox, however. They attempted to incorporate the new learning into the writing of a "new ethics." They spoke of "the whole man" unified in intellect, emotion, and will, mind and body, actively attending to his experience and putting thought into action. They located that wholeness of personality within a social consciousness newly aware of the bonds of persons in relationships or even in the social organism.

On the other hand, they did not give up the language of the older faculty psychology, and they heightened the will even more as an organ of moral choice and behavior. While they acknowledged the influence of one's environment on one's development, they insisted that the individual was responsible for his own moral character, attained through self-controlled exercise of the will. Only the person who had mastered himself could be an influence in a society struggling to master the forces of change.

A final paradox at the root of the other three lay in the presidents' whole consciousness of change. They were widely read in the literatures of the new disciplines. They were versed in the arts and steeped in the trends of philosophy. They were informed on social issues and recognized the forces of urbanization, industrialization, and immigration that were transforming American society. Everywhere they saw change. They were determined to see in all of it the beneficence of God. The old transcendent providence of a static dispensation they pulled down into an immanent revealing of

Good Will in every social improvement or advance in learning.[51] At times they made progress almost indistinguishable from the hand of God, so bent were they on rendering all change beneficent.

Yet always beating just aside the windows of their providential home were the dark wings of evil. Certainly the presidents did everything they could to sap its power. They made evil only the absence of good, evil in nature simply the conflict of neutral forces, evil in man simply the bad choice that could be corrected by the good one. They debunked the pessimism about human nature manifested in the poetry of James Russell Lowell, for example, and applauded the openness of science to change and possibility. They declared, in Tucker's phrase, that the normal man was "the successful good type."[52]

The very stridency of their claims to providence, though, revealed their fear that the moral consensus they ceaselessly invoked was no longer intact. Removing the grounds of obligation from obedience to a remote God to the more comfortable confines of contributions to social well-being may have made personal morality more palatable. But it could not delay the movement toward a world in which no one really knew for sure what was right and what was wrong. The presidents dug in against that movement, guarding the preserve of gentility, drilling their students on the imperatives of personal moral responsibility. They acknowledged that modern persons

---

[51]Good Will, of course, was but a translation of the more latinized word, benevolence (*bene* - well; *volare* - to will).

[52]Hyde, *Practical Idealism*, pp. 295-308; Tucker, "A Man's Soul and His World," in *Personal Power*, pp. 97-113. Both Hyde and Tucker quoted a speech by the naturalist Minot contrasting Lowell with the optimistic scientist Asa Gray; see Tucker, "Contemporary Greatness," in *Public-Mindedness*, pp. 336-56.

had to adjust to the demands and changes of society, but they were
determined that one should go forth to the battle for character armed with
moral resolution.

In both their unambiguous appeals -- to providence, to benevolence, to
the centrality of will, divine and human -- and their pervasive ambiguities of
rightarian and utilitarian views, the authors perpetuated the synthetic moral
philosophy of their predecessors. Both new and old stressed individual moral
responsibility based on universal common sense and social consensus about
moral matters. Both appealed to high motives as the inducement to moral
obedience. Ironically, but accurately, the new generation's books were
already being described as "old-fashioned teaching." Little did the authors
realize that "adjustment" would soon become the moral code of a society
overwhelmed by change.[53]

---

[53][anon.] "Theory and Practice of Public Life," *Nation* 91 (October 13, 1910):338. See also
Stow Persons, *The Decline of American Gentility* (New York: Columbia University Press, 1973),
and May, *End of Innocence*, pp. 9-19.

CHAPTER FIVE

THE SYNTHESIS IN PRACTICE: IDEALS AND REALITIES

At its fifth general convention in Washington, D.C., in February, 1908, the Religious Education Association took as the theme for its papers and addresses "The Relation of Moral and Religious Education to the Life of the Nation." Soon published as a volume entitled *Education and National Character*, the papers were introduced by the Association's presidential address, "Enlarging Ideals in Morals and Religion," given by one of the nation's leading college presidents, Henry Churchill King of Oberlin. The R.E.A. had been founded in 1903 at the initiative of William Rainey Harper, president of the new University of Chicago, and "was born out of a profound conviction," as King put it, "of the national need of a deeper and steadily deepening moral and religious life, if the nation was to be either great or permanent."

King's speech was a paragon of the rhetoric of religious progressivism. Calling for the nation "to conquer its own inner dangers" and "to face its unavoidable national and world duties," King took as his theme an interpretation of a sentence pieced together from the Lord's Prayer that had been adopted as the unifying statement at the World Parliament of Religions in Chicago in 1893: "Our Father, who art in heaven: Thy will be done, as in

heaven, so on earth." This prayer summed up all the hopes and convictions
of humanity as it entered the modern age, for it announced that God was on
the side of the ethical will seeking mastery of the world in behalf of "great
new enthusiasms, great devotions, and great causes." Modern men needed
to grasp the effects of science, technology, and social movements on their
conceptions of humanity's future. The world was vastly enlarged by science's
explorations of the universe, whether telescopic or microscopic; at the same
time the world was becoming more unified through a growing sense of its
lawfulness and an increasing appreciation for the basic likenesses of people
of all races and nationalities; and the world was evolving toward a goal
reflecting "the direction of the mighty ongoing of God's purposes." Through
an expanded, unified, and evolving conception of the will of God, modern
man could "catch the trend of the ages" manifested in the lawfulness of the
universe and of human society, and fulfill "the glorious promise of world-
mastery and self-mastery, of conquest of our highest ideals." Undergirded by
the conviction of God's working in the development of nature and society,
men could assume ambitions of "a titanic quality" as they undertook great
economic enterprises, social projects, and missionary movements. Such
ambitions dwarfed "all previous aims of common men," for they marked
progress toward achievement of "that rational, ethical democracy, which
seems to be the goal of all our earthly endeavor." So, King assured the
gathered educators, "we build again our heaven-scaling tower, but on
foundations laid by God himself; and the confused tongues give promise of
changing into a higher harmony in the unity of the will of God."[1]

---

[1]*Education and National Character*, pp. 7-15. For more about Harper's role in forming
the Association, see *Proceedings of the First Convention of the Religious Education Association*,
Chicago 1903 (Chicago: Executive Office of the Association, 1903).

Whether or not the inflated verbiage and grandiose manner of King's speech were simply part of the presidential raiment, they also reflected the dynamics of the new rational synthesis which he and his colleagues wished to evoke from a changing world. First, by holding forth in the broad, inclusive language of sweeping generalizations, the presidents continually strove to appeal to the common sensibilities of humanity. They attempted to describe the world and human responsibility in it in such a way that no right-minded person could possibly disagree. Who in a progressive age would want to hear that the world was coming apart or being overwhelmed with irresolvable dilemmas? The presidents insisted that rational persons everywhere would still affirm that earth was the stage on which the drama of human fulfillment would be played out.

For second, the world continued under the guidance of divine providence. The more humanity explored nature and human nature, the more evident God's plan became. The presidents baptized change itself as an unfolding of the divine will. Whether through the evolution of nature or the development of social institutions, the wisdom and benevolence of God was becoming more apparent.

If the world was ultimately sensible and purposeful through the divine reason and will, then it was, third, subject to the mastery of an educated mankind directed toward a universal moral goal. Every person living under rational self-control and benevolence would contribute to an emerging society of world unity and personal freedom. Such a world would exhibit a communion of values and interests sufficient to conquer differences of culture and tradition, to manage inequities and injustices, and to prevent conflict and war.

To the preparation and advancement of a rational, ethical world, the presidents wanted, fourth, to bring all the resources of an expanding higher education. They believed it possible and necessary to incorporate all the new learning under the aegis of their ideals, to put it all to work in the achievement of world purposes. They insisted that their own institutions, though small and limited by comparison with the burgeoning universities, would have a determinative effect on progress toward a rational, moral world. Their campuses were living expressions of the needed synthesis, microcosms of the universal effort to bring the new learning to bear on human problems while producing individuals capable of synthesizing knowledge into moral ends. The college ideal of broad exposure to every discipline from science to literature, unified under rationally determined moral purposes and giving fruit in personal character, was in effect an ideal at the foundation of any rational world; and to its advocacy the presidents devoted themselves in every speech and writing.

In this fourfold pattern integrating knowledge and action based on the common sense and educated character of rational persons, the presidents were, of course, perpetuating a model inherited from their earlier nineteenth century predecessors. The "old time" presidential authors had also insisted on the unity or concord of truth; they had articulated a natural theology in which any new discovery of "fact" could be expected to fit. They had structured a moral sphere of universal laws and immediate duties which would keep the individual conscience in harmony with the ultimate ends of God's reason and will. They had appealed to the common sense of mankind as their ground of knowledge, even while they strove to educate young people into the ways of thinking and acting that would build the personal character necessary to social order.

To the older synthesis the progressive presidents added the elements of dynamism and change. If truth had once been viewed as a static unity simply to be assembled like a puzzle with a fixed number of pieces, it now seemed open-ended, evolving toward new horizons of scientific discovery and natural law. If moral responsibility had once been circumscribed in a universe of eternal moral law by set patterns of righteous behavior, it now seemed expansive, stretching to incorporate social change into behaviors made acceptable by appeal to good will. The divine providence holding all in unity now seemed less a given structure than an unfolding one, as the governmental analogy gave way to the metaphors of training and educating mankind.

In short, the center of gravity of the synthesis was shifting from a preordained order to an unfolding one, from a handing down of laws to an educated discovery of appropriate forms, or more baldly, from an outlook that rested on the revealed reason and will of God to an outlook that appealed to the human apprehension of the natural and moral worlds. Inherited conceptions in theology or ethics would have to be discarded, or at least expanded to embrace the intellectual changes of the day; and the task of rethinking and revisioning the synthesis would fall to persons educated in the new learning and devoted to reconstructing the divine foundations.

Yet at the same time, the reconstruction of a rational synthesis was a profoundly conservative task. The new generation was determined to keep hold of divine providence by interpreting change as a manifestation of God's benevolent will. They were convinced as well that every social development could be subsumed under human moral responsibility and control. The order of things might be changing, but it was still an order, which the new writers sought to undergird by appeal to traditional concepts of divine will and human conscience.

The continuity of the new synthesis with the old showed itself not only in the theology and moral philosophy of ante-bellum and progressive presidents, but in the intended function of the synthesis on the college campus and in the society at large. Although the inherited liberal arts curriculum capped by Common Sense moral philosophy was now having to expand to include new sciences and disciplines, the progressive colleges still kept the moral purpose of knowledge at the axis of learning. A college education was still focussed on the shaping of moral character for responsible social leadership. Even while the colleges modernized their curricula and changed some of their rules of living to keep up with changing social mores, they did so on the grounds of building up the moral dimension of the college ideal. A college that put into action within its own community the practical idealism necessary to society at large, the new presidents argued, would also produce the kind of leadership needed in society.

The colleges thus saw themselves charged with the responsibility for maintaining what one of their critics, George Santayana, dubbed "the Genteel Tradition." They were exemplars of a national credo that rested on "the reality, certainty, and eternity of moral values" and their abiding relevance to contemporary problems. The progressive leaders of American culture viewed every issue of industry or politics or social change as essentially moral, and thought of America as "the leader in moral progress" and by providence the steward of moral judgment on itself and the world.[2]

The new collegiate moral philosophers had to resolve contemporary intellectual problems stemming from the advance of scientific materialism. They allied themselves with selected German Idealism in order to restrict science to phenomena, retain a sphere of moral freedom, and reinforce the grounds of theistic belief in moral ideals. Yet on the whole they were perpetuating an older "moral idiom" of informed voluntarism which D. H. Meyer described as comprising the belief that "complicated social problems could be solved by well-intentioned men, acting according to the highest principles, and clear-headedly reducing complex issues to their simple moral components, thus making them matters of ethical judgment and responsible choice." Presuppositions of individual morality and social control still underlay the new philosophy, which was fundamentally conservative in its impulse to manage social change.[3]

The social writings of the progressive presidents reflected the same inherent tensions that had marked the dynamics of the older synthesis. First, while they advocated reform and necessary social change, they did so within strictly defined limits of appropriate social behavior. Tucker promoted the settlement house, but for teaching hygiene and punctuality, not labor organizing. King called for racial justice, but so that individual Negroes could advance under an improved separate-but-equal system. Hyde protested the concentration of capital in trusts, but in order to insure a free market for the small businessman. Their reconstructed morality of benevolence was, in

---

[2]May, *End of Innocence*, pp. 9-11, 19.

[3]Meyer, *Instructed Conscience*, p. 143; see also Howe, *Unitarian*, p. 305.

keeping with its heritage, as much a social control as a basis for social reform.

In particular, second, the claims of social justice always seemed to be competing with, and ultimately were confined to, the practice of individual morality. As more and more individuals were trained in the moral ideals of self-control and disinterested benevolence, the argument ran, the problems of social maladjustments or inequities would work themselves out. The wealthy would learn to restrain themselves, the poor would learn to achieve, and a fair distribution of resources would result.

If such a rational Christian morality was at the foundation of American democracy, so much the more could it be the basis for an emerging world order, the authors argued finally. If nations, like individuals, acted on principles of self-control and disinterested benevolence, there would never be any reason for war, and the emerging traditional civilizations such as China could be welcomed into the family of Christian nations. If, on the other hand, a particular nation became greedy or aggressive, it was to be shunned and if necessary punished militarily in defense of Christian civilization. The presidential moralists were pacifists in a world of rational harmony; but if that harmony were disturbed by unruly people, a war to discipline them took on the nature of a moral crusade.

As their synthesis functioned in a world where ideals and realities often conflicted, then, it continued the older dilemma of rightarian and utilitarian morality that rendered it unstable and even arbitrary. The moralists were prone to falling back on their own common sense assumptions, asserting the universality of their viewpoint, but soon discovering the limitations of their claims relative to particular situations. They found it increasingly necessary to make judgments about the greater exigency and the greater good.

In the end, though, came not only a loss of moral consensus but a diminishing of the authority of those who by position and influence had once been the moral arbiters of American society. Following World War I, the Protestant Christian consensus began to evaporate in disillusionment, an "end of innocence." Social problems were not proving so amenable to solutions, nor a world devastated by war so receptive to God's coming Kingdom. The supreme confidence of America's educated moral leaders would soon come to seem naive, outdated, and consigned by its own simplicity to an idealistic past. Some liberals did recognize the need for a radical rethinking of the assumptions of Christian social progress; certainly not all were to be lumped together as sycophants, in William R. Hutchison's phrase, of a lawn-social Rotarian religion floating under the listless banner of normalcy. The three college presidents, though, continued to take the war only as a moral challenge to be mastered, and remained progressive idealists to the end.[4]

I. Advancing the College Ideal

When Tucker and King appeared together on the Oberlin platform at the latter's presidential inauguration in 1903, they each addressed the ideal at the heart of college education. Presenting his remarks under the rhetorical title, "Is Modern Education Capable of Idealism?" Tucker called for an "ethical revival at the heart of education." He was disturbed that the advance of specialized disciplines whether in science or literature threatened

---

[4]May, *End of Innocence*, pp. 393-94; Hutchison, "Liberal Protestantism and the 'End of Innocence'," *American Quarterly* 15 (Summer 1963):126-39.

to displace the centrality of the "idealizing process" of learning, in which the scholar moved from facts to relationships to the moral incentives within them. Tucker urged educators to think reverently of all knowledge, since knowing led to awe and thence to faith. He challenged them to see their intellectual work as a moral discipline in which they were taking responsibility for their own growth in character. He lifted up as the wider goal of education the social good to which all were obligated through their vocation and their duty of self-sacrifice. In conclusion, he quoted the epitaph of Eleazar Wheelock, the founder of Dartmouth and missionary to the Indians:

> By the Gospel he subdued the ferocity of the savage. And to the civilized he opened new paths of science. Traveler: Go, if you can, and deserve the sublime reward of such merit.

The same spirit and purpose was the moving force, Tucker concluded, even in modern education.[5]

King echoed similar themes in his own remarks, with his characteristic style of unilateral generalization:

> The goal of civilization, our sociologists tell us, is a rational ethical democracy. Our political students insist that the foremost danger of the nation is the lack of the spirit of social service. The greatest needs of the individual man are always character, happiness and social efficiency.

The liberal arts college, King declared, existed precisely to meet those needs and build that democracy. "*Just this, then, is the function of the college*:" he continued; "*to teach in the broadest way the fine art of living, to give the best preparation that organized education can give for entering wisely and unselfishly*

---

[5]In *Inauguration of President Henry Churchill King of Oberlin*, pp. 53-66.

into the complex personal relations of life, and for furthering unselfishly and efficiently social progress."[6]

The joining of knowledge and values, and their fulfillment in social service under the aegis of religion, were chords struck even more clearly by Hyde in his Noble Lecture at Harvard in 1898. "The Message of Christ to the Scholar" was to rise above mere uneducated idiocy, past the stage of mere technical or utilitarian knowledge, to the enlargement of the liberal arts and ultimately to the original contact with truth, and concomitant humility, characteristic of the scholar. Correspondingly one would rise from a knave to a respectable man of the world to a virtuous man and ultimately to a Christian who embodied the motive of self-sacrifice for the good of others. Just as a scholar found Universal Truth in the sphere of thought, so a Christian came in contact with Infinite Righteousness in the sphere of will.[7]

Hyde put it more succinctly in a 1909 article. Liberal education, he argued, was an ellipse with two foci: at one point was science uncovering the "immutable relations" of facts and events in the external world; at the other was religion, "an attitude of heart and will toward God" that gathered up all the virtues to which the study of nature, art, history, literature and life would attest: "reverence, gratitude, justice, kindness, sympathy, pity, courage, self-control, loyalty, and self-sacrifice."[8]

---

[6]"The Primacy of the Person in College Education," Inaugural Address reprinted in *Personal and Ideal*, pp. 1-70; see esp. pp. 12-13.

[7]In *The Message of Christ to Manhood*, William Belden Noble Lectures for 1898 (Boston: Houghton, Mifflin & Co., 1899), pp. 117-46.

[8]"The Place of Religion in a Liberal Education," *Homiletical Review* 58 (October 1909):286-87.

Thus all three presidents left little doubt that even as they brought their institutions into the twentieth century, accommodating the new learning and modernizing their campuses, they were determined that the historic unity of knowledge, values, and religious faith would be maintained and strengthened in the liberal arts college. In their administrative decisions, in their public defense of the college ideal, and in their exhortation to students, the three continually reinforced the unique nature of the college's living tradition which yielded the fruits of individual character and service to society.

No area of the college was more sensitive to change than the time-honored liberal arts curriculum. Cautiously, but with confidence that it could be done without threat to the unity of the college ideal, the presidents introduced coursework in the new learning, dropped or modified classics requirements, and opened moderate elective possibilities to students wishing to specialize in a given area. All of them lived in the shadow of Harvard's Charles William Eliot, whose radical notions of collegiate reform from an entirely elective curriculum to a proposed reduction of the Bachelor of Arts course from four to two years forced all college administrators to either defend what they were doing or show their openness to change.

Hyde had once said that he neither liked nor understood Eliot, who had been president of Harvard during Hyde's college years. When Eliot's Committee of Ten reported to the N.E.A. a plan for standardizing high school units for admission to liberal arts colleges, Hyde criticized it for failing to insist on certain content of the required units, in English, Mathematics, and Latin especially. Yet Hyde was mentioned as Eliot's successor, and published an article praising him in an 1899 *Atlantic Monthly* for modernizing the curriculum. The widespread sensitivity of this area, though, was evident in the curiously defensive tone of Tucker's comment which Hyde then quoted favorably: "President Eliot," said Tucker, "is the most religious man among us."[9]

In any case, Hyde was typically acerbic in his rejection of "the college of tradition" as a skeleton of dead languages propped up by textbook courses in elementary science and topped by Christian evidences "aiming to prove by what is in the world a God who never can be found outside it." However, he did not move so quickly away from what he had labelled "predigested intellectual food." Only at the turn of the century did he advocate dropping the admission and graduation requirements in Greek, and he was never much of a supporter of science or mathematics. He did develop a number of new specialized departments. When he arrived the old "chair" system in which one endowed professorship comprehended whatever its occupant was qualified to teach, was still in effect. One man was teaching mathematics, history and political economy. Hyde created specialized professorships of mathematics, French, physics, sociology, art and music, and by 1904 even allowed psychology to split off from his own moral philosophy course as a separate discipline. Meanwhile an elective system was instituted, along with an arrangement for tutorials, so that students could pursue their specific interests beyond certain basic requirements.[10]

During King's administration first as dean and then as president, Oberlin moved to consolidate its dual liberal arts courses into one standard curriculum. The "philosophical and science" course had been less rigorous

---

[9]Hyde, "President Eliot as an Educational Reformer," *Atlantic Monthly* 83 (March 1899):348-57; Burnett, *Hyde*, pp. 39, 190, 194.

[10]Hyde, "College and Seminary," p. 264; Burnett, *Hyde*, pp. 116-26, 161-82; Hatch, *Bowdoin*, pp. 185-88.

than the "classical" course; admissions requirements and basic coursework were now standardized as of 1901. The preparatory Academy which had once thrived with over five hundred students readying themselves for college admission had been declining as the high school movement spread, and was closed in 1916 as the institution tried to concentrate its resources on the college. Elective possibilities were increased for liberal arts students, while classical requirements were reduced.[11]

Tucker sponsored a similar modernization of Dartmouth, reorganizing the faculty into departments rather than chairs of instruction, developing fields such as biology, sociology, economics, and modern languages, and opening up elective possibilities. The Dartmouth curriculum was divided into three major sections -- science and mathematics, languages and literature, and history, philosophy, and social and political science -- and students were required to distribute their coursework among the three with concentration in one particular area. Answering criticism that such broad options were not in keeping with the collegiate tradition of mental discipline, Tucker justified electives as a contribution to "the college discipline . . . understood as set to the task of developing the art of thinking." He considered a more disciplined capacity for self-determination to be good preparation for any field.[12]

The presidents continued to believe that religion was the soul of the college, though they gradually moved their institutions away from the inherited forms of religiosity. All three colleges had been Congregational in origin and through most of the nineteenth century maintained those ties

---

[11]Barnard, *From Evangelicalism*, p. 83; United States Commissioner of Education, *Annual Report, 1884-85* (Washington, D.C.: Government Printing Office, 1885), p. 192; *Annual Report, 1917*, p. 319; Love, *King*, pp. 159-60.

[12]Tucker, *My Generation*, pp. 299, 314, 337-39; Richardson, *Dartmouth*, 2:700-1.

through the clergy serving on their boards or in their presidencies. Oberlin and Bowdoin both dropped the remaining vestiges of church relationship in order to qualify for pension money from the Carnegie Foundation for the Advancement of Teaching. Tucker withheld Dartmouth from the plan but not because of wishing to retain church ties. His college had been chartered in 1769 as an independent institution, but from 1816 to 1819 had had to fend off in court the state legislature's attempt to take it over. Steadfast for independence, Tucker was not about to allow the institution to be tied up with one of the nation's major, and in Tucker's view notorious, capitalists. At the same time, during Tucker's tenure the Dartmouth governing board shifted to alumni control with only one clergy remaining by 1906; thus the college was completely removed from Congregational oversight.[13]

A parallel development was the abolition of the long-standing requirement for student attendance at Sunday church services. The Oberlin faculty abolished it in 1905, Dartmouth even earlier, in 1903; but Sunday vespers and other chapel talks continued, of course, as a faculty and presidential forum within the colleges. Hyde seemed determined to prove that such changes were not detrimental to the religious devotion of his student body. He still taught his senior religion class and published their class creed in a 1903 *Outlook*:

> I believe in one God, present in nature as law, in science as truth, in art as beauty, in history as justice, in society as sympathy, in conscience as duty, and supremely in Christ as our highest ideal.

---

[13]Hatch, *Bowdoin*, pp. 184-85; Richardson, *Dartmouth*, p. 2:697; see also for a recounting of the Dartmouth College case, pp. 1:287-346.

Whatever may have been the corrosive force of change on the mind of the students, the seal of the presidential mind was indelible.[14]

The presidents defended and celebrated the college ideal at every opportunity. Hyde and King appeared on the same program on a September afternoon of the 1904 St. Louis Universal Exposition. Both were at the height of their careers, having just turned forty-six years of age (Hyde that very day, King less than a week earlier), and both spoke avidly of the college. Hyde even said he meant "the real college," neither a school nor a university, neither a school-college (preparatory school) nor a university-college (such as Harvard). With its unique sense of community, its stress on teaching by personal contact, its aim of building character in the Christian spirit, and its contribution, in King's words, to "social progress," the college was fitting itself for social leadership in the new century.[15]

In his theology of *God's Education of Man*, Hyde suggested that the law was the school stage of compulsion, grace was the college stage of being won to an Ideal, and character was the university stage of service to humanity. He was always blocking off that center stage as the preserve of the liberal arts college, where students would learn that every field of study revealed God's expression of himself, and that seeking truth was a form of worship. He developed this middle ground in an 1888 *Atlantic Monthly* article, "The Future of the Country College," establishing a three-fold role for the college. Intellectually, it permitted the student to develop an interest in a field beyond the rote and drill of high school but not yet at the level of indepen-

[14]Love, *King*, p. 154; Richardson, *Dartmouth*, pp. 2:715, 744; Hyde, "The Creed of a College Class," *Outlook* 74 (June 27, 1903):510-12.

[15]Hyde, "The College," and King, "The Function of College Education," in Rogers, ed., *Congress of Arts and Sciences*, 8:119-32 and 8:151-54, respectively.

dent research in the university. Morally, the college encouraged development of personal ethics and standards beyond those inherited from childhood, but still within a community of support not available in the university. Religiously, it nurtured growth of personal beliefs and practical faith beyond memorized doctrines but not yet at the point of critical investigation and reinterpretation. He was not concerned if such an education did not appeal to everyone, asserting in a 1902 *Forum* that "the highest education must be aristocratic." His point was simply that the college had, and would retain, its place in the American system.[16]

Tucker considered the college unique for its "corporate consciousness"; campus traditions blended together with academic and social activities to create a spirit of community past and present. Far from being a provincial ideal, such a spirit made an important contribution to the public mind. Educators had been too preoccupied with impressive university research, utilitarian technical school growth and reorganization of elementary and secondary education, he told the New England Association of Colleges and Preparatory Schools in 1897. The continuing distinction of the college should not be overlooked, for the liberal arts milieu served to bring out the cultural contribution and moral influence of the new fields. As public high schools replaced private academies, he told them, the residential college niche would become even more significant as a stage between secondary schooling and professional training, allowing more personal development in a homogenous community and preventing a premature leap into a specialty.

---

[16]Hyde, *God's Education*, pp. 197-98; Burnett, *Hyde*, pp. 127-29, quotes Hyde's address to the New York State Regents' Convocation in Albany, July, 1886, where the speaker the previous year had been Daniel Coit Gilman; Hyde, "The Future of the Country College," *Atlantic Monthly* 62 (December 1888):721-26; "Problems of Our Educational System," *Forum* 32 (January 1902):551-65, esp. 561.

In its exposure of students to a wide range of learning, the college
provided training toward vocations, but not in them, Tucker wrote some years
later. Educators should not allow the spirit of commercialism to invade the
college, for it would defeat the basic purpose of nurturing moral maturity and
independence of thinking. He thus resisted efforts to bring more business
courses into the curriculum, even though it was becoming a more popular
career, and the percentage of students entering the professions of law,
medicine, teaching, or the ministry had dropped from 86 percent in the years
from 1821-1870 to only 51 percent in the last ten years of his term.[17]

Throughout his presidential career King struck the recurring chords of
the revolutionary changes in human thought in the last years of the
nineteenth century and the consequent demands for adjustment in "moral and
religious education." But he was confident that the Christian colleges had
made the transition "not indeed without change, but without breach with the
very best in their past, and without sacrifice of truth, of ethical ideals, or of
religious faith." In fact, he thought that the colleges were leading the way
toward absorbing and unifying the scientific spirit, the historical spirit, the
social consciousness, and the idealist philosophy in one comprehensive view
of "a larger, more unified, more evolving, more law-abiding world" that gave
"greater reason for faith in God and in our possibilities of sharing in his
purposes."[18]

---

[17]Thwing, *Guides*, p. 397; Tucker, *My Generation*, pp. 249-66, 354; "The Integrity of the
College Unit," *School Review* 5 (December 1897):683-96; "Administrative Problems of the
Historic College," *Educational Review* 43 (May 1912):433-48, esp. 441; "The Historic College:
Its Place in the Educational System," Inaugural Address at Dartmouth, 1893, reprinted in
Public Mindedness, pp. 204-33.

[18]"Importance of the Christian College," pp. 28-48.

Warning against the temptation to become "just like all the rest," King persistently urged the colleges to stand firm on their unique and ideal inheritance. They had always stood for an education moral and religious in nature, yet open to freedom of thought "within the broadest Christian lines." They had always been democratic institutions, resisting any "aristocracy of sex, of color, of wealth," and King worried that the modern increase in wealth might make the colleges domains of the privileged less committed to unselfish social service. They had always been builders of character, and must renew that task under a "new Puritanism" of "self-discipline" and "personal efficiency" (resistance to liquor and tobacco or general dissipation that was "illogical and out of date"). In sum, if the colleges met the challenge of educating the whole person, in preparation for service, with a national and world-wide outlook, they would continue to prove "a factor in the making of a better America" and produce in their young men and women the "living seed of the great oncoming kingdom of God."[19]

With his colleagues, King defended the place of the college as a necessary and essential stage between secondary and university education. The former could not absorb the tasks of the college, for its youth were too young and could not possibly digest enough of the vast new learning and its complex demands on life. The latter was too specialized, lacking the breadth of aim and capacity of the college. Nor was liberal arts education to be confused with training for jobs or technical skills. Rather it offered the unique opportunity of developing qualities of "judgment, adaptability, discernment, and interpretive power" characteristic of the "thinking man" who

---

[19]"The Future of Moral and Religious Education," *Religious Education* 4 (October 1909):293-304.

acquired an appreciation for the civilization in which he lived, as well as for the laws of life, physical and spiritual, by which he could contribute rationally to the mastery of modern problems.

The heart of the college was its community, which King understood along the lines of one of his favorite definitions. Borrowing Herrmann's summary of the moral law, "mental and spiritual fellowship among men, and mental and spiritual independence on the part of the individual," King suggested that the college provided "a rich, chosen, ordered environment" in which students could experience the whole of life in "hastened living." They were exposed to historical traditions, academic disciplines, and responsible social life in such a way as to "get a fused and assimilated sense of the world" in which they lived. King fretted that the social aspects of college life were too predominant, possibly a reflection of his continuing battles with students over such matters as the smoking rule. He encouraged individuality, not conformity, independence of thinking, not going along with the crowd, but an independence always addressed to certain ends, of course.[20]

King extended his conclusions from modern psychology to the life of the college. The complexity of life and relations needed to be reflected in the college experience so as to call out "the entire man -- physical, intellectual, aesthetic, social, moral and religious." Likewise the need for expressive activity and work should be met through physical education, writing and speech activities, social service, and participation in community life as a college citizen. Third and most important, the personal associations foundational to building character were at the center of the college ideal.

---

[20]"Primacy of the Person," pp. 1-70; "What the College Stands For," Presidential Address, January 11, 1917, *Association of American Colleges Bulletin* 3 (February 1917):3-23.

King drummed into his students the psychological fact that one learned by imitation, and that to be at one's best one must associate with the best -- the best books, the best art, the best persons. College associations offered the possibility of "character by contagion" as students came into personal contact with teachers of "character-begetting power" who could shape their charges by the ideals of the moral life. Not so much the professors' "individual propositions" but more their trend of thought, spirit, tone, and atmosphere were what influenced students in the shaping of great convictions and deep faiths. The resulting spirit of the college was catholic in breadth, receptive to new learning; objective in mood, recognizing lawfulness everywhere in the world and in human relationships; and social in consciousness, reverent of persons and dedicated to serving society. The great ends that "the true college must set before itself," King concluded in his inaugural, were "culture, character and social efficiency."[21]

Hyde put equal stress on the hiring of teachers with sufficient character to be a shaping force in the life of the college. He wrote to *The Nation* his six preferred qualities of an instructor: sound health, high character, thorough scholarship, genial personality, artistic appreciation, and contagious enthusiasm. He always took great care with his choices of faculty, and particularly wanted to hire younger scholars who would have immediate influence for good on students. In return, he gave the faculty wide

---

[21]"Primacy of the Person," pp. 42, 61, 69; *Rational Living*, pp. 246-50; *Personal and Ideal*, p. 111.

responsibility for administration and curriculum and did what he could to elevate their salaries.[22]

In his thoughts on *The Teacher's Philosophy In and Out of School*, Hyde addressed teachers at all levels with the comprehensive maxim that good teaching was simply "democracy, Christianity, good-will, incarnate in the teacher, and diffused like an atmosphere throughout the school." At the college level the teacher's aim was to develop the social interests of students, that is, their will to take account of the aims, interests, rights, and preferences of others. Both the curriculum in its breadth and the social life of collegiate activities in athletics, fraternities, or interest groups, were calculated to build a social will. The individual was definitely not, however, to become purely a social creature, but rather to learn how his own interests fitted in with those of others.

The miniature democracy of the college had its impact on teachers as well, for they needed to respect the rights of others, particularly the trustees and benefactors of the school. Every professor was "at perfect liberty to give dignified and moderate expression to whatever views on political and social questions he might hold," but should demonstrate courtesy to the institution, since aggressive promotion of views contrary to those of the wider constituency would limit "his largest usefulness as a professor." Thus students, faculty, and administrators enjoyed the rights and undertook the duties of living responsibly together in the community.[23]

---

[22]"The College Administration and the College Instructor," *Nation* 102 (April 20, 1916):434-35; "Personality and College Professors," *Outlook* 92 (August 21, 1909):931-37; Burnett, *Hyde*, pp. 142-49.

[23]*The Teacher's Philosophy In and Out of School*, Riverside Educational Monographs, ed. Henry Suzzallo (Boston: Houghton Mifflin Co., 1910), pp. vi, 25-37; Burnett, *Hyde*, pp. 195-96,

Hyde encouraged the students to use their college opportunity to build an individuality. He warned them against social conformity that might lead them down the path to smoking, drinking, gambling, and licentiousness, and cautioned them more generally against putting college life before their studies. He was not humorless about the "transformation" that undergraduates went through in their four years; he composed what he thought would be a typical letter home in each of the years, mirroring the wide-eyed innocence of the freshman, the defiance of all traditions of the sophomore, the egotistical and abstract idealism of the junior, and the discovered duties of social service undertaken in love by the senior. Hyde realized that football, romance, contention with parental values, and social -- sometimes socialist -- idealism were part of college experience. But he wanted his charges to see that the college years were their chance to develop independent character based not on rules and discipline but on freely chosen ideals and virtues. They would be exposed to the full range of life in "all lands and all ages" under the guidance of "professors who are Christians." Thus they could grow in initiative, in the desire to give their best and not take anything without paying the full price for it, and ultimately in their capacity for following Christ according to the will of God into paths of self-sacrificing service to society. Hyde collected these exhortations over the years into a volume which he dedicated

> To Theodore Roosevelt
> Who as legislator, commissioner, secretary
> colonel, author, governor
> vice-president, president and peacemaker
> has wrought in the world
> what he was taught in college

---

quoting from Hyde's 1901 address at Boston University.

and shown the power for good
a college man can be.[24]

Tucker was concerned to bring the historic Eastern colleges into the atmosphere of the new learning, and constantly denied their provincialism. He also recognized the difficulty, though, of recruiting a cosmopolitan and productive teaching force that would exhibit the necessary college sympathies and ideals. The scholars coming out of advanced university education were not always well matched to the generalist's or beginner's interests of undergraduates, nor well suited to participation in the governance of the institution. Finding teachers who combined quality of scholarship with ability to influence student character was the supreme presidential challenge.[25]

Collegiate education was intended to develop the humanity of a student, in Tucker's view, not only his individuality but his sense of unity and responsibility in social relationships. With the other two presidents, Tucker constantly sought to keep the balance between the individual and the social. In his collection of speeches to students titled *Personal Power*, he suggested that the college ought to quicken the mental and moral senses of its undergraduates to the end of personal power and development of virtue. Each year from 1905 to 1908 he opened the school year with an address on one aspect of "The Moral Training of the College Man." The "gentleman" was the man of efficiency, honor, and devotion who upheld his duty of

---

[24]"An Address to Freshmen," Bowdoin College, September 1908, *Independent* 65 (October 1, 1908):746-48; *College Man*, see esp. Preface, "The Transformation of the Undergraduate," pp. 4-45, "The Continuity and Contrast of College and the World," pp. 114-28, and "The More Excellent Way," pp. 129-49.

[25]"Undergraduate Scholarship," in *New Reservation*, pp. 23-49; "The Administration of the Modern College," in *Public Mindedness*, pp. 234-51; "Administrative Problems of the Historic College," pp. 433-48.

service to society with refinement and sensitivity. The "scholar" learned to appreciate truth and beauty in its widest expressions, gaining from a general exposure to various fields a sense of the power of the true. The "citizen" learned in the college how to participate in forming responsible public opinion and how to subordinate private interests to the public good. The "altruist" went beyond that to a moral motive equivalent to religious consecration, but had the valiant struggle of overcoming the modern tendency toward accumulation of money. With more and more graduates entering the business world, the altruist's values of honesty and benevolence would be all the more important.[26]

Tucker was aggravated by that false social life which applauded popularity and not service. He warned against the ballooning repute of football players and other athletes who were becoming models of leisure and glamor, and who might be tempted to take undue financial advantage of the publicity. Society was losing its respect for scholarship, Tucker cautioned, to the extent that it failed to reward study with acclaim equal to that of more ostentatious pursuits. The scholar was also a man of "effective personality," he assured his undergraduates, and should keep to the task even while enjoying reasonable participation in sports, fraternities, and social companionships.[27]

Thus the three presidents sought to bring their colleges into effective relation with the progressive era by defending their place in the educational system and by articulating and refining the college ideal. First, by revising

---

[26]*Personal Power*, Preface, "The Moral Training of the College Man," pp. 195-262, "The Capacity for the True," pp. 114-28; *My Generation*, pp. 249, 254-56.

[27]*Personal Power*, "The Training of the Gentleman," pp. 195-211, "The Well-Bred Man," pp. 140-41; "Undergraduate Scholarship," in *New Reservation*, p. 44.

the curriculum, reorganizing the faculty, and reforming academic regulations, they hoped to incorporate the new learning into a traditional ideal of the unity of seeking truth. They were almost defensive at times in insisting that the trend away from classics and moral philosophy did not entail a loss of the religious centering of the college. They wanted to argue both that the colleges were progressive and that they were maintaining the cohesion of all learning in a rational, divinely grounded world.

Second, the presidents wanted their institutions to continue to produce men of character (King occasionally referred also to women), individual, independent, and devoted to the social good. Character was to be the practical fruit of educating young people into a rational and moral synthesis of knowledge and action, yielding verities and ideals to guide their lives. To the end of character the colleges were to bring all their resources, curriculum, teaching staff, administration, physical plant, and activities.

Finally, the presidents advocated the college community as a microcosm of personal and social idealism, both a model for training the young and a pattern for the larger world to pursue. Growth, changes in student life, and new trends such as athletic prominence, were reshaping the college community; but it was still an exemplary democracy for the practice of individuality, benevolence, and social service.

All the changes created tensions, to be sure. The presidents were not unaware of the secularity pervading all the fields from science to literature. King noted with alarm the college philosophers teaching without reference to historic revelation. Hyde flagged any cynicism or stoic pessimism he perceived in literature. Tucker cautioned against academic specialization that would push character-building into the background or reduce respect for the educated generalist devoted to the social good. Yet they promised their audiences that the college would remain dedicated to its inherited and appropriate goals. Addressing the Union League Club of Chicago, a progressive organization of unfaltering allegiance to Teddy Roosevelt, Tucker proclaimed that the colleges would continue their training in conscience and moral leadership, giving distinction to the national character. His address was titled with a question, "What Has Patriotism the Right to Demand of Education?" He answered by quoting Phillips Brooks's cry of the nations to each other: "Show us your man!" The colleges stood ready to the task.[28]

II. Encounter with a Changing World

The presidents grounded the college ideal of service in a progressive vision that incorporated economic and social changes in America and the world. All three were persuaded that the old system of laissez-faire individualism was morally inadequate to new social conditions. All three advocated a new social consciousness that would intelligently grasp the conditions of urban life, industrial growth, expanding technology, and a growing sense of the closeness and interconnectedness of the whole world. Yet reverence for the person was for them still the heart of any social awareness, as individual responsibility was the backbone of any social reform. Their stress on the reform, uplift, and moral accountability of the individual tied them closely to their predecessors, as did their resistance to any social reform cast in the mold of political coercion rather than ethical persuasion.

---

[28]*Public Mindedness*, pp. 195-203. Theodore Roosevelt had close political ties with the Union League, and his portrait still hangs prominently in the main lounge of the Club in Chicago. See Bruce Grant, *Fight for a City; The Story of the Union League Club of Chicago and Its Times* (Chicago: Rand McNally & Co., 1955), pp. 184-88.

They continued and rather more intensified the belief that democracy was
the fullest fruit of the Gospel and that American Anglo-Saxon culture would
be the basis for a new Christian world civilization.

As they brought the idealism of their new synthesis into encounter with
social realities, then, the presidents perpetuated three fundamental tensions
that had been endemic to the older synthesis as well. First, while they
advocated social reform, they also conceived of it as a mode of social control.
Second, while they spoke for a new social consciousness, they resisted any de-
emphasis on individual moral responsibility. Third, while they presented
themselves as pacifists in a world of rational harmony, they were also moral
crusaders who could promote war as a necessary weapon in the defense of
Christian civilization.

A. Reform and Control

If an older generation had been able to view American society
somewhat monolithically as a community ordered to the predominance of
white, Anglo-Saxon Protestant males, the new moralists were forced to cope
with major population shifts of immigrant peoples into American cities as
well as demands for reform among women and blacks. The progressive
response to social change, while humanitarian and charitable, was fundamentally conservative of the traditional social order. Immigrants were to be
inculcated with values of individual responsibility and self-control, women
were to keep their rightfully ordered place in the home, and blacks were to
seek advancement within the given structures of an increasingly apartheid
society.

King and Hyde both advocated humane social reform, especially relief of oppressive working conditions and abuse of women and children. King saw in the rise of the cities one of the major challenges to morals and religion, and a test of democracy's resistance to corruption. He was encouraged, though, by social scientific studies of the new human conditions and was hopeful that they would lead to "increasing discernment of the laws of life." At any rate the obvious evils of twelve-hour work days, child labor, and low pay were being recognized as detrimental to personal health and growth as well as to that thread of the social fabric, the home and family. Hyde was particularly interested in the "birthrights" of children, and applauded the urban child welfare movement. Progressive reforms such as child labor laws, industrial education and training, vocational guidance, playground development, youth interest clubs and associations, and juvenile laws and courts, all were in the interests of the greater welfare of children and ultimately of society. Many of these reforms fell to the public schools, which Hyde extolled as the training ground in Christian civilization, especially for immigrant children.[29]

Of the three presidents, Tucker was the staunchest advocate of the settlement house and the social reforms related to it. While decrying the economic greed that encouraged importation of cheap immigrant labor, leading to "disturbed social conditions and . . . debased moral standards," he was tireless in his call for the churches and public institutions to take account of changing economic conditions and needs, especially in the cities. Having come to Andover in homiletics, he soon added a course in pastoral theology

---

[29]King, *Moral and Religious*, pp. 26-30, 104, 337; Hyde, *Quest*, pp. 233, 255, 259; *Practical Idealism*, pp. 196-202.

which he used as a forum for teaching "social economics." He led his students in the study of labor, crime, and pauperism in successive years, and one of his graduates, Robert A. Woods, returned from field research in England to start the South End Settlement House in Boston under Andover's auspices. Tucker's commitment to developing "Andover House" partly accounted for his resistance to the Dartmouth presidency, and helped him weather the whole Andover trial controversy. He announced in 1893 the goals and principles of the new settlement house; it would go far beyond charity in addressing the causes of inhuman social conditions by creating a center of community pride and neighborhood identity; it would conduct its work on a personal, not an institutional level, undertake nothing already being done by other organizations, avoid religious proselyting, and strive to awaken its neighborhood to work for its own self-improvement.[30]

Twenty-five years later, Tucker summarized the work of the house under three headings. It had worked specifically with immigrants and their children, upbuilding neighborhood unity and spirit; it had made a contribution to social reform through studies of urban life and proposed housing and child labor legislation; and it had provided field training for a new corps of professionals devoted to social change. The whole settlement house movement, Tucker suggested, had proved itself second only to the public schools in the Americanization of immigrant peoples.[31]

Tucker also encouraged the work of combined churches and community centers such as Berkley Temple in Boston, coining the term "institutional

---

[30]"The Goal of Equality," in *New Reservation*, pp. 50-78; *Function*, p. 4; *My Generation*, pp. 161, 172-76, 181, 184; "The Work of Andover House in Boston," *Scribner's Magazine* 13 (March 1893):357-72.

[31]"Twenty-five Years 'In Residence',"*Atlantic Monthly* 119 (May 1917):640-49.

missions" to describe their organization. Here the church could exercise its long overdue sympathy for the poor working classes who could hardly be blamed for turning to socialism if the Christian businessmen and other laymen ignored their cries for justice. Through institutional missions and settlement houses the immigrants could learn Christian values of reverence, hard work, thrift, and cleanliness, and know that someone cared about them. Otherwise, the poor would continue to drift, to dirty their new houses as they destroyed their old, without the vitality of Christian values to enable them to make their own unique contribution to American society.[32]

Speaking to an audience in his former home of Manchester, New Hampshire, in 1896, Tucker offered his vision of "The Spiritual Life of the Modern City." Beyond the statistics and material production and consumption of a city was a spiritual life either dissipated by vice, corruption and poverty or fulfilled in unity. Through Christian values permeating all levels of city life -- high standards of business, purity in the home, a sense of charity and sympathy -- the city could achieve a collective righteousness characterized by love of the neighbor, self-restraint, and self-sacrifice for the community.[33]

Responsibility for social righteousness lay at the door of every citizen. Tucker lifted up some traits of "great citizens" before his listeners at the New York Federation of Churches in 1905. They would move imaginatively from duty to action, guided by intelligent allegiance to needed reform, with the courage to stand against corruption, and the consecration to endure for their

---

[32]Aaron I. Abell, *The Urban Impact on American Protestantism 1865-1900* (Cambridge: Harvard University Press, 1943), pp. 137, 154; Tucker, *Function*, pp. 67-94; "Some Present Questions in Evangelism," *Andover Review* 1 (March 1884):233-44, esp. 236.

[33]*Public Mindedness*, pp. 38-57.

principles to the end. The next year Tucker told the Religious Education Association meeting in Boston that citizenship was sacred, for in the face of organized power all too often leading to self-aggrandizement, true citizenship demanded justice in behalf of the public good.[34] King and Hyde certainly agreed on the importance of citizenship, the latter calling for well-informed voters who would serve the public interest while retaining independence of thinking against any political machinations of the wealthy.[35]

The presidents struggled mightily, however, over the issue of extending full citizenship to either women or blacks. They unanimously opposed the organized movement for "woman's rights," King particularly attacking the "militant suffragettes" for trying to emancipate women by force. Invoking his favored sin of selfishness, King insisted that women acting in "selfish force" would only produce a cheap and insecure "forced victory" for themselves. Moreover, their movement was being undermined by the Feminists among them who vitiated marriage by advocating "'free alliance'" or free love. On the contrary, King asserted that social progress was achieved "by the patient and persistent processes of education and moral enlightenment," eventuating in laws "enthroned in the reason and conscience of the community" and obeyed by all out of "free self-control."

Yet he and Tucker did recognize, in King's words, that "it cannot be justly claimed that women have a fair representation in organized society to-

---

[34]Ibid., "Good Citizenship Dependent Upon Great Citizens," pp. 1-6, "The Sacredness of Citizenship," pp. 7-15.

[35]Hyde, *God's Education*, pp. 182-83; "The Abolition of the House of Lords," *Outlook* 93 (December 18, 1909):866-68.

day."[36] Tucker thought it unfair to universally confine the woman's role to the home when many were not even married; and he praised the influence of women in building up the social conscience through their work in settlement houses. On the other hand, Hyde was adamantly opposed to the whole movement of changing sexual roles. If every individual served society in his or her proper and most fitting place, the woman should limit herself to the home. Cultural and philanthropic activities for women were constructive so long as they were not an end in themselves, but were brought back to the home as "rich acquisitions in literary and aesthetic taste, social life and philanthropic and religious fervor." Hyde told college women to take advantage of their "comparative economic freedom," not to become idle aristocrats, but to broaden their interests and contribute thereby to the social good.[37]

All three men acknowledged, in Tucker's phrase, a duty to the colored race in the South. King called for America to "face its great peculiar problem of relation to the negro race." Hyde composed a plan for governing race relations on which he was sure North and South could agree. All these approaches, of course, reflected a presidential viewpoint of speaking for the white, Anglo-Saxon Protestant majority who assumed the duties and initiatives in resolving such social dilemmas.

Hyde and King pointed to racial differences that had to be taken into account in any constructive race relations. These distinctions were "deeper than the skin," said Hyde; King named some of them: Negroes were more

---

[36]*Fundamental Questions*, pp. 155-62, 168.

[37]Tucker, "Notes on the Progress of the Social Conscience," in *New Reservation*, pp. 79-118, esp. 112, 116; Hyde, *Practical Idealism*, p. 172; "The Choice of the College Woman," in *College Man*, pp. 175-93.

"individual" with unique endowments in music and emotional range, combined with a "positive genius" for religion, and a "tendency to content" and avoidance of frantic haste. Moreover, Negroes were possessed of some noble qualities; King pointed to the fidelity of Livingstone's Negro attendants in carrying his mortal remains all the way back from interior Africa to return them to England. Negroes had much cause for self-respect and self-sufficiency. On the other side, whites would undermine their own self-respect if they callously repressed Negroes and gave them no opportunity for self-improvement. Neither side could gain anything from bitterness, suspicion or hatred of the other.

The segregated system of separate but equal facilities and opportunities, Hyde and King agreed, was in "the interest of racial integrity and racial progress." Hyde went on to advocate industrial opportunity for Negroes "of trained and approved efficiency," as well as educational opportunities in leadership and technical skills. He warned, however, that "the North must appreciate the tremendous burden such education, involving as it does a double school system, lays upon the resources of the South," and extended his support of the General Education Board established in 1902 to funnel northern philanthropy to southern schools.

King pleaded with Negroes that it was "wiser and more self-respecting not to fight separate schools, separate cars, etc., provided only that the accommodations are the same, and that the separation of the races is truly maintained, in that the schools and cars of the blacks are not made a dumping ground for the less desirable whites." He was sure that a self-respecting Negro would not "press the demand . . . for so-called social equality" or more particularly would not want "social mixing." He recommended as a parallel the suggestion for the Jews published in *The Indepen-dent*: "'Jews can make their own social world like other people . . . Where they are not wanted they will not want to go.'" The demand for justice was preeminent, though, for it was in the nation's interest to bring the Negro "to self-knowledge, to self-reverence, to self-control," and finally to bring everyone to "the white flower of the moral and Christian spirit -- reverence for the person."[38]

In summary, then, the progressive social idealism of the presidents aimed at the extension of Christian civilization through the dedicated service of educated citizens and the moral improvement and uplift of the "uncivilized races," in Hyde's phrase. The three men advocated proper legislative resolution of social conflict, and decried the politicizing of the women's rights movement. They believed that immigrants, Negroes, and Indians needed for their own welfare the moral benefits of Christian society: "the inculcation of a desire to hold property; the capacity for steady industry; an interest in good pictures and good music and good books; a regard for personal comfort and personal cleanliness." To that end they supported "the social settlement and the industrial school" and separate but equal opportunities for the Negro.[39]

In all this they were in continuity with their collegiate predecessors, who, while they had not had to cope with rapid industrialization, immigration, and urbanization, had been equally resistant to the politicizing of social change and every bit as fervent in their desire to spread Christian civilization through missions to the Negro and the Indian. When Rhode Island was

---

[38]King, *Moral and Religious Challenge*, pp. 283-308; Hyde, "A National Platform on the Race Question," *Outlook* 77 (May 21, 1904):169-70; Tucker, "The Estimation of Power," in *Personal Power*, pp. 15-30.

[39]Hyde, *Outlines*, p. 219.

rocked in 1842 by the Dorr Rebellion, which sought rights of citizenship for the unpropertied class of men, Francis Wayland was outraged at such a forceful revolt undermining the very social order to which it wanted admission. Their legitimate rights would come in due time through rational means, he assured those in rebellion, but civil disorder would only set back their cause.

Wayland and his presidential generation belonged to the gradualist mainstream of the anti-slavery movement. Even at Oberlin, where anti-slavery convictions had been instrumental in its inception in 1834 and 1835, and where free blacks had been admitted from the beginning, the college's most famous sponsor, later president during the immediate ante-bellum period, Charles Finney, was a gradualist. He warned the anti-slavery organizers who had come to Oberlin in 1835 after their schism from Lane Seminary in Cincinnati, that they should avoid a "denunciatory spirit" in attacking slavery, and work for conversions to moral benevolence. Finney considered slavery a sin to be repented, not an economic institution to be abolished politically. Only when war seemed inevitable did he and his presidential colleagues generally warm to the cause of the North against the South, whose actions Wayland typically interpreted as a rebellion which must be suppressed. Finney had once even professed a "constitutional" distaste for blacks, protesting the elimination of the "nigger heaven" balcony of the revivalist Chatham Street Church in New York where he often preached; he was rumored to practice discrimination at Oberlin as well.[40]

---

[40]Wilson Smith, *Professors*, pp. 134-35, 141, 194-96; Timothy L. Smith, *Revivalism and Social Reform; American Protestantism on the Eve of the Civil War* (Gloucester, Mass.: Peter Smith, 1976 [orig. publ. 1957]), pp. 180, 215; Gilbert H. Barnes, *The Antislavery Impulse, 1830-1844* (New York: D. Appleton-Century Co., 1933), pp. 76-77, 162; Bertram Wyatt-Brown, *Lewis Tappan and the Evangelical War Against Slavery* (Cleveland: Press of Case Western

Thus the typical sensitivities and moral idiom of the presidential moralists were continuous into the progressive era. All appropriate personal and social behavior was to be defined and ruled by the basic principle of disinterested benevolence: the unselfish effort to seek the good of others, even while pursuing a modest self-interest that worked indirectly for the good of all. The method of moral persuasion was the appropriate avenue of justifiable social change; moral improvement was the purpose of preaching the Gospel to slaves and later to immigrants; and moral supremacy was the only means of victory in social conflict. Such fundamental attitudes kept reform bound within strict limits of propriety while largely perpetuating the traditional social order. Control was to remain in the hands of educated, rational, morally upright individuals, as defined by their spokesmen and educators.

B. Social Consciousness and Individual Morality

The new progressive social consciousness consisted of a heightened awareness of the interdependence of all in the social organism. The presidential moralists, though, did not think so much in terms of social systems as the locus of both problems and reforms. They tended rather to conceive of society as shaped by its interdependent parts, namely, the individuals of which it was composed. They continued to insist that if all individuals were self-controlled, moderate, and devoted to the good of all, society itself would be improved. Whether laborer or capitalist, worker or professional, everyone was to play his role with restraint and benevolence, and a just society would be the certain result.

Reserve University, 1969), pp. 177-78.

In his Phi Beta Kappa address at Harvard in 1894, Tucker described
"A New Movement in Humanity" from a perspective centered on liberty and
personal freedom to a viewpoint of the unity and mutual relatedness of
persons in society. Education was moving away from sheer individualism to
the training of students to see their relations to others and their social duties.
"To whom amongst us would more liberty be a greater good?" he asked his
listeners. "What conditions of present suffering or distress would it satisfy?"
The power of liberty had run its course, in Tucker's opinion, and rising to
replace it was the force of unity as "cooperation, partnership, sympathy,
fellowship . . . [the] new principle in adjusting industrial relations and
ennobling social relations."[41]

Five years later Tucker elaborated his theme in a speech to Union
Seminary students on "Social Righteousness." A morality of personal
goodness was insufficient to meet modern conditions, he argued. The
suffering created by current urban and industrial problems could only be
alleviated by reforming institutions and changing the environments in which
people were living. He lifted up the settlement house as a prime example
of putting human sympathy into concrete action by creating neighborhood
centers where immigrants and the poor could be exposed to the refinements
of education and culture. Attacking the gross accumulation and vulgar
display of wealth as a cause of much social suffering, Tucker told his
Dartmouth students that power should be judged by its capacity for restraint
and refinement accompanied by sacrifice in behalf of social justice. "Keep
then the balance," he admonished them, "keep the proportion, keep the
perspective. Start in with righteousness and you shall come out with your

---

[41]*New Reservation*, pp. 195-213.

nation great, your cities safe, your corporations strong, your social life clean, your personal lives honorable in the sight of all men."[42]

King and Hyde agreed that a new social consciousness gave promise of ameliorating social ills even while heightening the personal. King invoked a "socialized individualism" that would work for the common good of the community while respecting individual rights and initiatives. He believed that the evils of present conditions would be overcome by the "positive growth of the good" as righteous persons exercised the values of love in society. Hyde was equally persuaded that evil would be redeemed by service and sacrifice. The public arena should belong to those with a strong sense of public good, and unfit men should be excluded from politics. For democracy was "the great practical corollary" of the spirit of Christ, and those who lived and advocated Christian values embodied the Kingdom of God "here and now." Through "happy homes, cheerful school-rooms, faithful work, honest trade, wholesome food, healthful dwellings, beautiful pictures, refined social intercourse, vigorous out-door life, abundant recreation," the Kingdom was coming to realization in American society.[43]

Francis Wayland had once declared that "those nations have always enjoyed the most perfect freedom, who have been most thoroughly imbued with the doctrines of Jesus Christ." Exemplary of the political economy taught by the old moral philosophers, Wayland extended those doctrines to economic conduct. Morally upright individuals, unselfishly pursuing the right,

---

[42]"Social Righteousness," in *Public Mindedness*, pp. 16-37; "The Estimation of Power," in *Personal Power*, pp. 15-30.

[43]King, *Moral and Religious*, p. 341; "Good Thoughts in Bad Times," *Biblical World* 50 (November 1917):267-75; Hyde, *Outlines*, pp. 223-25, 254; *God's Education*, p. 101; *Good Will*, p. xv.

even while advancing their private interests, would unconsciously contribute to the public good through the harmony of all economic interests under the divine benevolence. Wealth was not to be pursued directly, but would inevitably bless the nation devoted to the Christian virtues of work, thrift, charity, unselfishness, and responsible ownership of property.[44]

The late nineteenth century economy, choked by monopolies and trusts, marred by conflicts of labor and capital, and dominated by wealth unscrupulously gained, demolished any theories of simple harmony. Yet the progressive moralists largely advanced the same principles as their predecessors and believed that a return to fundamental economic morality would solve the problems and restore equilibrium.

Tucker was somewhat more skeptical of the benevolence of capitalist men of fortune than the other two. He issued a response to Andrew Carnegie's *Gospel of Wealth* in an 1891 *Andover Review*, calling it a gospel of patronage, and arguing that economic inequities should be corrected at the point of the distribution and accumulation of wealth in the first place, and not be left to the charity of those who had gotten rich by dubious means. He applauded legislation aimed at breaking up monopolies and the control of political parties by the wealthy few.

On the other hand, Tucker was as critical of the politicizers of labor problems as of the captains of industry. He was persuaded that labor reform should be accomplished economically, not in the political realm. Thus he opposed socialism as a political platform, yet at one point proposed that since the morale problem of industrial workers was their lack of interest in

---

[44]"The Duties of an American Citizen," p. 41. See also D. H. Meyer, *Instructed Conscience*, pp. 99-107.

their products, they be allowed to participate in the ownership of the companies employing them.[45]

King decried the "aristocracy of wealth" by which a handful of men with "barbarically stupendous fortunes" threatened to achieve control of the economy and practically of the government. He protested monopolistic gains protected by tariff legislation and achieved at public expense through land grants, railroads, and utilities. He blamed the wealthy for blocking legislation to protect laborers, especially women and children, and for standing in the way of protection of natural resources. He considered them the cause of a general demoralization in which the common man no longer thought he could obtain justice in the courts and found himself humiliated by the "'conspicuous waste'" and "cynical indifference" of the irresponsible rich.

On the other hand, King did not wish to fuel a senseless class warfare. "Invective of the rich is little to the point," he asserted; strife between capitalists and laborers was not in the national interest. He pleaded instead for national reform in the public good, comprised by legislation protecting labor and establishing a tribunal for settling labor disputes. He was disturbed by the tendency on both sides toward "increasing combination" or organized activities such as strikes and lock-outs. Against the "syndicalists" or unionizers he urged not "violent emancipat[ion]" through "selfish force" but rather gradual reform through moral persuasion and progressive legislation. Any resort to "mob violence" would be a foolish effort to answer "the selfish lawlessness of the capitalistic class by a like selfish lawlessness on the part

---

[45]"The Gospel of Wealth," *Andover Review* 15 (June 1891):631-45; "The Goal of Equality" and "Notes on the Progress of the Social Conscience," in *New Reservation*, pp. 50-118.

of the working class." Democracy required restraint, self-control, and self-sacrifice on everyone's part.[46]

Hyde's opinions of the wealthy were ambivalent to the point of contradiction. In a 1909 *Outlook* he demanded "The Abolition of the House of Lords," that is, the lords of industry who were monopolizing the economy through tariff controls. He railed against dishonesty and stealing in high places, and attacked the "effeminate irresponsibility" of the idle rich who contributed nothing to public service. At the same time, he hardly opposed wealth as such, finding it in the hands of a Christian the means to beneficence, refinement, charity, and even sponsorship of movements to solve social problems. The rich Christian was "God's finest masterpiece in the world today," holding in his hands the means to greater ends. Money did not equate with materialism; one should see that "the president of a railroad, the corporation attorney cannot live their lives and do their work effectively without comfortable homes, enjoyable vacations, social connections, educational opportunities, which cost a great deal of money."[47]

The greatest good of all in society was achieved, in Hyde's opinion, by each person doing his work well in his particular place. The health of the organism depended on the devotion to duty of each part, the whole benefiting from the rational relations of its constituent elements. The merchant's duty was to have just regard for his customers, the professional's to keep up with advances in his field to the benefit of his clients, and the worker's to produce durable, sound goods in honest and loyal service to his

---

[46]*Moral and Religious*, pp. 309-42; *Fundamental Questions*, pp. 155-57.

[47]"Abolition of the House of Lords," pp. 866-68; *God's Education*, pp. 85-90; *From Epicurus*, pp. 192-93; *Abba Father*, p. 52; *Sin*, p. 36.

employer. Hyde wanted everyone -- producer and consumer, employer and
worker -- to see that they all belonged to one social system in which each
contributed to the good of all. The laborer in particular was to see that
"work is worship"; Hyde composed a worker's prayer in his volume, *Abba
Father*, a petition to be fair to one's employer, loyal to fellow workmen, and
"a sound member of the economic order." Similarly he rated workers in his
scale of *Self-Measurement* according to their dedication, excellence, and
initiative, asking "Do you work just enough to draw your pay?" If so, he
replied in his typical we-language, "then we cannot deny that you are
industrious . . . But we can give you a mark of only plus one." The highest
mark of plus three was reserved for the worker of industry, fidelity, and
innovation. Thus the greatest social good was achieved neither by selfish
individualism nor by impersonal socialism, but rather by a social consciousness of bearing one another's burdens through individual initiative and
common social service.[48]

Thus the presidents sought a synthetic middle ground between
individualism and socialism, placing the moral onus squarely on the person
even while pleading for wider sensitivity and compassion for social inequities
and injustices. They put forward no platform of fundamental economic
reform. On the contrary, their views, and those of much of the social gospel
movement, as Ralph Luker has observed, reflected "a conservative's growing
awareness that it is industrial capitalism which has been the radical force in
American society, generating social change of unforeseen consequence,

---

[48]*God's Education*, pp. 179-84; *Practical Idealism*, pp. 204-5, 208-10; *Abba Father*, p. 27;
Self-Measurement, p. 33.

heedlessly disruptive of human community."[49] The presidents were determined to keep order and unity, and to do so by invoking again the traditional
values of individual morality.

C. The Crusade for Peace and World Order

The progressive era presidents confronted a radically changing world.
Improved communications and extensive commerce were bringing all peoples
into closer interconnectedness and cultural contact. In the world arena, as
at home, chaos threatened if humanity did not achieve moral mastery of
economic and social change. The only assurance of future order, in the
presidential view, lay in extending Christian civilization beyond its base in
Europe and America to embrace the whole world. If a rational, moral
synthesis was broad enough to incorporate changes at home, it could certainly
also sweep into its grasp the economic and cultural conflicts rampant in the
world at large. Such expansion was a trend of the universe, and those who
resisted it would have to be overcome.

"What is taking place among men," King was so bold as to tell the
National Education Association in 1915, "is the gradual spread of Western
civilization over the world." Modern educators should take as a primary task
the building up in their students of a "world-wide vision" that looked beyond
racial prejudices to an "intelligent and unselfish cooperation on a world-wide
scale" based on "those moral and religious convictions that form the spiritual
roots of all that is best in Western civilization." Of course, those convictions
rooted in Christianity, which Hyde called the absolute form of religion. The

---

[49]"The Social Gospel and the Failure of Racial Reform," *Church History* 46 (March
1977):80-99.

Christian mission to the world was based, he suggested, on the assurance that if the Gospel of Good Will was "good for me, it is good for my neighbor . . . if it is good for my country and my race, it is good for every country under heaven, and for all races of the earth."[50]

Tucker celebrated the fact of Christianity's possession of the Anglo-Saxon race and eagerly awaited its adoption of other peoples, though not of those feebler races of which Mohammedanism was possessing itself. He told the Yale students in 1898 that "the Christian nations are moving under an irresistible momentum" that exhibited the operation of a great moral law: to him that has shall more be given. As rising Christian civilization advanced, drawing its power from the lower civilizations, it would achieve both higher culture and greater responsibility for the moral order of the world. He later wrote that "we of the more virile Christian peoples have outgrown the lower and more cruel sins of the primitive races," but he also decried the exploitation of backward peoples that evidenced a continuing lower instinct in people of Western nations.[51]

In one of his rhetorical flourishes Hyde had once illustrated the relation of means to noble ends by claiming that "if, like Cecil Rhodes, we undertake for instance to paint the map of Africa British red, we shall want a monopoly of the product of the Kimberley and adjacent diamond mines." But on the whole the presidents were more attuned to Tucker's call for sympathetic love of other peoples beyond crass commercialism. After his tour of the Orient in 1909-1910, King thought it little wonder that the Chinese had joined in the

---

[50]King, "Education for World-Living," *Journal of Proceedings and Addresses of the National Education Association* 53 (1915):251-52; Hyde, *Good Will*, p. 240.

[51]"Some Present Questions in Evangelism," pp. 233-44; *Making and Unmaking*, pp. 215-16; *Function*, pp. 105-6.

Boxer Rebellion, given the "bulldozing methods, the systematic exploitation" typical of Western commercial interests.[52]

If the moral and religious convictions of Christianity accompanied economic expansion into the Orient, though, King thought the Eastern peoples could overcome their lowly status and achieve a higher civilization. Under the Christian concept of reverence for the person, Orientals could retain their "peculiar contribution" to world culture, preserving the best in their "historical inheritance." At the same time, they would find "the only hopeful basis" for their civilization in the threefold convictions of Christianity. First, Christianity stood for freedom of investigation, thus stimulating the scientific spirit that was producing so much advanced technology. Second, Christian faith not only had nothing to fear from historical criticism, but encouraged it as it continued to demonstrate the historical supremacy of Jesus and the religion he founded. Third, Christianity was the faith underlying the whole social consciousness of human interrelatedness and mutual reverence. Oriental religions, whether the Emperor cult or Shinto or Buddhism, had neither the openness nor the historicity nor the moral impetus of Christianity, which was in that sense "a survival of the fittest." The Orient no longer had any use for anti-worldly, pessimistic, impersonal religion; in the Christian faith it would find the means of moral progress and the avenues to economic and social advancement as well.[53]

The presidents were confident that in a world moving by the will of God, all nations were called to be great and to give their best to their common duties. Among those duties was the responsibility of the stronger

---

[52]Hyde, *From Epicurus*, p. 194; King, *Moral and Religious*, pp. 349, 366-69.

[53]*Fundamental Questions*, pp. 190-211, esp. 203-4.

nations to the weaker, degenerate peoples, Tucker argued. On this basis he justified U.S. intervention in Cuba in 1898, for in a limited, unselfish war, neither self-aggrandizing nor fortune-seeking, the U.S. could help restore order and dignity to the downtrodden Cubans. Hyde concurred that Americans had "not a particle of animosity or resentment against the poor Spaniards," but only wished to guarantee the political independence of the Cubans and Filipinos, establishing a benevolent trust so that they could develop their own customs, institutions, and self-expression. This international good will on the part of America Hyde considered a fruit of "The New England Conscience."[54]

Thus the fundamental moral precept of disinterested benevolence was to govern international relations as well. Wayland's generation had been convinced that nations practicing the virtues of justice, benevolence, and unselfishness would remain in peace. The progressive presidents also believed that nations adhering to basic Christian morality, summed up by the great commandment and golden rule of Jesus, would never have reason to go to war. Hyde judged war among the civilized Christian nations to be "unnecessary and inexcusable" and as early as 1897 called for a federation of such nations to advance mutual cooperation.[55]

When much to their chagrin Europe fell into war, eventually drawing in the U.S.A. as well, the three men ironically recast the events as a great moral struggle, a contest of civilization against barbarism. Germany had been reduced to a morality of sheer tyrannical power, Tucker asserted in a

---

[54]Tucker, *Public Mindedness*, p. 15, "The Conscience of the Nation," pp. 58-70; Hyde, *God's Education*, pp. 96-101; "The New England Conscience," *Outlook* 78 (December 31, 1904):1088-90.

[55]Wayland, *Elements*, pp. 359-64; Hyde, *Practical Idealism*, pp. 211-12.

1915 *Atlantic Monthly*. No Christian nation could exhibit such swaggering militarism, such failure of self-control. King accused the Germans of a "*conscious, deliberate, and stupendous . . . attempt to reverse the moral standards of the race*." In one of his last public addresses Hyde assured the Germans that Americans had only the kindliest good will toward them, and would welcome them back into the family of nations as soon as they got over their "obsession of autocracy at home and ruthlessness abroad."[56]

In their moral condemnations the presidents were forced to turn against the very country from whose philosophers and educators they had learned so much. Tucker did not want German language study banned from the public schools, for Americans needed to be knowledgeable about German *Kultur*; knowing one's enemy was only intelligent patriotism. King now found in *Kultur* the roots of the German apologetic for being a super-race that had evolved a State above all moral obligations to other peoples.[57]

Against such barbarism America could enter a war with clear conscience and high ideals, the presidents assured their listeners. "Wherever the good of all is better served by war than by peace," penned Hyde, "there the Christian . . . nation . . . will prepare for and engage in the horrors of righteous war." The soldier for the good could be certain that he was "fighting for the real good even of the nation against which he is compelled to wage war." Before the U.S.A. actually entered the fray, Tucker spoke out for military preparedness as necessary to an aggressive and defensible peace;

---

[56]Tucker, "The Ethical Challenge of the War," in *New Reservation*, pp. 119-45; King, *A New Mind for the New Age*, Cole Lectures for 1920, Vanderbilt University (New York: Fleming H. Revell Co., 1920), p. 26; Burnett, *Hyde*, pp. 256-57.

[57]Tucker, *My Generation*, pp. 434-35; King, *New Mind*, pp. 24-25, 86-87.

for peace was not a weaker stance than war if the righteous nation stood firmly for alleviation of social conflict.[58]

King praised the moral mission of America in entering the war, calling the selfless national idealism of saving civilization the "highest moral achievement" of the American people. By fighting for moral ideals America had aligned itself with the very will of God, by whose laws all violations of universal moral rule were inevitably punished. He argued that righteous force for a righteous cause would necessarily be victorious. Here again was an echo of Wayland's argument, developed in consequence of the Civil War, that offending force must be met with force if a righteous cause were to prevail. Just as war had caused Wayland to give up his theoretical pacifism, so it stimulated King to charge that pacifism in its extremist form would have turned Jesus' death into a suicide.[59]

The presidents were undaunted by any conflicting moral claims of the nations; Hyde even quoted a German on one side who asserted that his people were doing all they could "to humble and tame thoroughly and for its own good that lower England that is now in power," then quoted an Englishman on the other to the effect that the Germans had "adopted a cause for which they must suffer." But Hyde was convinced that this only revealed how all nations would work toward ultimate conciliation under the Universal Good Will.[60]

---

[58]Hyde, *Best Man*, pp. 75, 93; Tucker, "The Crux of the Peace Problem," in *New Reservation*, pp. 146-71.

[59]King, *New Mind*, pp. 56, 86; *The Way to Life*, rev. and enlarged ed. of *Ethics of Jesus* (New York: Macmillan Co., 1918), added two chapters on the war question; Wayland, *Elements* [1865 Edition], pp. 408-13.

[60]*Good Will*, pp. 39-40.

By the time the war was over, Hyde's voice had been stilled. Tucker and King continued, however, to preach moral progress through Christian world civilization. Tucker concluded his autobiography with a plea to the incoming generation to make peace its ruling idea and dominant purpose, through the achievement of a moral equilibrium and balance of power in the world. Only so would justice and humanization for all peoples come about.[61]

King worked with the Y.M.C.A. in Paris during the war, and in 1919 issued a booklet, *For a New America in a New World*, condemning the impenitence of the Germans but celebrating the moral and religious accomplishments of the Allies. He urged the soldiers to take home with them the moral stamina and democratic social vision that had motivated them to fight. A few years earlier he had advocated the immediate reconstruction of world missions as soon as the war had ended.[62] Now he plunged into the activities of the Federal Council of Churches aimed at building a Christian social order. He wrote optimistically of *A New Mind for the New Age* that would carry the moral and religious challenge valiantly into a new day.

His awareness of post-war disillusionment and cynicism only made King more emphatic about the need for Christian ideals in world affairs. He was indignant at Congressional treatment of President Wilson, which he viewed as a decline into self-serving party degeneracy when an opportunity for putting moral principle into international law was presenting itself. The

---

[61]*My Generation*, p. 449.

[62]*For a New America in a New World* (Paris: Young Men's Christian Association, 1919); "Missions and the World-War: A Kingdom That Cannot Be Shaken," *American Journal of Theology* 21 (January 1917):1-14.

whole treaty process capped by the proposal for a League of Nations had been destroyed by the selfish scramble of the nations for advantages and privileges.   America's refusal to participate indicated an isolationist abdication of responsibility for building a Christian world civilization.

King was troubled by the universal ignorance about the new world that lay ahead. But if moral and religious men did not forge on to interpret the new, he wondered,

> Who shall declare, for example, the real significance of the Russian revolution and the Bolshevist movement? Who shall lay the foundations in righteousness of a Balkan settlement? Who shall point the sure way to industrial righteousness and peace? Who, in short, knows the road to that diviner world for which we really fought this war?

Above all, King feared a "paralysis of will" in the face of such questions; for him the answer lay in an even more intensified commitment to a morality of willful self-control and self-sacrifice in behalf of the great causes and great ideals of progress.[63]

For many others, though, the unanswered questions of the war had no ready solution. At the very least, the old progressive answers were undone. "Who . . . knows the road to that divine world . . .?" No outcome of that quest would soon be apparent to the nascent twentieth century world.

III.   The Lost Consensus

In December 1900 *The Outlook* asked Tucker and Hyde, among others, to name the greatest books of the preceding century. The two differed somewhat in their selections of literature and poetry. Hyde preferred the American poet and essayist Ralph Waldo Emerson, the English artist and

---

[63]*New Mind*, pp. 50-51, 54.

critic John Ruskin, and Romantic poet Robert Browning. Tucker chose the
last great German Renaissance man, J. S. von Goethe, the American author
National Hawthorne, and two Romantics, French novelist Victor Hugo and
Victorian poet laureate Alfred, Lord Tennyson. On five authors, however,
the presidents agreed: a German, philosopher G. W. F. Hegel, three
Englishmen, scientist Charles Darwin, philosopher Herbert Spencer, and
essayist and historian Thomas Carlyle, and one American, novelist Harriet
Beecher Stowe. Hegel, Darwin, and Spencer were all foundational figures
in the nineteenth century encounter with evolution and its absorption into the
idea of progress revealing an immanent God. Carlyle and Stowe were major
voices of the century's enlightened moralism that advocated idealistic uplift
for all of humanity. To the practical achievement of these two broad ideals
the presidents devoted their careers.[64]

"Religion is life, or neither is anything," King liked to say, and the
presidents took it upon themselves to show that all of life had spiritual
significance, whether through the activities of social progress or the education
of social leaders. Everywhere they saw advancement in human nobility they
saw God revealed; as Hyde put it in his poem, "The Friendship of the Good,"

> I see thy features in each human face;
>   I hear thy mandate in each civic call;
> I own thy kindred in the lowliest race;
>   I love thy likeness in the souls of all.[65]

In their "Progressive synthesis of righteousness, social service, and
scholarship," as one historian of Oberlin put it, the presidents were exemplars

---

[64]"The Greatest Books of the Century," *Outlook* 66 (December 1, 1900):800-802.

[65]King, *Personal and Ideal*, p. 107; Hyde, "The Friendship of the Good," *Outlook* 85 (March 9, 1907):563.

of a wider cultural effort to infuse all new learning and social advance with a religious atmosphere. John D. Rockefeller gave the money for a chapel at the University of Chicago in 1910 with this charge:

> As the spirit of religion should penetrate and control the university, so that building which represents religion ought to be the central and dominant feature of the university group. Thus it will be proclaimed that the university in its ideal is dominated by the spirit of religion, all its departments are inspired by religious feeling and all its work is directed to the highest ends.

If such was the university ideal, so much the more was it the ideal of the liberal arts colleges, the shapers of individual and national character.[66]

King once proclaimed of his times that "no other generation ever had so little excuse for cherishing prejudice, and for turning aside from the path of utter intellectual integrity." He and his colleagues welcomed new disciplines to their curricula, celebrating the spirit of science and history. They urged individuality in the quest for truth even as they invoked a social consciousness that professed sacred respect for every person.[67]

Yet the presidents were open to scientific study as to social change only within the confines of certain moral and social assumptions. Their books were criticized for giving "conservative interpretation" to psychological investigations, or for treating modern industrialism in much too individualistic a way. In continuing to insist on personal morality and on moralistic analysis of complex social and political problems they were increasingly viewed as reactionary. In their ideal of "religiously consecrated education and genteel

---

[66]Barnard, *From Evangelicalism*, p. 127; Rockefeller's statement may be found on a plaque in the narthex of Rockefeller Chapel at the University of Chicago.

[67]King, *Fundamental Questions*, p. 115.

culture" they had more in common with their predecessors than with the rising generations.[68]

When Randolph Bourne reviewed Tucker's collection of addresses titled *The New Reservation of Time* in a 1917 *New Republic*, he blamed the book's stilted weightiness on the confinement of Tucker's mind to the prison of institutionalism.   Bourne lamented the fact that "our civilization could apparently find no other way of using such a mind than to put it for the best years of its life into the routine of a New England college, where the horrifying prestige of the higher education kept it in a state of torpor."   A later *Dial* reviewer agreed that Tucker's potential to be a true public philosopher had been wasted at Dartmouth, and he confessed that in a bitter mood he thought of Tucker's *My Generation* more as "Our Unregeneration."[69]

Such comments only indicated the cultural pluralism that would be ever more predominant in the postwar world.   In the years to come the new academic fields would detach themselves deliberately from moral and religious assertions, and students, like the citizenry at large, would shape their personalities in a context less definitely Christian or even religious.   One of his biographers concluded that King was "never comfortable" in that postwar society, and in the last eleven years of his life he published nothing more.[70]

---

[68]Henry D. Sheldon, Review of King's *Personal and Ideal Elements in Education*, *Dial* 38 (April 16, 1905):272; [anon.] "The Social Leadership of the Church," review of Tucker's *Function of the Church in Modern Society*, *Independent* 70 (May 11, 1911):1010-12; Barnard, *From Evangelicalism*, p. 110.

[69]Bourne quoted in Tucker, *My Generation*, pp. 445-46; [anon.] Review of *My Generation*, *Dial* 67 (November 1, 1919):386.

[70]Barnard, *From Evangelicalism*, p. 110.

In his final book, *Seeing Life Whole* (1923), King continued to press, if in a more insistent or even peevish tone, his progressive idealist response to the question, "Have the world and life abiding meaning and value?" But if that was still the question of youth, King's vision of "the ideal life" was now woefully and embarrassingly inadequate. In perhaps his most brilliant address, Tucker had already hinted at a malaise that was making "the control of modern civilization" so difficult. Tucker described a

> strange contradiction in the experience of the modern man; on the one hand, a sense of power rising at times to arrogance, and on the other hand, a sense of helplessness involving at times an abject surrender to the environment. In our more confident moods we vaunt our alliance with the forces of nature, but not infrequently we are made to feel that we have to do with things which are irresistible and inevitable.[71]

The presidential architects of a progressive synthesis holding learning, action, and faith in productive unity could only chide the new paralysis of will in American culture. They were not in a position to contribute to yet another new synthesis nor to absorb the coming revolutions in the economic and social life of their nation. They feared a world of disorder, but could see no answer for it but the dominance of the Christian civilization of the West. They belonged, in short, to the last years of the nineteenth century, and if they themselves thought of their century as divided by Darwin's meridian, they nevertheless in their very drive to synthesize sustained and expanded the rational and moral universe of their old-time predecessors.

---

[71]King, *Seeing Life Whole*, p. 1; Tucker, "On the Control of Modern Civilization," in *New Reservation*, pp. 172-91, esp. 173.

SELECTED BIBLIOGRAPHY

I. William DeWitt Hyde

A. Works

1. Books

Abba Father, Or, The Religion of Everyday Life. New York: Fleming H.
Revell Company, 1908.

The Best Man I Know; Developed out of the will for the good of all. New
York: The Macmillan Company, 1917.

The College Man and the College Woman. Boston: Houghton Mifflin
Company, 1906.

The Five Great Philosophies of Life. 2nd ed. of *From Epicurus to Christ.*
New York: The Macmillan Company, 1911, 1914.

From Epicurus to Christ. Haverford Library Lectures. New York: The
Macmillan Company, 1904.

God's Education of Man. Boston: Houghton, Mifflin and Company, 1899,
1901.

The Gospel of Good Will, As Revealed in Contemporary Scriptures. The
Lyman Beecher Lectures on Preaching at the Yale School of
Religion for 1916. New York: The Macmillan Company, 1916.

Jesus' Way; An Appreciation of the Teaching in the Synoptic Gospels.
Boston: Houghton, Mifflin and Company, 1902.

Outlines of Social Theology. New York: The Macmillan Company, 1895,
1900.

Practical Ethics. New York: Henry Holt and Company, 1892, 1893.

Practical Idealism. New York: The Macmillan Company, 1897.

The Quest of the Best; Insights into Ethics for Parents, Teachers, and Leaders of Boys. New York: Thomas Y. Crowell Company, 1913.

Self-Measurement; A Scale of Human Values with Directions for Personal Application. The Art of Life Series, Edited by E. H. Griggs. New York: B. W. Huebsch, 1908, 1916.

Sin and Its Forgiveness. Modern Religious Problems, Edited by A. W. Vernon. Boston: Houghton Mifflin Company, 1909.

The Teacher's Philosophy In and Out of School. Riverside Educational Monographs, Edited by Henry Suzzallo. Boston: Houghton Mifflin Company, 1910.

2. Addresses

"The College." *Congress of Arts and Science, Universal Exposition, St. Louis, 1904*. Edited by Howard J. Rogers. 8 vols. Boston: Houghton, Mifflin and Company, 1906-7, 8:119-32.

"The Definition of a Good Man." *The Message of the College to the Church*. Addresses in Old South Church, Boston, Lent 1901. Boston: The Pilgrim Press, 1901, pp. 41-66.

"The Message of Christ to the Scholar." *The Message of Christ to Manhood*. William Belden Noble Lectures for 1898. Boston: Houghton, Mifflin and Company, 1899, pp. 117-146.

3. Articles

"The Abolition of the House of Lords." *Outlook* 93 (December 18, 1909):866-68.

"An Address to Freshmen." *Independent* 65 (October 1, 1908):746-48.

"The Adjustment of the Small College to Our Educational System."
　　Outlook 71 (August 2, 1902):886-89.

"The Cardinal Virtues." *Atlantic Monthly* 88 (July 1901):108-21.

"The Case System in the Ministry." *Homiletic Review* 57 (February
　　1909):95-96.

"The Christ of Criticism and the Christ of Faith." *Independent* 52 (May 31,
　　1900):1297-98.

"Church or Sect?" *Outlook* 66 (December 8, 1900):889-94.

"The College Administration and the College Instructor." *Nation* 102
　　(April 20, 1916):434-35.

"College and Seminary." *Independent* 61 (August 2, 1906):264-68.

"The Cross of Christ in the New Theology." *Outlook* 64 (March 24,
　　1900):678-79.

"Cost and Consecration." *Outlook* 62 (July 29, 1899):713-19.

"The Creed of a College Class." *Outlook* 74 (June 27, 1903):510-12.

"The Essentials of Christianity." *Outlook* 81 (November 4, 1905):567-69.

"The Friendship of the Good." *Outlook* 85 (March 9, 1907):563.

"The Future of the Country College." *Atlantic Monthly* 62 (December
　　1888):721-26.

"The Greatest Books of the Century." *Outlook* 66 (December 1,
　　1900):800-802.

"Impending Paganism in New England." *Forum* 13 (June 1892):519-28.

"Life's Promise and Fulfillment." *Independent* 69 (December 8,
　　1910):1281.

"The Minister Who is Wanted." *Independent* 55 (August 20, 1903):1960-62.

"Mystic Morality." *Independent* 54 (January 9, 1902):74-78.

"Mystic or Christian?" *Independent* 54 (January 2, 1902):10-12.

"A National Platform on the Race Question." *Outlook* 77 (May 21, 1904):169-70.

"New Century Ideals." *Outlook* 67 (January 5, 1901):73.

"The New England Conscience." *Outlook* 78 (December 31, 1904):1088-90.

"The New Ethics." *Atlantic Monthly* 90 (November 1902):577-89.

"The New Standard of College Teaching." *Nation* 90 (February 3, 1910):107-8.

"Personality and College Professors." *Outlook* 92 (August 21, 1909):931-37.

"The Place of Religion in a Liberal Education." *Homiletical Review* 58 (October 1909):286-87.

"A Poisonous Phrase." *Outlook* 101 (May 18, 1912):122.

"President Eliot as an Educational Reformer." *Atlantic Monthly* 83 (March 1899):348-57.

"Problems of Our Educational System." *Forum* 32 (January 1902):551-65.

"Reform in Theological Education." *Atlantic Monthly* 85 (January 1900):16-26.

"The Strenuous Life." *Outlook* 74 (May 9, 1903):119.

"What Is Salvation?" *Andover Review* 13 (April 1890):372-79.

B. Biography and Criticism

Burnett, Charles T. *Hyde of Bowdoin; A Biography of William DeWitt Hyde.* Boston: Houghton Mifflin Company, 1931.

Hatch, Louis C. *The History of Bowdoin College.* Portland, Maine: Loring, Short and Harmon, 1927.

Patton, C. H. and W. T. Field. *Eight O'Clock Chapel; A Study of New England College Life in the Eighties*. Boston: Houghton Mifflin Company, 1927.

Thwing, Charles Franklin. *Guides, Philosophers and Friends; Studies of College Men*. Freeport, N.Y.: Books for Libraries Press, 1971. Originally published, 1927.

Review of *From Epicurus to Christ*. *Independent* 58 (May 11, 1905):1075.

Review of *Outlines of Social Theology*. *Critic* 27 [n.s. 24] (October 5, 1895):211.

Review of *Practical Ethics*. *Critic* 21 [n.s. 18] (September 24, 1892):163.

Roosevelt, Theodore. "The Search for Truth in a Reverent Spirit." *Outlook* 99 (December 2, 1911):819-826.

II. Henry Churchill King

A. Works

1. Books

The Ethics of Jesus. William Belden Noble Lectures for 1909. New York: The Macmillan Company, 1910, 1912.

For a New America in a New World. Paris: Young Men's Christian Association, 1919.

Fundamental Questions. New York: The Macmillan Company, 1917.

Letters on the Greatness and Simplicity of the Christian Faith. A Revised Edition of *Letters to Sunday-School Teachers*. Boston: The Pilgrim Press, 1906.

The Moral and Religious Challenge of Our Times; The Guiding Principle in Human Development: Reverence for Personality. New York: The Macmillan Company, 1911.

A New Mind for the New Age. The Cole Lectures for 1920, Vanderbilt University. New York: Fleming H. Revell Company, 1920.

An Outline of the Microcosmus of Hermann Lotze. Oberlin: Pearce and Randolph, 1895.

Personal and Ideal Elements in Education. New York: The Macmillan Company, 1904, 1908.

Rational Living; Some Practical Inferences From Modern Psychology. New York: The Macmillan Company, 1905, 1918.

Reconstruction in Theology. New York: The Macmillan Company, 1901, 1907.

Seeing Life Whole; A Christian Philosophy of Life. The Deems Lectures for 1922, New York University. New York: The Macmillan Company, 1923.

The Seeming Unreality of the Spiritual Life. The Nathaniel William Taylor Lectures for 1907. New York: The Macmillan Company, 1908, 1911.

Theology and the Social Consciousness; A Study of the Relations of the Social Consciousness to Theology. 2nd ed. New York: The Macmillan Company, 1902, 1907.

The Way to Life; A revised and enlarged reprint of those portions of the author's Ethics of Jesus, dealing with the Sermon on the Mount, with a special discussion of war and the teaching of Jesus. New York: The Macmillan Company, 1918.

2. Addresses

"Enlarging Ideals in Morals and Religion." King, Henry Churchill, et al. *Education and National Character.* Papers of the Fifth General Convention of the Religious Education Association, February 11-13, 1908. Chicago: The Religious Education Association, 1908, pp. 7-15.

"The Function of College Education." *Congress of Arts and Science, Universal Exposition, St. Louis, 1904.* Edited by Howard J. Rogers. 8 vols. Boston: Houghton, Mifflin and Company, 1906-7, 8:151-54.

"The Fundamental Nature of Religion." *Congress of Arts and Science, Universal Exposition, St. Louis, 1904.* Edited by Howard J. Rogers. 8 vols. Boston: Houghton, Mifflin and Company, 1906-7, 8:243-55.

"The Importance of the Christian College in the Making of America." Welch, Herbert, Henry Churchill King, Thomas Nicholson. *The Christian College.* New York: The Methodist Book Concern, 1916, pp. 28-48.

3. Articles

"Difficulties Concerning Prayer." *Biblical World* 46 (September 1915):131-34, and *Biblical World* 46 (November 1915): 281-84.

"Education for World-Living." *Journal of Proceedings and Addresses of the National Education Association* 53 (1915):251-52.

"The Future of Moral and Religious Education." *Religious Education* 4 (October 1909):293-304.

"Good Thoughts in Bad Times." *Biblical World* 50 (November 1917):267-75.

"It's All in the Day's Work." *Biblical World* 45 (May 1915):259-67.

"Missions and the World-War: A Kingdom That Cannot Be Shaken." *American Journal of Theology* 21 (January 1917):1-14.

"Some Modern Interpretations of Christianity." *Outlook* 73 (April 25, 1903):972-76.

"What the College Stands For." Presidential Address, January 11, 1917. *Association of American Colleges Bulletin* 3 (February 1917):3-23.

B. Biography and Criticism

Barnard, John. *From Evangelicalism to Progressivism at Oberlin College, 1866-1917.* N.p.: Ohio State University Press, 1969.

Cockerell, T. D. A. Review of *Rational Living. Dial* 40 (March 1, 1906):151.

Foster, Frank Hugh. *The Modern Movement in American Theology; Sketches in the History of American Protestant Thought from the Civil War to the World War.* New York: Fleming H. Revell Company, 1939.

Gladden, Washington. "Henry Churchill King: Leader in Theological Thought." *Outlook* 85 (January 26, 1907):222-28.

Love, Donald M. *Henry Churchill King of Oberlin.* New Haven: Yale University Press, 1956.

Sheldon, Henry Davidson. Review of *Personal and Ideal Elements in Education. Dial* 38 (April 16, 1905):272.

III. William Jewett Tucker

A. Works

1. Books

Divinity of Jesus Christ; an exposition of the origin and reasonableness of the belief of the Christian church by the authors of Progressive Orthodoxy. Boston: Houghton, Mifflin and Company, 1893.

The Function of the Church in Modern Society. Modern Religious Problems, Edited by A. W. Vernon. Boston: Houghton Mifflin Company, 1911.

The Making and Unmaking of the Preacher. Lectures on the Lyman Beecher Foundation, Yale, 1898. Boston: Houghton, Mifflin and Company, 1898.

My Generation; An Autobiographical Interpretation. Boston: Houghton Mifflin Company, 1919.

The New Reservation of Time, And Other Articles Contributed to the Atlantic Monthly During the Occupancy of the Period Described (1910-1916). Boston: Houghton Mifflin Company, 1916.

Personal Power; Counsels to College Men. Boston: Houghton Mifflin Company, 1910.

Progressive Orthodoxy; A Contribution to the Christian Interpretation of Christian Doctrines by the Editors of the Andover Review. Reprint Edition with a New Introduction. Hicksville, N.Y.: The Regina Press, 1975. Originally published 1886.

*Public Mindedness; An Aspect of Citizenship Considered in Various
    Addresses Given While President of Dartmouth College.* Concord,
    N.H.: The Rumford Press, 1910.

2. Addresses

"The Church of the Future." *The New Puritanism.* Introduction by
    Rossiter W. Raymond. New York: Fords, Howard, and Hulbert,
    1898, pp. 223-29. Reprinted from *Outlook* 57 (November 27,
    1897):755-59.

"The College Graduate and the Church." *The Message of the College to the
    Church.* Addresses in Old South Church, Boston, Lent 1901.
    Boston: The Pilgrim Press, 1901, pp. 147-70.

"Is Modern Education Capable of Idealism?" Inauguration of President
    Henry Churchill King of Oberlin College. Oberlin: Oberlin
    College, 1903.

3. Articles

"Administrative Problems of the Historic College." *Educational Review* 43
    (May 1912):433-48.

"The Gospel of Wealth." *Andover Review* 15 (June 1891):631-45.

"The Greatest Books of the Century." *Outlook* 66 (December 1, 1900):802.

"The Integrity of the College Unit." *School Review* 5 (December
    1897):683-96.

"'Life in Himself': A Meditation on the Consciousness of Jesus Christ."
    Andover Review 17 (February 1892):186-95.

"The Problems Which Confront Our Colleges at the Opening of the
    Twentieth Century." *Education* 20 (June 1900):585-87.

"The Relation of the High School to the Higher Education." *Education* 18
   (June 1898):579-87.

"Some Present Questions in Evangelism." *Andover Review* 1 (March
   1884):233-44.

"Small Vs. Large Colleges." *School Review* 14 (December 1906):717-25.

"Twenty-five Years 'In Residence'." *Atlantic Monthly* 119 (May 1917):640-
   49.

"The Work of the Andover House in Boston." *Scribner's Magazine* 13
   (March 1893):357-72.

B. Biography and Criticism

Buckham, John Wright. *Progressive Religious Thought in America; A Survey
   of the Enlarging Pilgrim Faith.* Boston: Houghton Mifflin Company,
   1919.

Hill, Ralph Nading, Editor. *The College on the Hill; A Dartmouth
   Chronicle.* Hanover, N.H.: Dartmouth College, 1964.

Leavens, Robert F. and Arthur H. Lord. *Dr. Tucker's Dartmouth.*
   Hanover, N.H.: Dartmouth Publications, 1965.

Review of *My Generation. Dial* 67 (November 1, 1919):386.

Richardson, Leon B. *History of Dartmouth College.* 2 vols. Hanover,
   N.H.: Dartmouth College Publications, 1932.

"The Social Leadership of the Church." *Independent* 70 (May 11,
   1911):1010-12.

"Theory and Practice of Public Life." *Nation* 91 (October 13, 1910):337-38.

Thwing, Charles Franklin. *Guides, Philosophers and Friends; Studies of College Men.* Freeport, N.Y.: Books for Libraries Press, 1971. Originally published 1927.

IV. Ante-bellum Anglo-American Authors

Butler, Joseph. *The Analogy of Religion, Natural and Revealed, to the Constitution and Course of Nature.* New York: Ivison, Blakeman, Taylor and Company, 1878. Originally published 1736.

Fairchild, James H. *Elements of Theology, Natural and Revealed.* Oberlin: Edward J. Goodrich, 1892.

Finney, Charles Grandison. *Lectures on Systematic Theology.* Revised by the Author, Revised and Edited by George Redford. London: William Tegg and Company, 1851.

Hopkins, Mark. *Evidences of Christianity.* Lectures before the Lowell Institute, Revised as a Textbook. Boston: T. R. Marvin and Son, 1909. Originally published 1863, Revised 1880.

McCosh, James. *The Method of Divine Government, Physical and Moral.* Edinburgh: Sutherland and Knox, 1850.

Mahan, Asa. *Science of Moral Philosophy.* Oberlin: James M. Fitch, 1848.

_____. *The Science of Natural Theology; or, God the Unconditioned Cause, and God the Infinite and Perfect, As Revealed in Creation.* Boston: Henry Hoyt, 1867.

Paley, William. *Works.* Philadelphia: J. J. Woodward, 1831.

Lehrer, Keith, and Ronald E. Beanblossom, Editors. *Thomas Reid's Inquiry and Essays.* The Library of Liberal Arts. Indianapolis: The

Bobbs-Merrill Company, Inc., 1975. Includes *An Inquiry Into the Human Mind on the Principles of Common Sense* (1764); *Essays on the Intellectual Powers of Man* (1785); *Essays on the Active Powers of Man* (1788).

Upham, Thomas C. *Elements of Mental Philosophy, Embracing the Two Departments of the Intellect and the Sensibilities.* 2 vols. New York: Harper and Brothers, 1840, 1841.

Wayland, Francis. *The Elements of Moral Science.* Edited with an Introduction by Joseph L. Blau. Cambridge, Mass.: The Belknap Press of Harvard University Press, 1963. Originally published 1835.

_____. *Occasional Discourses.* Boston: James Loring, 1833.

_____. *Sermons to the Churches.* New York: Sheldon, Blakeman, and Company, 1859.

Wayland, Francis [Jr.] and H. L. Wayland. *A Memoir of the Life and Labors of Francis Wayland, D.D., LL.D.* 2 vols. New York: Sheldon and Company, 1867.

V. Studies of Scottish Common Sense Philosophy and Its Influence in America

Ahlstrom, Sydney E. "The Scottish Philosophy and American Theology." *Church History* 24 (September 1955):255-72.

Bozeman, Theodore Dwight. *Protestants in an Age of Science; The Baconian Ideal and Antebellum American Religious Thought.* Chapel Hill, N.C.: The University of North Carolina Press, 1977.

Grave, S. A. *The Scottish Philosophy of Common Sense.* Oxford: The Clarendon Press, 1960.

258

Holifield, E. Brooks. *The Gentlemen Theologians; American Theology in Southern Culture, 1795-1860*. Durham, N.C.: Duke University Press, 1978.

Hovenkamp, Herbert. *Science and Religion in America, 1800-1860*. N.p.: University of Pennsylvania Press, 1978.

Howe, Daniel Walker. *The Unitarian Conscience; Harvard Moral Philosophy, 1805-1861*. Cambridge: Harvard University Press, 1970.

Lundberg, David and Henry F. May. "The Enlightened Reader in America." *American Quarterly* 28 (Summer 1976):262-93.

May, Henry F. *The Enlightenment in America*. New York: Oxford University Press, 1976.

Mead, Sidney E. *The Lively Experiment; The Shaping of Christianity in America*. New York: Harper and Row, 1963.

Meyer, D. H. *The Instructed Conscience; The Shaping of the American National Ethic*. Philadelphia: University of Pennsylvania Press, 1972.

Persons, Stow. *American Minds; A History of Ideas*. New York: Henry Holt and Company, 1958.

Riley, I. Woodbridge. *American Philosophy: The Early Schools*. New York: Russell and Russell, Inc., n.d.

Schneider, Herbert W. *A History of American Philosophy*. 2nd ed. New York: Columbia University Press, 1963.

Seth, Andrew. *Scottish Philosophy; A Comparison of the Scottish and German Answers to Hume*. 2nd ed. New York: Burt Franklin, 1971. Originally published, 1890.

Sloan, Douglas. *The Scottish Enlightenment and the American College Ideal*. Teachers College, Columbia University: Teachers College Press, 1971.

Smith, Wilson. *Professors and Public Ethics; Studies of Northern Moral Philosophers Before the Civil War*. American Historical Association. Ithaca, N.Y.: Cornell University Press, 1956.

VI. Studies of the Progressive Era
in American Society and Liberal Protestantism

Abell, Aaron Ignatius. *The Urban Impact on American Protestantism, 1865-1900*. Cambridge: Harvard University Press, 1943.

Averill, Lloyd J. *American Theology in the Liberal Tradition*. Philadelphia: The Westminster Press, 1967.

Bryson, Gladys. "The Comparable Interests of the Old Moral Philosophy and the Modern Social Sciences." *Social Forces* 11 (October 1932):19-27.

_____. "The Emergence of the Social Sciences from Moral Philosophy." *The International Journal of Ethics* 42 (April 1932):304-23.

_____. "Sociology Considered as Moral Philosophy." *The Sociological Review* 24 (1932):26-36.

Buckham, John Wright. *Progressive Religious Thought in America; A Survey of the Enlarging Pilgrim Faith*. Boston: Houghton Mifflin Company, 1919.

Cauthen, Kenneth. *The Impact of American Religious Liberalism*. New York: Harper and Row, 1962.

Foster, Frank Hugh. *The Modern Movement in American Theology; Sketches in the History of American Protestant Thought from the Civil War to the World War.* New York: Fleming H. Revell Company, 1939.

Hall, G. Stanley. "On the History of American College Textbooks and Teaching in Logic, Ethics, Psychology, and Allied Subjects." *Proceedings of the American Antiquarian Society* n.s. 9 (April 1894):137-74.

Herbst, Jurgen. "From Moral Philosophy to Sociology; Albion Woodbury Small." *The Harvard Educational Review* 29 (1959):227-44.

_____. *The German Historical School in American Scholarship; A Study in the Transfer of Culture.* Port Washington, N.Y.: Kennikat Press, 1965, 1972.

Holifield, E. Brooks. "Reading the Signs of the Times." *Reviews in American History* 5 (March 1977):14-20.

Hutchison, William R. "Cultural Strain and Protestant Liberalism." *American Historical Review* 76 (April 1971):386-411.

_____. "Liberal Protestantism and the 'End of Innocence'." *American Quarterly* 15 (Summer 1963):126-39.

_____. *The Modernist Impulse in American Protestantism.* Cambridge: Harvard University Press, 1976.

Lotze, Hermann. *Microcosmus: An Essay Concerning Man and his Relation to the World.* Translated by Elizabeth Hamilton and E. E. Constance Jones. 2 vols. 4th ed. Edinburgh: T. and T. Clark, n.d. [1885].

Luker, Ralph E. "The Social Gospel and the Failure of Racial Reform." *Church History* 46 (March 1977):80-99.

May, Henry F. *The End of American Innocence.* New York: Alfred A. Knopf, 1959. Quadrangle Paperbacks, 1964.

Persons, Stow. *The Decline of American Gentility.* New York: Columbia University Press, 1973.

Roberts, David E. and Henry P. Van Dusen, Editors. *Liberal Theology; An Appraisal. Essays in Honor of Eugene William Lyman.* New York: Charles Scribner's Sons, 1942.

Santayana, George. *Lotze's System of Philosophy.* Edited with an Introduction and Lotze Bibliography by Paul Grimley Kuntz. Bloomington, Indiana: Indiana University Press, 1971.

Schlesinger, Arthur Meier. "A Critical Period in American Religion, 1875-1900." *Proceedings of the Massachusetts Historical Society* 64 (June 1932):523-47.

Williams, Daniel Day. *The Andover Liberals; A Study in American Theology.* Morningside Heights: King's Crown Press, 1941.

Wright, Conrad. *The Liberal Christians; Essays on American Unitarian History.* Boston: Beacon Press, 1970.

VII. Studies in American Higher Education

American Education Society. *Quarterly Register and Journal* 1 (Andover: Flagg and Gould, 1829).

Barnes, Sherman B. "The Entry of Science and History in the College Curriculum, 1865-1914." *History of Education Quarterly* 4 (March 1964):44-58.

_____. "Learning and Piety in Ohio Colleges, 1865-1900." *The Ohio Historical Quarterly* 69 (October 1960):327-52.

Brubacher, John S. and Willis Rudy. *Higher Education in Transition; An American History, 1636-1956.* New York: Harper and Brothers Publishers, 1958.

Butts, R. Freeman. *The College Charts Its Course.* New York: McGraw-Hill Book Company, Inc., 1939.

Cremin, Lawrence A. "The Revolution in American Secondary Education, 1893-1918." *Teachers College Record* 56 (March 1955):295-308.

Curti, Merle and Roderick Nash. *Philanthropy in the Shaping of American Higher Education.* New Brunswick, N.J.: Rutgers University Press, 1965.

Godbold, Albea. *The Church College of the Old South.* Durham, N.C.: Duke University Press, 1944.

Koos, Leonard V. "College Aims Past and Present." *School and Society* 14 (December 3, 1921):499-509.

Morison, Samuel Eliot. *The Founding of Harvard College.* Cambridge: Harvard University Press, 1935.

Rudolph, Frederick. *The American College and University.* New York: Alfred A. Knopf, 1962.

Schmidt, George P. *The Old Time College President.* New York: Columbia University Press, 1930.

Smith, Charles Forster. "Southern Colleges and Schools." *Atlantic Monthly* 54 (October 1884):542-57, and *Atlantic Monthly* 56 (December 1885):738-50.

Snow, Louis F. *The College Curriculum in the United States.* Columbia University Contributions to Education. Teachers College Series, No. 10. New York: Teachers College, Columbia University, 1907.

Snyder, Henry Nelson. "The College Under Fire." *The Methodist Quarterly Review [South]* 62 (July 1913):532-45.

Tewksbury, Donald G. *The Founding of American Colleges and Universities Before the Civil War.* New York: Teachers College, Columbia University, 1932.

Trow, Martin. "The Second Transformation of American Secondary Education." *International Journal of Comparative Sociology* 2 (1961):144-66.

United States Commissioner of Education. *Annual Reports.* Washington, D.C.: Government Printing Office.

INDEX

266

Idealism (German), 70-71, 82, 84, 97
Immortality, 140-41
Infinite, 97, 100
Jesus Christ, 119-27
Kant, Immanuel, ix, 33-34, 66-67
King, Henry Churchill
    activities, 28-29, career, 26,
    personality, 23-24, writings,
    30-31, 85, 153; on atonement,
    123-24, biblical criticism,
    115-16, character, xi, xii, 129,
    175, Christ, 119-20, 122-23,
    126, church, 139, college ideal,
    198-99, 206-209, colleges, 35,
    conscience and duty, 168-69,
    creeds, 118-119, curriculum,
    201-202, ethics, 161-64,
    evolution, 99, friendship,
    103-105, God 100-101,
    immortality, 140, labor reform,
    228-30, materialism, 95, 98,
    miracles, 113, moral
    philosophy, 153, morality, 180,
    natural theology, 94-95, new
    world order, 238-39, new
    learning, 70, the Orient, 233-
    34, progress, 189-90,
    psychology, 171-74, Puritanism,
    141-42, 207, race relations,
    221-23, religion, 73, 240,
    science, 106-107, sin and
    salvation, 128-29, social
    consciousness, 111-12,
    227,spirituality, 134-36, 33-34,
    war, 236-37, wealth, 229,
    women's rights, 220, work,
    179-80
Liberal Arts, 39-40

Liberalism, 9-10
Locke, John, 44
Lotze, Hermann, 95-98, 100
Luker, Ralph, 231-32
Mahan, Asa, 50-51, 55, 58-59
May, Henry, 71
McCosh, James, 49, 60-61,147
Mead, George Herbert, 83
Mental discipline, 13
Miracles, 52, 113
Modernism, 7-9
Moral philosophy, 13, 41, 56-65,
    149-50, 154-66, 184-88
Moral judgment, 46
Moral law, 55
Moral science, ix
Moral sense, 47
Munger, Theodore, v
Natural theology, vi, 40, 49-51,
    54-55, 87-107
Natural science, vi, 69, 50, 71,
    89-90, 98-100, 106-107
Natural law, 89-90, 93, 96, 99-100,
    105
New world order, i, 196, 232-39,
    243
New learning, xi, 6, 13-15
"New Theology," v
Oberlin College, 26-27, 197-98,
    201-202
Paley, William, 50, 51, 53, 57, 59
Palmer, George H., 80-81
Park, Edwards A., 79,80
Personalism, 98, 100-105
Practical idealism, 19, 89
Pragmatism, 16
Progress, 7, 8, 10, 19, 72, 75, 108,
    189-90, 197, 232-33, 238
Providence, 145-46, 187, 191, 193

DDS